African Philosophy

American University Studies

Series V
Philosophy
Vol. 134

PETER LANG
New York • San Francisco • Bern
Frankfurt am Main • Paris • London

Segun Gbadegesin

African Philosophy

Traditional Yoruba Philosophy and Contemporary African Realities

PETER LANG
New York • San Francisco • Bern
Frankfurt am Main • Paris • London

Library of Congress Cataloging-in-Publication Data

Gbadegesin, Segun,
 African philosophy : traditional Yoruba
philosophy and contemporary African realities /
Segun Gbadegesin.
  p. cm. — (American university studies. Series
V, Philosophy ; vol. 134)
  Includes bibliographical references and index.
  1. Philosophy, Yoruba. 2. Philosophy, African.
3. Yoruba (African people)—Social life and customs.
4. Africa—Economic conditions—1960- 5. Africa—
Social conditions—1960- I. Title. II. Series.
B5619.N6G33   1991   199'.66—dc20   91-864
ISBN 0-8204-1770-X   CIP
ISSN 0739-6392

Die Deutsche Bibliothek-CIP-Einheitsaufnahme

Gbadegesin, Segun:
African philosophy : traditional Yoruba philosophy
and contemporary African realities / Segun
Gbadegesin.—New York; Berlin; Bern; Frankfurt/M.;
Paris; Wien : Lang, 1991
  (American University Studies Ser. 5, Philosophy ;
Vol. 134)
  ISBN 0-8204-1770-X
NE: American university studies / 05

The paper in this book meets the guidelines for permanence and
durability of the Committee on Production Guidelines for
Book Longevity of the Council on Library Resources.

© Segun Gbadegesin, New York 1991

All rights reserved.
Reprint or reproduction, even partially, in all forms such as microfilm,
xerography, microfiche, microcard, offset strictly prohibited.

Printed in the United States of America.

To Adetoun and the children,
in love and appreciation

ACKNOWLEDGEMENTS

This work has benefitted from the good will, support and encouragement of several institutions, friends and colleagues. Obafemi Awolowo University, Ile-Ife, Nigeria granted me a sabbatical leave during 1989/90 academic year and leave of absence during 1990/91 academic year. As a visiting professor at the University of Wisconsin-Madison during 1989/89, I had access to excellent facilities for research. Colgate University provided the intellectual and social environment which facilitated the completion of the work, as well as some financial assistance for its publication. I am grateful to these institutions. The following persons deserve special thanks for the encouragement and inspiration I received from them: Dean Don Crawford; Michael Byrd; Linda Hunter and Fred Hayward; Andrew Levine, who encouraged me to embark on the project; Terrence and Rosemary Penner; Marcus Singer; Haskell Fain; Bill Hay; and Daniel Wickler, all of the University of Wisconsin, Madison. Chris Willard, Julie Fellenz and Jacqueline Crystal helped with the preparation of the manuscript at the initial stages. I appreciate the encouragement I received from Gene Blocker, Albert Mosley and Roland Abiodun, and an anonymous reader of the manuscript. Kwasi Wiredu read the entire manuscript and offered extensive comments which enabled me to clarify my position on some of the issues. I appreciate his time and encouragement. I am also grateful to Professor Elliot Skinner who read Chapter 5 and gave very useful comments. At Colgate, several colleagues made my year a pleasant one. Dean Selleck encouraged me with the provision of vital facilities for my work. Harvey Sindima read the entire manuscript and offered very helpful suggestions. I am also grateful to Chris Vecsey and Carol Ann Lorenz, Roy Bryce-Laporte, Charles Rice and Elleni Tedla for their support in various ways. I acknowledge, with gratitudes, the encouragement I got from the faculty of the Department of Philosophy and Religion at Colgate. Among my graduate students at Wisconsin, I should mention in particular, Akuwa, Bob, Cuca, Anthony, Ludora, Pearl, Tokunbo, and Sauda and Joseph Smith. Joseph helped with the technical production of the chart in Chapter 2. Finally, my wife, Adetoun, has always been a loving and loyal wife and sister; and this has been an important source of strength for me. This time, she not only took up additional responsibilities for the family, but while I was away from home, I lost my dear father; and Adetoun played the role of a daughter, son and wife. To her and our loving children, I dedicate this volume.

Contents

Preface — xi

Part I Traditional Yoruba Philosophy

1. On the Idea of African Philosophy — 1
2. *Eniyàn*: The Yoruba Concept of a Person — 27
3. Individuality, Community and the Moral Order — 61
4. Traditional African Religiosity: Myth or Reality? — 83
5. Causality and the Concept of Health and Illness — 105

Part II Contemporary African Realities

6. The Concept of Ultimate Reality and Meaning and Contemporary African Realities: The Religious View — 137
7. Contemporary African Realities: The Cultural View — 161
8. Contemporary African Realities: The Politico-Economic View — 189
9. The Ethics and Politics of Work — 215
10. Concluding Remarks: Development and Human Values — 255

Endnotes — 263

Bibliography — 283

Index — 295

PREFACE

My position in this book has been greatly influenced by two central beliefs, derived from my own experience of the social, economic and cultural dimensions of life in Africa, and reinforced by years of active teaching and research in philosophy. First, I am convinced of the reasonableness of the belief that, if philosophy as an academic discipline is to mean anything to Africa in the present situation of its existence, it has to be made relevant to the realities that confront Africans. Though I have not argued directly for this view here, it represents, for me, a foundation upon which a lasting structure of an African philosophical tradition can be built. Second, from the vantage point of research in the areas of social and political philosophy and ethics, it has become clear to me that no one can ignore the importance of the cultural dimensions of philosophical reflections. Indeed, the relationship between the two is one of mutual influence. Culture influences philosophy by providing it with the basic materials for reflection, while philosophy influences culture by posing a critique, in various ways, of its foundation. This connection between philosophy and culture is not confined to modern philosophizing alone. I am convinced that if we look well enough, we will find it in all ages and all contexts. The denial of philosophical reflection to traditional Africans therefore appears to me to be a "modernist" bias without an adequate justification.

From this perspective, therefore, I believe that we may approach African philosophy rewardingly by looking at the presuppositions and foundations of traditional philosophy as well as posing a critique of the foundations of our contemporary realities. This accounts for the two parts into which this study is divided. Part I deals with the foundations of traditional Yoruba philosophy by an examination of its conceptual scheme. I also attempt a comparison of some of the concepts with those of traditional Akan philosophy. In Part II, I develop a critique of contemporary African realities from three perspectives: religious, cultural and politico-economic, focusing on the available literature in these areas. I end with some remarks on the tension between the goal of development and the respect for human values which are generally acknowledged as the foundation of African social life.

The approach I have adopted here represents my own understanding of the distinctive nature of African philosophy and the way to advance its frontiers. Of course, I also recognize the value of diversity and I respect other view-points. What I consider to be counter-productive, however, is what appears to be an unending dispute about the nature of the subject itself and the continued insistence by some on the myth of philosophy as something alien to traditional Africa. I am convinced there is a need to rethink that position. We need to get on with the positive task of reconstructing an authentic African philosophy which will be distinctive in the contributions it makes towards the resolution of the crisis of African existence. There will be problems along the way. Confusions will need to be clarified. There are a lot more issues to deal with, a lot more confusions to clarify and a lot more ideas that call for reconstruction. But such clarifications and reconstructions cannot be done unless we have made a start from somewhere. I therefore expect that a study such as this will provide a basis for moving forward in the kind of interest that it generates and, I think, that is how African philosophy will advance.

Hamilton, New York
July, 1991.

African Philosophy

Part I Traditional Yoruba Philosophy

1

ON THE IDEA OF AFRICAN PHILOSOPHY

Definitions of African philosophy

There are at least four schools of thought regarding the question of the nature of African philosophy. For one group, it is the philosophical thought of traditional Africans as could be sifted from their various world-views, myths, proverbs, etc. In this sense, it is the philosophy indigenous to Africans, untainted by foreign ideas. To attain a deep understanding of this philosophy, then, one needs to go to its roots in the traditions of the people without the mediating influence of the westernized folks. For another group, African philosophy is the philosophical reflection on, and analysis of, African conceptual systems and social realities as undertaken by contemporary professional philosophers. The basic idea here is that African traditional thought, like any traditional thought, raises issues of great philosophical interest, and that this makes it fit for philosophical investigation. Such investigations may be rewardingly carried out by professionally trained philosophers with the collaboration of those traditional thinkers with good knowledge of traditional beliefs, values and conceptual systems. For yet a third group, African philosophy refers to a combination of these two approaches, without suppressing or looking down on any. The point of this is the presupposition that philosophical thought cannot be ruled out of court wherever the existence of a community of rational beings is conceded or acknowledged. Thus, traditional societies must have had their own share of philosophers and philosophical reflections. Such reflections take on the form of beliefs and values, concerning life and its meaning which later passed through generations of survivors to become part of the communal ethos. These can now be examined by trained philosophers for contemporary relevance. Finally, there is a fourth group for which African philosophy is none of the above, but just any collection of texts produced by Africans and specifically described by their authors as philosophy. This group is also responsible for the view that African philosophy, as presented by ethnographers and philosophers adopting their methods, is a myth. The trend of the debate thus generated by these seemingly incompatible views of African philosophy appeared to have, perhaps unwittingly, identified the substance of African philosophy with the issue of its meaning and method. It is not unusual, for instance, to find a course in African philosophy dealing with only the debate on its meaning. My objective in this opening chapter, is to re-examine the issue of meaning and method, and identify the view I consider most appropriate for an adequate understanding of the subject and content of African philosophy.

African philosophy as the traditional African philosophical thought.

First, then, we need to re-examine the positions listed above, starting with the first which sees African philosophy as *the* philosophical thought of traditional Africans. This is the view attributed to the so-called ethno-philosophers, prominent among whom is Placide Tempels the author of *Bantu Philosophy*. Strictly, Tempels does not offer a definition of African philosophy in general, or even Bantu philosophy with which he concerns himself. The closest he goes in this direction is in his appeal to his fellow Europeans to "try above all to *understand* Bantu philosophy, to know what their beliefs are and what is their rational interpretation of the nature of visible and invisible things."[1] One may see this as a view of what Bantu philosophy is: the beliefs of the Bantu and their rational interpretation of things. And though Tempels says this much, there is nowhere in his book, in which he suggests that this is all there is to either Bantu philosophy or African philosophy. In other words, for all we are entitled to infer, Tempels may, without contradiction, accept the idea of a contemporary African philosophy alongside his account of Bantu philosophy. At least, he does not say anything to suggest otherwise.

Yet he says enough to suggest to critics that he is on the wrong track. The very idea of a Bantu *philosophy* is a misconception because it suggests the possibility of a collective philosophy based on recollections of oral traditions and this is unacceptable to his critics. We either have an individualized and written philosophy or we have none at all. So in spite of what he does not expressly affirm [that African philosophy is *the* philosophy of traditional Africans], for conceiving Bantu philosophy as the philosophical thought of traditional Bantus, Tempels belongs to the first category. So does Kagame, one of his African collaborators. This is how professional philosophers see Tempels; and to describe his approach to the matter of African philosophy, the term "ethnophilosophy" is coined.[2] Other authors placed in the same category include Leopold Senghor and J. S. Mbiti.[3]

There is need for a clarification of the position of these people. As observed earlier, it seems quite compatible with Tempels' position that in addition to the traditional philosophy of the Bantu, there are also modern philosophies elaborated by individual Bantus. So he does not need to insist on a monolithic sense of Bantu philosophy. We may imagine Senghor and Mbiti maintaining similar positions. Indeed, Mbiti goes out of his way to suggest that what he refers to as African philosophy "may not amount to more than simply my own process of philosophizing the items under consideration...."[4] The point, then, is that these authors may be willing to admit that the exposition of world-views is not all there is to African philosophy; in which case they will not be properly located in our first category above. Indeed, for Tempels, Bantu philosophy, among other things, is the rational interpretation of things by the Bantus.

Is there anyone who has maintained the position suggested by our first category then? There is a sort of ambiguity in the suggestion itself. While it may be interpreted [as has been done above] as making the claim that African philosophy is *the* philosophy indigenous to traditional Africans, it may also be interpreted as the claim that the most authentic source of African philosophy is the traditional thought and world-view indigenous to Africans. The difference between the two seems clear. The first is claiming that African philosophy is either traditional world view or nothing; the other is making a weaker claim that even if African philosophy exists in other forms, its most authentic source is the world-view of the people. This second one is my own interpretation of the first category above and I think it is a claim that those grouped in that category may be willing to defend.

Even this weaker claim has not been spared by critics. Professor Hountondji, for instance, has insisted that world-view cannot be a source of African philosophy because (1) it is communal or collective thought and (2) it is unwritten. I will have more to say on this below. For now, the problems I have with this first view are two. First, the idea of defining an *authenthic* African philosophy in terms of *only the* traditional will not do. It cannot be defended because it would then follow that contemporary African philosophy is not authentic. In other words, it would appear to mean virtually the same denial as contained in the first interpretation: that African philosophy means only traditional philosophy. Yet we need to come to terms with the fact that even in its traditional form, we cannot expect any philosophical thought to be static. The thinkers of traditional societies have their ways of responding to problems that arise for them. They could be, and indeed have to be creative and innovative in their responses even when the majority of the members of such societies believe that they are still doing things according to laid down traditions. Without such creativity, no society can survive. So we have to assume that creativity is an integral part of the endowment of the traditional philosophic sages. If so, then it cannot be expected that their philosophical ideas will be static. Therefore, identifying what is authentic with what is traditional may amount to a misplaced focus.

The second problem I have with this position as interpreted above is that it tends to assume that, once we have identified these authentic philosophical ideas, we need only report them without posing any critique. In other words, because they are regarded as authentic, they provide us with the correct thought forms of the people and all we need to do is to learn them, and perhaps be guided by them. This discounts the fact that such ideas are responses to the realities that confront the people at one time or the other and may not be adequate to contemporary problems. Some of the ideas may need to be superseded because they are not even morally adequate; while it is even possible that, though they now seem part of the traditional ideas, they have in fact been taken over from other sources or assimilated into the traditional world-view from the people's confrontation with other realities. Take the case of proverbs, for instance. It is generally agreed that proverbs are good sources of a people's traditional beliefs. But some proverbs find their ways into the world-view of a people as a result of their contact with other peoples. Many Yoruba proverbs now include references to money, to wealth and poverty, and to master-servant relationship, all of which developed out of the colonial experience of the people. According to one such proverb, "even if the eyeballs of the laborer are as red as the palm fruit, the farm owner is his master and he will have his way." This may be interpreted as a realistic way of looking at the master-servant relationship. But two points need to be noted. First, it is not a saying that is indigenous to traditional Africa because the kind of master-servant relationship it depicts is not indigenous to Africa. Second, it is not a saying that reflects the attitude of traditional Africans to the wrongness of such a relationship. Rather, it is a saying which reflects the ideology of the ruling class at the dawn of colonialism. Those natives who were recruited as interpreters for the colonial masters and who were made to believe that they had joined the class of the masters had a way of putting across the harsh realities of the colonial exploitative and oppressive relationship to their unfortunate kith and kin. If we now look at proverbs as sources of authentic African philosophy, we have to be fully aware of this dynamic aspect of language. We cannot therefore just be contented with a report of such thought forms. We also have to pose a critique of their adequacy. Indeed, it is my view that such an uncritical report does not do justice to the fact that traditional thinkers too must have reflected critically on those ideas among themselves, reflections which, unfortunately, are not now available to us in writing. This is one reason it seems to me that we cannot insist too much on the exposition of world-view as *the* only authentic approach to African philosophy. It is, in effect, a matter of orientation. World-view, in the sense it features in the work of Tempels and others appears to be conceived as a static category. It endures over time. That is, in spite of the dynamic concept of vital force attributed to the Bantu, the general context of the world-view in which this concept features is static, unshaken by experience. This is one problem with Tempels. If this idea implicit in the exposition of Bantu philosophy is removed, the whole edifice may crumble, for that is its foundation. Notice that the problem is not so much with the collective nature of the world-view as with the conception of it as static. Cultural experience is, on the other hand, a dynamic one. Bantu beliefs and values must therefore be conceived of as changing over time with their different experiences. This is why we need to acknowledge the existence of contemporary African philosophy, both seen as reflections on cultural experiences at particular points in time and space. As Gene Blocker rightly observes in his very useful contribution to this issue, "[a]s modernity spreads and the traditional shrinks, there comes a point when it is just silly to refer only to the traditional as culturally authentic."[5]

Let me now summarize the observations thus far. As far as I know, nobody has maintained the extreme position that African philosophy consists *only* of the indigenous thoughts and world-views of traditional Africans. The closest to this view is that the only authentic source of African philosophy is the world-views, beliefs, proverbs, myths, etc. of traditional Africans. The problem I have with this is not so much with the collective or unwritten nature of world-views, as with its apparent refusal to come to terms with the dynamic nature of culture and world-view and to acknowledge the authenticity of contemporary thought as a source of African philosophy. This refusal is perhaps also responsible for the reluctance to pose a critique of the reported world-view, as if doing so will damage its status. Clearly, such an orientation does not help towards the building up of a tradition of African philosophy that can be relevant to the present and future circumstances of Africa. What I have said here does not suggest that the idea of a traditional philosophy is incoherent. From what I have said, all that follows is that we should also give room for the idea of modern African philosophy which needs not be regarded as foreign or unauthentic. I should point out here that some professional philosophers have persisted in the denial of the very idea of traditional philosophy even in the modified sense of philosophical reflections of traditional Africans on their cultural experience.[6] So much for the first view.

African philosophy as works of African professional philosophers.

The second view of African philosophy identified above sees African philosophy as the philosophical reflections on, and analyses of African conceptual systems as undertaken by professional philosophers. This also has its drawback. For, seen exclusively, it seems to imply that philosophical thought in Africa started with the emergence of professional philosophers in Africa less than a century ago. On this view, the African philosophical mind was a *tabula rasa* before the first group of Africans set out on their voyage to Europe and America to study philosophy. But it is a view which cannot be sustained because though there is the technical aspect of philosophy as an academic discipline, it is also true that our technical philosophizing takes place within a historical tradition and is informed and guided by the ideas and values of such a tradition.[7]

I would like to combine my discussions of this view with the last view identified above -- the view that African philosophy is a set of written texts by Africans and specifically intended by their authors as philosophy, because they both seem to rest on a common presupposition -- that the very idea of traditional African philosophy is incoherent. While the former relates African philosophy to African cultural experience and therefore identifies it as the philosophical reflections on such experience, it seems to deny the possibility of such reflections in the past. On the other hand, the latter view relates African philosophy to anything that occupies the attention and interests of professional philosophers and which are clearly documented in writing. The emphasis in both is on writing and individuality as preconditions for philosophy in the real sense. This is what I would like to take up here.

The idea of traditional African philosophy has been contested on two grounds: (i) regarded as 'communal' thought, it has been construed as falling outside the mainstream philosophy of the West which is mainly individualistic, (ii) as mostly deriving from oral traditions, it has been considered as impossible to attain the exalted image of written (Western) philosophy. That is, the idea of an unwritten philosophy is considered a gross misunderstanding of the philosophic enterprise.[8] There is one more important view of this denial, arising from a view of philosophy as consisting of epistemology and logic. Traditional thought, in general [and not just African traditional thought], is considered to be lacking in logic and epistemological foundations which are regarded as the bedrock of philosophy. Therefore it cannot be philosophy, though it may be treated as subject matter for philosophical reflections. Thus while we could have a philosophy of traditional thought, we could not have traditional philosophy.[9]

From my earlier comments, it is clear that I do not intend to limit African philosophy to indigenous 'communal' thought. It seems to me, though, that critics of African philosophy who have focused on the 'communal' nature of traditional thought, and have on this ground rejected the idea of traditional African philosophy, have not given us the last word on this matter. The issues are these. Suppose 'ethnophilosophers' have focused on 'communal' thought, but instead of merely exposing such thoughts, they have also subjected them to critical analysis, it is not clear to me what is wrong with that and why it could not be philosophy. Second, it is also not clear why 'communal' thought, in virtue of its being 'communal' cannot be philosophy. It is at least not a self-evident truth that philosophy must always be an individualistic enterprise. It is true, historically, that western academic philosophy has been individualistic, but we should also not forget that such individualized philosophizing has always taken place in the bosom of some communal traditions, with the presuppositions of certain ideas which are not now easy to trace to any one individual. We need not deny the fact that we are all children of our traditions, try as we may to fantasize individuality.

Of course, there is no communal thought in the sense of a group mind because there is no group with a single mind. But from this, it does not follow that we cannot talk intelligently of the cultural beliefs and values of a people, arising from their common reflections on their common experiences. I hear someone saying: "Well, precisely, and those are beliefs and values, you see, not philosophy!'' Yet the point is that this kind of response begs the question of what reflections are philosophical. Presumably, critical reflections that are traceable to particular individuals are, as opposed to those traced to culture groups. This will do only if we accept the original view which is being questioned: that philosophy is an individualistic enterprise. But assume that this is a view attributable to a particular group of people (Western) and a particular tradition of doing philosophy, it is not clear why it must hold for all times and all places? Indeed, it seems to me that we have in this very view a 'communal' view about philosophy which may be cashed out as follows:

(a) It is the view or belief of [some] Western philosophers that *philosophy must be an individualistic enterprise.*
(b) Traditionally, in the West, *philosophy is conceived as an individualistic enterprise.*

It seems true that the italicized parts of (a) and (b) may be offered as common [indeed, communal] beliefs of some, if not most, Western philosophers. If this is so, we have to see how they differ from the so-called communal beliefs that have been condemned as unphilosophical. Suppose, we are confronted with such views as the following:

(c) It is a common belief among Africans that *children ought to take care of their aged parents.*
(d) Traditional Africans believe that *the meaning of a person's life is determined, in part, by the message of destiny they brought into the world.*
(e) Americans believe that *freedom is a value which should not be compromised.*

The major difference I see here is that the former set of "beliefs" {[a] and [b] above} may be traced to the writings of a few Western philosophers while (c) and (d) in the latter set may not, because even if they were recorded in some forms of writing in the past, those forms are not now available to us. Notice that (e) is also in the same category of a communal belief, with the difference that it has been articulated by some individuals and preserved in writing. But now, it appears that our inability to trace the italicized parts of (c) and (d) in western forms of writing is the ground for our regarding them as unacceptable. Yet, the impression we are given is that communal beliefs cannot be philosophical because of their nature as 'communal.' The problem of writing is different. If we are able to identify (a), (b) and (e) as communal in a sense, and they are not rejected because of that, then we are saying, in effect, that the communal nature of a belief does not render it unphilosophical. Consider this point: the various 'communal' beliefs may have their origins in particular individuals who either accepted them, internalized them, or were responsible for initiating them in the first place. If we make the effort, perhaps we may discover this, just as we may be able to trace the first set of beliefs to the writings of individual philosophers. The idea of a communal thought without individual thinkers does not make much sense. But this is what has been assumed in the critique of ethnophilosophy- that it looks for philosophy in a group mind. Why does this seem so? Why is it not reasonable to assume that the so-called communal thought is not group mind, but a result of the common reflections [i.e., individual reflections on the common experiences of life] of a people subjected to similar realities. The mistake of ethnophilosophy will not then be that it looks for philosophy where there is none. Rather, it will be that it does not itself do justice to such philosophies by way of critical reflections. I am assuming that the so-called originators of communal beliefs must have reflected critically and probably criticized each other and that what seem to have become communal thought are products of critical reflections of a people making effort to understand life. The ethnophilosophers could continue in that tradition of reflection [which we have no good ground to suppose did not exist] by using their own 'modern knowledge' to subject such 'communal' thought to necessary understanding and criticism. Their mistake is that they do not; they merely describe and present the 'communal' views to their audience.

Of course, this view of the issue is not acceptable to Hountondji because, for him, the object of analysis [or description] of the ethnophilosopher simply does not exist, or at least exists, only in his imagination. So, however critical the latter is with regard to his subject-matter, he is only fooling himself, since he is concerned with an "implicit, unexpressed world-view, which never existed anywhere but in the anthropologist's imagination. Ethnophilosophy is (therefore) a pre-philosophy mistaking itself for a metaphilosophy, a philosophy which, instead of presenting its own rational justification, shelters lazily behind the authority of a tradition and projects its own theses and beliefs on to that tradition."[10] Now, there is certainly a problem here. I appreciate the main direction of Hountondji's criticism of ethnophilosophy, namely as a misguided *descriptive* account of world-view for an audience outside Africa. But it seems this is not all he is saying. Indeed, his quarrel seems to be more with the very idea of a world-view as collective philosophy than with the literature which describes or criticizes it. For while he is willing to admit the literature of ethnophilosophy produced by Africans, he is not willing to admit the world-view described.[11]

Why? This question is relevant in view of Hountondji's acknowledgement of two uses of the word 'philosophy', though he regards one as the 'vulgar' use and the other as the strict (theoretical) use. According to the first [popular, ideological] meaning, philosophy is any kind of wisdom, individual or collective, any set of principles presenting some degree of coherence and intended to govern the daily practice of an individual or a people.[12] In the stricter sense, however, "philosophy, like chemistry, physics or mathematics, is a specific theoretical discipline with its own exigencies and methodological rule."[13] I think Mudimbe also shares this view in his claim, also without any argument, that "strictly speaking, the notion of African philosophy refers to contributions of Africans practicing philosophy within the defined framework of the discipline and its historical tradition.[14] He then goes on to suggest that "it is only metaphorically or, at best, from a historicist perspective, that one would extend the notion of philosophy to African traditional systems of thought, considering them as dynamic processes in which concrete experiences are integrated into an order of concepts and discourses."[15] I am willing to accept the need for people to be clear about the two usages; but I am not sure that we should, without argument, reject one as vulgar and the other as authentic. But it is clear that, though, Hountondji acknowledges that there are these two uses of the word; he has no serious argument to reject the popular 'vulgar' usage. So, one expects that the two uses are in order as long as a speaker or writer does not confuse them. Suppose that the ethnophilosopher is concerned with the elaboration and critique of the philosophy of a people in the popular sense. Why should s/he be castigated for that? If philosophy no longer refers to the wisdom or principles that shape the lives of a people, then of course, we have to do away completely with that sense of the word and perhaps the English dictionaries should strike it off from record. The problem is that if one recognizes two senses of a word and one then turns around to cast aspersion on the effort of those who take seriously one of those senses, there is need for more justification than has been offered.

The main argument that Hountondji gives against the first sense seems to me to beg the question. He says, "for if we want to be scientific, we cannot apply the same word to two things as different as a spontaneous, implicit and collective world-view on the one hand and, on the other, the deliberate, explicit and individual analytic activity which takes that world-view as its subject."[16] I find it difficult to accept this position for several reasons. First, suppose it is even true that the same word cannot be applied to two different things, then since historically we have always understood these two senses of the word, if we now have to shed one of them, we need an argument to determine which. That argument cannot be based on the history of usage without begging the question. Neither can it be based on the claim of strict versus popular usages. That it has always been applied to a theoretical discipline will also not do because we may discover, indeed, that it got attached to that discipline by attending to what it means in its popular usage which may then be seen as its more fundamental usage. In short, while it is possible that Hountondji is right, he has not done justice to this claim and certainly not enough to convince us of his rejection of world-view as philosophy. Second, rather than reject "spontaneous, implicit, world-view" as philosophy, is there no other way out? If the problem is the application of the same word to two "different" things, perhaps this is one reason why even professional philosophers mark a distinction between analytic philosophy and speculative philosophy. Perhaps we could mark a distinction between academic or theoretical philosophy and cultural or national philosophy, between 'strict philosophy' and philosophy as world-view. As Gene Blocker also observed, "in the case of the more professional, academic sense of *philosophy*- philosophy as defined by the tradition of Plato, etc. This, too, can be variously defined- rather narrowly in analytic terms, or more broadly to include metaphysics and a practical guide to life and, may be, even a bit of religiosity."[17] Third, is the idea of a spontaneous, unconscious philosophy itself not a myth deliberately urged by the critic to discredit some activity which may have been consciously undertaken? It is true that Tempels said much about Bantu philosophy. The reason for this seems obvious. For, though he tried to transcend the ethnocentrism of Levy-Bruhl, we know that Tempels was not entirely open-minded. His denial that "Bantus are capable of presenting us with a philosophical treatise complete with an adequate vocabulary" is one among several which betray his ethnocentrism. Are we to believe, then, following Tempels, that there are no Bantu traditional thinkers capable of elaborating a philosophical treatise? Perhaps, Hountondji does not hold this kind of position. But the strict conditions- including writing, which he stipulates for a discourse to be recognized as philosophy, seem to entail some such position. Yet it is a dangerous position for what it entails: that we must throw out the baby of traditional philosophy with the bath-water of ethnophilosophy. This point is forcefully and, in my judgment, rightly made by Olabiyi Yai in his critique of this approach.[18]

One can go further to show that implicit in this denial itself is an ethnocentric view of philosophy, a view which surprisingly betrays the unique humility of the philosophic mind. For instance, Hountondji asserts:

> The distinction between the two ideas of philosophy should lead not to the consecration of the vulgar meaning but to its destruction. It should compel a philosopher to reject as null and void the pseudo-philosophy of world-views and make him see clearly that philosophy in the strictest sense, far from being a continuation of spontaneous thought systems, is constituted by making a clean break from them.[19]

If we eliminate the idea of spontaneous thought system as a contradiction in terms [and thus a myth in itself], and if we agree that without an adequate basis for representing one as pseudo and the other as genuine [save that one is academic and the other, perhaps, not], the imperative of destroying one or the other of these senses of philosophy has certainly not been demonstrated. Perhaps academic, theoretical philosophy is the genuine one, but it is at least not obviously so, once we set up this kind of competition. And as Yai has queried, "are we certain that we are not still confusing genres by forcing the texts concerning African oral tradition into pre-established genres and categories, because they exist within the European cultures whose languages we use as an instrument for analysis, by calling them cosmogonies, myths, proverbs, apothegms, etc.?"[20] Indeed, it appears that the emphasis on this so-called abstract, theoretical 'strict' philosophy is being down-played even in the west which is supposedly its original home.

We may go further. The contrast that is thus drawn between 'pseudo-philosophy of world-view' and 'strict philosophy' rests on the contrast that has often been drawn between 'folk thought' and 'philosophic or scientific thought.' As has been noticed earlier, for Hountondji, philosophy and science are first cousins and folk thought happens to be alien: it is superstitious, pre-logical, mythical thought. This contrast has been rightly challenged even by professional philosophers on the ground that folk thought is not alien to scientific thought, that judgments of logicality are theory-dependent, and that African traditional thought is not as unscientific as is usually assumed. Thus Sandra Harding, reviewing recent contributions in this area, sums up as follows:

> the definition of logical and rational thinking is itself a cultural artifact that has changed even within the history of Western thought. Judgments of logicality and rationality are 'theory-dependent': what counts as a logical statement depends upon other views a society holds about self, community, nature, and their relationships. The beliefs that appear logical to one who conceptualizes species as related to each other through evolutionary patterns will differ from those of one who conceptualizes species as all created by God in the first week of the universe.[21]

Furthermore, Robin Horton, in one of his useful contributions on this matter, attempts a comparison between African traditional thought and Western science, showing that the spiritual entities that occur in African thought function as explanatory strategies just as theoretical entities in science. Both are therefore attempts [perhaps in differing degrees of adequacy] to make sense of the world.[22] Finally, Kwasi Wiredu has called attention to the existence of folk thought in Western philosophical thought and, according to Sandra Harding, '[m]ost of the beliefs of the average or even extraordinary Western scientist or intellectual are grounded in the "authority of the ancients" rather than in critical, individual evidence gathering.'[23] The point to note, then, is that western philosophical thought is not wholly critical. That is, apart from the existence of various traditions of philosophizing in the West; even those that we are made to understand are critical, analytical and scientific may be seen to rest on some deep commitment to some unquestioned traditions of folk thought.

I should probably clarify my position at this point. I am not defending ethnophilosophy. Rather I am making two claims. First, Hountondji's criticism of ethnophilosophy has not been as convincing as one would wish. By rejecting ethnophilosophy because it deals with world-view [which for him is not philosophy], Hountondji has not articulated a distinction between philosophy and worldview. Second, by supposing that ethnophilosophy deals with an imaginary, illusory object, Hountondji unjustifiably denies the objective reality of cultural forms. Anthropologists do not just present figments of their imagination as the beliefs of the people. Perhaps, sometimes they are to be criticized for sweeping generalizations; but if we look well enough, we will find certain aspects of their conclusion in the beliefs common to the people. If ethnophilosophy is mistaken, therefore, it is in two ways: First, it mostly describes without criticizing and this does not do justice to the conceptual schemes it elaborates. Second, by assuming that authentic African philosophy can only be *the* traditional philosophic worldviews of the people, or nothing, it presents a narrow view of African philosophy.

But critics have also rejected 'ethnophilosophy' on the allegation that it focuses attention on mythical thought which it presents as philosophy. Thus Oruka, in a passage quoted approvingly by Hountondji, is critical of the fact that "what in all cases is a mythology is paraded as African philosophy."[24] If this objection is that ethnophilosophy presents myth as philosophy without sorting out its philosophic import, then, of course, one has to agree with Oruka. Yet it seems to suggest something more, namely, that mythical thinking is all there is to traditional African thought. There is no good basis for this kind of suggestion and so even if we dismiss myth as the opposite of philosophy it does not thereby follow that the idea of traditional philosophy becomes invalid. Indeed, in view of our strong commitment to development, there is an urgent need for us to expose some of the negative effects of some aspects of such mythical thinking, through serious philosophical appraisal.

Another problem that has been raised with the idea of a traditional African philosophy is the absence of written texts. It has been argued that there can be no philosophical tradition without a tradition of writing. This is, of course, true. But it does not then follow that people cannot engage in philosophical discourse in the absence of writing, and so there could have been philosophical reflections and thus philosophers, in traditional African societies. The problem that has been raised on this is how to identify them, and it seems to me that this is no longer an insurmountable problem in view of the developments of such methods of approach as philosophic sagacity.[25] Besides, the results of such reflections are contained in the 'books of life' in various societies. It seems to me, however, that this issue of writing has not been given adequate thought. It is true that as a result of our colonial experience, there is a tendency for us to now see every aspect of our lives from the perspective of what is acceptable to the west. But writing, as Niangorah-Bouah has rightly observed, "is the representation of word and thought by agreed signs."[26] Surely, we do not want to argue that traditional Africans had no means of representing their words and thought in writing. I do not think anyone would disagree with the claim that "black Africans have always known graphic signs for writing" and that "writing is therefore a habitual and familiar activity in black Africa with its roots in prehistory."[27] If we try hard, we may be able to discover some fragments of this tradition of writing as Niangorah-Bouah has succeeded in doing for the Akan. And since a philosophical expression does not require elaborate essay, we may also discover fragments of what we have been denying. The point is this: if we consider philosophy in the first sense identified by Hountondji and we are able to overcome the myth of "strict-philosophy-or-nothing", we are immediately confronted with the question: does the African have anything to offer to the world by way of a philosophy of life? We should all be willing to go along with the view that our focus should be more on contemporary problems of social life and less on the archaeological excavations of past ideas. But this is an orientation, and it should not rest on the assertion that there was no philosophical thought worthy of examination in traditional thought.

Finally, on this same issue, there is the problem raised by Robin Horton regarding the non-philosophical nature of traditional thought. Several authors have responded to Horton's views and there is no point repeating what has been said by others.[28] I only want to make a couple of points here. First, Horton admits that traditional world-view "is by no means static" and concedes the existence of "creative thinkers" who "are constantly making re-adjustments in response to the challenge of new and puzzling situations."[29] But, of course, to make his point in a dramatic fashion, he rejects the full implication of this acknowledged existence of creative thinkers by encircling such creative efforts within the bounds of tradition, so that "re-adjustments are by and large piecemeal, within the framework."[30] In other words, though there are creative thinkers who rise to the challenge of new situations, even when such new situations demand dynamic changes in tradition, they refuse to change! This is another myth about traditional societies, the myth of creative thinkers who do not create; the myth of a non-static world-view which is nonetheless not dynamic. Must we force such contradictions on traditional cultures just by the application of the word 'traditional'? If we recognize the existence of creative thinkers, how else are we to describe them other than as the philosophically minded individuals within a traditional society? What percentage of the members of the so-called modern cultures are either philosophically or scientifically conscious? Wiredu has succeeded, I think, in laying the ghost of this kind of unhelpful dichotomization.[31]

Horton also concedes that traditional cultures are eminently logical (against the Levy-Bruhlian tradition), but of course, they "have never felt the need to develop logic."[32] I understand this as the development of logic as a theoretical discipline as opposed to organizing one's practical life logically. But why must this be required of traditional philosophy? If we grant that such thought systems are "eminently logical", what else is required to demonstrate their philosophical nature? Gyekye has rightly pointed out that pre-Socratic Greek philosophy did not develop epistemology, and that formal logic developed with Aristotle. Yet we do not deny the existence of philosophical thought to pre-Socratic and pre-Aristotelian Greece. Indeed, some philosophers have argued that philosophy in the real and original sense of the word should be restricted to efforts to find answers to the fundamental questions of life: destiny, purpose and meaning of life; that is, questions which address the issues facing humanity and answers to which provide the guide of life for humanity.[33] Again, then, there seems to be no one conception of philosophy that dominates the scene and objecting to traditional philosophical thought on the allegation that it fails to develop formal logic and epistemology seems to beg the question at issue, ironically a crime made possible by logic itself. And it is interesting that, even in the West, the idea of defining the *essence* of philosophy as logic, epistemology and analyticity is no longer taken seriously by philosophers. But, as Godwin Sogolo has observed, "ironically, the rate at which the attitude is dying out in the West is the same rate at which African philosophers are picking it up."[34]

African philosophy as body of texts produced by Africans

I have discussed the negative aspects of Hountondji's position, that is, what he rejects. I now want to discuss the positive aspect, that is, what he recommends as the reference of African philosophy: a set of texts, specifically the set of texts written by their authors themselves.[35] From this perspective, the important condition is that the author is African and the text is characterized as philosophy.

It does not matter whether it has an African focus or not. There are two issues here. First, the philosophical nature of a text is to be determined by the declaration of its author. Second, the whole body of such philosophical texts produced by Africans constitute African philosophy. To take the last issue first, while I appreciate the reasoning behind it, I still think it has problems. On the one hand, it seems to limit the production of African philosophy to Africans. But does this mean that a foreigner cannot make contributions to African philosophy or produce works that may be included in the tradition? I do not think that Hountondji will want to make this claim. Yet this seems to be a consequence of this definition. Secondly, one major problem is the inclusion of all works produced by Africans as African philosophy as long as it is supposed to be philosophy. If we adopt this criterion, I wonder why we should want to have different labels in the first place. But perhaps this is its virtue: the elimination of labels. If every philosophical work in Africa is African philosophy, then we have no need for any further criterion for marking distinctions between them, except as they fall into the traditional branches of epistemology, ethics, logic, metaphysics, etc. Another virtue of the criterion is that it seems to conform to the practice of labelling in other places. For instance, Professor Bodunrin has argued that the expression British philosophy "does not mean the philosophy of the average Englishman nor a philosophy generally known among the British people."[36] He insists that "British philosophy is not a monolithic tradition" and that "British philosophy is not a body of thoughts that had its origins in the British Isles."[37] Finally, Bodunrin makes the point that "the philosophy of a country or a region is not definable in terms of the thought-content of the tradition nor in terms of the national origins of the thinkers."[38]

While I agree with Bodunrin's characterization of British philosophy, it seems to me that he also should have explored further the origins of that distinctive temperament which characterizes British philosophy and which still remains a solid core of the tradition. Why, for instance, is empiricism a predominant feature of the tradition? How has that tradition been appropriated and made relevant to British life so that even the average British can identify with it? Pragmatism is a predominant feature of American philosophy, even in its various branches. But we must ask what accounts for this if there is such a distinction between the average persons' orientation and the professional philosophers'. And though it may be true that the average American is not aware of Pierce's pragmaticism, there seems to be no doubt that the essential features of that philosophy appropriate the cultural forms that are typically American. It seems correct to observe that the phrase "British philosophy" or "American philosophy" does not refer to just any collection of texts in Britain or America, but rather to the tradition of philosophy which, by its uniqueness, has been identified with those regions: empiricism in Britain, pragmatism in America, idealism in Europe, etc. This uniqueness may be in the matter of method of approach or content. It is therefore not strange that several traditions may be identified in a place at one time. A tradition may be built around a unique method of approach or around a cluster of issues. The question that should bother us at this stage in our development is whether an African philosophical tradition can be adequately built around borrowing and appropriating. A tradition that is appropriated is the better for it because it does not thereby lose its distinctiveness. But the appropriator does not thereby have a distinctive tradition of its own! Western philosophy appropriated Greek philosophy; but there is still a unique tradition of Greek philosophy.

The issue here is whether it is desirable that a tradition of African philosophy should be built around borrowing and appropriation. Professor Wiredu has observed that "for a set of ideas to be a genuine possession of a people, they need only appropriate them, make use of them, develop them and, if the spirit so moves them, thrive on them."[39] I do not think anyone will disagree with this view. Yet it seems to me one should feel uneasy if the most we could do is to borrow and appropriate to build our own tradition of philosophy when in fact we could build several traditions around issues and approaches that our peculiar realities throw up for us. Wiredu further argues that "the work of a philosopher is part of a given tradition if and only if it is either produced within the context of that tradition or taken up and used in it."[40] I take this to mean that there could be a Kantian tradition in African philosophy, which is where Wiredu's own work on Kant would come in as African philosophy. If a Kantian methodology is taken up and used by several Africans, then we could have a tradition of African philosophy which is Kantian. While I do not reject this totally, I cannot imagine what it would look like if every philosophical work in Africa were to be an appropriation of Kant. Of course, it may not all be, but why not and suppose it all is? Wiredu's point, made to me in private correspondence, that we need to fashion out a desirable direction for African philosophy is very well taken. This is why I am in favor of a more distinctive Africa-centered approach, one which, in methodology and content, is relevant to the African condition, and why I am still uneasy about treating as African philosophy, texts which, even if produced by Africans, neither have African realities as their focus nor care about the relevance of their productions to the advancement of Africa. This, of course, raises the question of how to determine what is relevant and I guess there is a lot of room for accommodation here. Thus Wiredu's work on Kant will qualify as one which advances our knowledge of mathematics and science which are crucial to development. But of course, there are problems. Wiredu himself identified one such problem. For him, the problem is that "[i]f an interest in the sort of problems in the philosophy of mathematics which [he] discussed in that article never develops in African thought so that no tradition emerges on our continent into which [the] article might naturally be fitted, then it would not be unjust to exclude it from African philosophy." [41] My point, though, is that we need to mark a distinction between African philosophy which emerges from contemplations of the African cultural, social, economic and political conditions, and African literature in philosophy which is neither Africa-centered nor relevant to the African condition.

The second criterion of Hountondji, that a work is philosophy if its author intends it as such, can be quickly dealt with. Simply put, leaving it to the subjectivity of the author to determine the philosophical identity of such texts is inadequate because an author may intend or describe anything as philosophy. But an intention may not be realized; and a description of one's work as philosophy does not make it philosophy. Indeed, following this criterion, it is not clear why Tempel's work should be rejected as unphilosophical.

My own view is that African philosophy is first and foremost a philosophical activity and is addressed to issues relating to African realities - traditional or contemporary. By the latter, I mean that it satisfies any or all of the following:

(i)   it focuses on African conceptual systems,
(ii) it deals with problems and issues African in nature,
(iii) it is based on contemporary African experience
(iv) it is a comparative study and analysis of African realities vis-a-vis other regions of the world.

By being a philosophical activity I mean that it is marked by a critical reflection on its subject matter. Therefore, a report of a communal world-view without an attempt to evaluate will not qualify.

African philosophy should be African in orientation by attending to problems which arise in the context of African experience and probing other problems from an African perspective. Relevant issues can be found in almost all areas of philosophy. The relevance of traditional thought cannot be denied. Contemporary philosophers can learn a lot by probing into the philosophical foundations of traditional thought and the philosophical issues in the views of traditional philosophers, some of whom can still be identified. However, all of these must be done with a view to throwing light on the resolution of contemporary problems. Africa is currently undergoing a deep crisis in its existence. Philosophy can help in the clarification of the issues in that crisis, if not in its final resolution. And judging from the way we have carried on the debate on the reality of African philosophy thus far, I cannot but agree with Arthur Murphy that "[t]he trouble with professional philosophy has not been its lack of popular success, but its actual irrelevance to the conditions of life....."[42] Yet, more than anywhere else, contemporary Africa requires the nurturing of a philosophical preoccupation that is relevant to the condition of life in Africa; a philosophy that is resolved to raise issues crucial to the resolution of the present crisis. I belief that, on this, the various schools of thought on African philosophy must agree.

Comparison with American philosophy

To round up this chapter, I would like to make a comparison between the conception of African philosophy which I believe to be adequate with a conception of American philosophy as identified by one of its leading experts, Marcus G. Singer. For my purpose here, I will focus on Singer's lead-off piece for the volume *American Philosophy* which he edited a few years ago on the basis of lectures given at the Royal Institute of Philosophy in London.[43] Going through that piece, I was struck by the similarity between my conception of African philosophy and his conception of American philosophy. It is this similarity that I would like to underscore here to again show that the idea of a national or cultural philosophy is is not something that exists only in the imagination of Africans.

Marcus Singer on the Point of American philosophy

The first notable point which Singer made is that the "only reason for having a lecture series on or for studying American philosophy, as such, is the idea that there is some significant connection between the philosophers in question, identified somehow and on some criterion as American, and the American scene, culture, or setting. Otherwise the philosopher in question, if worth further consideration at the present day, can be studied under some more orthodox heading, such as epistemology, ethics, metaphysics, or logic."[44] Singer's point here is that the term 'American philosophy' is specific in its application to what may be referred to as the philosophy of American culture and certain philosophers have been identified with that unique tradition. I could go on quoting from Singer's characteristically excellent paper, but it is not necessary since we are here dealing with African and not American philosophy. Nevertheless, let me end by making reference to Singer's most salient point. After citing Royce's similar characterization of the point of American philosophy as illustrated in the works of its historical figures like Edwards, Emerson, and James, he ends with Morris Cohen's conception as presented in his *American Thought*. Cohen had declared that the book "would focus not on technical philosophy [strict philosophy?] but rather on the general ideas which are taken for granted in various fields of thought and thus come to constitute the philosophy of a period and a country even before they have been systematically articulated."[45] And Singer concludes "If there are such general ideas commonly or generally presupposed in a given nation or culture, they would constitute the philosophy of that culture, and one then could not adequately understand that culture without being able in this sense to pinpoint and understand its philosophy. This then would be the focal point for the study of American Philosophy, and this is in fact how I conceive it."[46] This is also part of my conception of African philosophy as highlighted above. No one, I think, will deny that certain general ideas are commonly presupposed among African peoples; ideas which govern their attitudes to life and without which they cannot be understood, ideas which some creative intellectuals have captured and reproduced in literary works. Professor Sodipo's lucid account of the two senses of philosophy is helpful here. In the first sense,

> the general intellectual temper of a culture-its characteristic mode of thought, its pervasive world outlook, its unquestioned assumptions-constitutes its philosophy. These assumptions, beliefs and sentiments do not always rise to the level of consciousness and they may not be formulated explicitly, but they nevertheless exercise considerable influence in a culture. For they make it possible for the members of that society to communicate and exchange ideas, and to live in some agreement and common expectation of what is good and right or bad and wrong. Second, some members of that culture attempt to give a systematic expression to its world-view or to analyze and modify some of its aspects.[47]

Of course, in traditional cultures like Africa, we do not have such general ideas neatly documented in writing forms. But they are also not always explicitly documented in modern cultures. They have to be decoded by great thinkers familiar with the national character of the people. They are presuppositions, even unconscious foundations of common practice. Those who reject the very idea of a traditional African philosophy will probably not be able to make sense of this because they focus attention on the explicitly and consciously expressed views forgetting that behind every such views are unexpressed assumptions which need decoding. Again, the following quotation by Marcus Singer from one of the greatest American philosophers may be of help to put the foregoing in proper perspective:

> When criticizing the philosophy of an epoch, do not chiefly direct your attention to those intellectual positions which its exponents feel it necessary explicitly to defend. There will be some fundamental assumptions which adherents of all the variant systems within the epoch unconsciously presuppose. Such assumptions appear so obvious that people do not know what they are assuming because no other way of putting things have ever occurred to them. With these assumptions a certain limited number of types of philosophical systems are possible, and this group of systems constitutes the philosophy of the epoch.[48]

Notice here, the admission of implicit assumptions, unconscious presuppositions and the idea of limitation of available conceptual frameworks. So it is not just traditional cultures that have shortage of options, contrary to Horton. And if we can have a philosophy of an age, then as Singer rightly infers, there can be a philosophy of a nation or a people.

In African traditional cultures, such general ideas include conceptions of God, the human person, destiny, community, the moral life and causation. Contemporary African cultures also demonstrate the presuppositions of new ideas resulting from new experiences of slavery, colonialism, racism, science, technology and development. Thus themes of freedom and rights, independence and liberation now feature as constituents of African philosophies.

A pertinent question, then, may be raised: if contemporary African cultures generate new ideas resulting from new experiences, why focus on ideas from past experiences? This is probably at the heart of the controversy. But advocates of philosophy of contemporary African experience have put the matter wrongly. For, having new experiences which deserve more attention does not negate the fact of past experiences. Indeed, could it not be that these new experiences may be accounted for by appeal to the past? Can we really be relieved of the historical junctions in our existence? While therefore it is true that we need to focus attention on our needs in the next century, an African orientation in philosophy that recalls and examines the thoughts arising from past socio-economic realities is not doing the wrong thing. Without knowing where we are coming from, it may be difficult to resolve the contradictions in our understanding of the direction in which we are heading.

2

ENIYAN: THE YORUBA CONCEPT OF A PERSON

In this chapter, we are concerned with the issue of human existence. I would like to address the question 'what is a person'? Deriving either from introspective reflections or from observations of life, this question is a crucial one which any rational human being is bound to raise at some point. That some traditional thinkers in African cultures must have raised such a question should be obvious from an examination of the traditional conceptual schemes. I will limit myself here to the Yoruba traditional thought, while drawing out similarities and differences through comparison with the Akan conceptual scheme. The reason for this should be obvious. I have an intuitive understanding of the Yoruba language; and this makes it easier for me to investigate the conceptual scheme derived from it. Second, the problem created by generalization for all traditional African societies has been demonstrated by several studies and should be avoided. However, a comparison of the Yoruba and Akan views on these issues is perfectly in order, fortunately because there are philosophical studies of the Akan conceptual schemes on the same subject.[1]

The Yoruba word for person is *èniyàn*. However, *èniyàn*, has a normative dimension, as well as an ordinary meaning. Thus it is not unusual, referring to a human being, for an observer to say *"Ki i se èniyàn"* [He/She is not an *èniyàn*]. Such a comment is a judgment of the moral standing of the human being who is thus determined to fall short of what it takes to be recognized as such. I will come back later to the requirements of being, morally speaking, an *èniyàn*. In the language, greater emphasis is placed on this normative dimension of *èniyàn*, perhaps more than is placed on the concept of person in English language. For now, however, I would like to address the issue of the structural components of the human person.

Among the terms that feature in discussions of the Yoruba concept of *ènìyàn*, the following are prominent: *ara, okàn, èmí, orí*, though there is a lot of confusion about what each of these means and what relationship exists among them. One way to avoid or, at least, minimize confusion is not to start with English equivalents of these terms, but rather to describe their usages among the Yoruba and to relate them to each other in terms of their functional interdependencies. Beside helping us to avoid any inadequate prejudgments concerning resemblances between English-language and Yoruba-language philosophical discourses, this approach will also help throw light on the distinctiveness of Yoruba philosophical language.

Ara is the physico-material part of the human being. It includes the external and internal components: flesh, bone, heart, intestine, etc. It is described in physical terms: heavy/light, strong/weak, hot/cold, etc. Of course, sometimes its usage seems to suggest that it refers to the whole of the person, as when it is said: *Ara re lo mò* [She knows herself only - She is selfish]. In such a usage, however, we can be sure that the intention is to convey the message that the person under reference is judged as having concern for his/her own body - without caring for others or even for his/her own real self. *Imotara-eni-nìkan* is the Yoruba word for selfishness. The idea is that a selfish person is more concerned with the well-being of his/her body only [as opposed to the spirit]. This suggests that if human beings were to be concerned with their spirits, they would not be selfish. It is ignorance of what is required for true well-being that makes people selfish. The body is like a case which houses the senses which also constitute its most important elements. It is also the window to the world. Through the senses, a person is acquainted with the external world. There is, indeed, no serious controversy on the nature of the body. It is also significant that the question whether a human person is all body or something else is not seriously raised by typical Yoruba thinkers because it appears too obvious to them that there is more to a person than the body.

However, reference to *ara* as a material frame does not do justice to its conception as the totality of the physical organs. Further, and perhaps resulting from this, because different human beings have different bodily constitution, they naturally adapt differently to different situations. A heavily built person will absorb external pressures differently than a lightly built person. Illness and health are functions of bodily constitution, and this is an important consideration in the traditional diagnosis of illness and counselling. Traditional healers take account of the physico-chemical constituents of the human body.

Internal organs of the body are conceived to have their roles in the proper functioning of the person. For instance, the intestine plays a role in the physical strength of a person. A weak person is described as having only one *ifun* [intestine] or none at all. This is on the basis of an understanding that the intestine has an important role in building strength through its part in the metabolic activity of the body. A weak person is thus one whose intestine is not functioning well or who has none. In the same way, *opolo* is recognized as the life-wire of logical reasoning and ratiocinative activities. Located in the head, *opolo* controls the mental activities of human beings. A person who misbehaves is described as having no *opolo* or whose *opolo* is malfunctioning. The mentally retarded is one whose *opolo* is not complete, the insane is one whose *opolo* is disrupted. *Opolo* is thus a material component and the functions and activities it performs are carried out and recognized on the physical plane. It can also be located in the head and traditional psychiatrists generally identify a disruption in its functioning as a physical cause of mental illness. This, of course, does not rule out their also looking for extra-natural causes for such illness if, after a period of medication based on the theory of physical cause, the patient does not improve.

Okàn is another element in the structure of the human person. In the language, it appears to have a dual character. On the one hand, it is acknowledged as the physical organ responsible for the circulation of blood and it can be thus identified. On the other hand, however, it is also conceived as the source of emotional and psychic reactions.[2] To encourage a person, one is asked to *Kií lókàn* [strengthen her heart]. A person who is easily upset is described as having no *okàn*; and when a person is sad, it is said that her *okàn* is disrupted. In this usage, then, it appears that the emotional states of persons are taken as functions of the state of their *okàn*. Is *okàn* then the seat or center of conscious identity equivalent to the English concept of "mind"? This is a difficult question for the reason that the Western concept of mind is itself ambiguous.

If we attend to the non-technical conception of mind, it means "that which feels, perceives, wills, thinks"; or that from which thought originates." This is how the *Webster's New International Dictionary* defines it, reserving the technical sense for "the conscious element in the universe [contrasted with matter]." In the non-technical sense, the mind may be an entity but not necessarily in the Cartesian sense of "that entity whose essence is thought." That which is "the subject of consciousness" may be a material entity. The dictionary does not give any clue as to its nature. On the other hand, the philosophic sense of mind which contrasts it with matter makes it more of an immaterial entity whose essence is thought. Since we are interested here in the question whether the Yoruba language entertains the concept of mind, we should attend to the non-technical sense.[3] The question then is whether *okàn* is construed as "that from which thought originates" in the language. This is an especially pertinent question since *okàn* is recognized as a material component of the body. So is it just that *okàn* is a material component whose activities have consequences for the psychic and emotional, and thinking states of a person and is therefore responsible for them? Or is it that beyond the physical and visible *okàn* there is something invisible and perhaps non-physical which is responsible for all forms of conscious identity?[4]

It appears to me that something of the latter is involved. The Yoruba word *okàn* translates as heart. Following the former suggestion, it would mean that the pumping and circulation of blood by the physical heart is construed as so crucial that its results are connected with the state of a person's thoughts and emotions at any point in time, and that, therefore, between *opolo* [brain] and *okàn* [heart], conceived in physical terms, we may account for the mental activities and emotional states of persons. Though reasonable, I think this is a far-fetched hypothesis for understanding the Yoruba views on the matter. The reason is this. Drawing this kind of connection between the activity and/or state of the physical heart and the mental states of persons requires more than an intuitive understanding and this requires adequate scientific knowledge which is not available to everyone whether Africans or Westerners. This accounts for the non-physical conception of heart in the English language. Thus, after entering a technical zoological definition as "a hollow muscular organ which keeps up the blood circulation", *Webster's New International Dictionary* gives the following, among others: "the heart regarded as the seat of spiritual or conscious life; consciousness, soul, spirit. Hence, a faculty or phase of consciousness or its seat." This suggests that beyond the physical organ, there is a source of conscious identity which is construed to be invisible and more or less spiritual. In Yoruba language, *ìgboiyà* [bravery], *èrù* [fear], *ìfé* [love], *ìkórira* [hate], *ayò* [joy], *ìbànújé* [sadness], *ojora* [cowardice] are different manifestations of the state of the person and the *okàn* is identified as the basis for such conditions. A coward is an *aláèlókàn* [a person without a heart]. But this cannot be taken literally as "a person without the physical organ." A stubborn person is *olókàn líle* [a hard-hearted person]. In these cases, the reference is to the state of the person's conscious feelings which is not identified with the functioning of the physical heart. Of course, it may not also be identified with a spiritual entity beyond the physical organ. There is no necessity about such identification and reference to *okàn* in such statements may just be a manner of speaking, a metaphorical twist on language.

Yet, there appears to be a stronger evidence for suggesting that in Yoruba language and thought, *okàn* is conceived as the source of thought, and that therefore it makes sense to speak of something like an invisible source of thought and emotions which is quite distinct from the physical heart. Referring again to *Webster's New International Dictionary*'s definition of mind in the non-technical [non-philosophical] sense, mind is "that from which thought originates", "the subject of consciousness", "that which feels, perceives, wills, thinks." Interestingly, Webster's adds the following: "formerly conceived as an entity residing in the individual" which seems to suggest that it is no longer conceived as such. For the technical [philosophical] sense, the following is given: "the conscious element in the universe [in contrast to matter]." If we focus on the non-technical sense, it would appear that mind refers to something which is the source of thought in a broad sense. Since the existence of thought in this sense is recognized in Yoruba language, it would appear that we may indeed locate its source too.

The Yoruba word for thought is *èrò*. To think is to *ronú*; thinking is *irònú*. Etymologically, to *rò* is to stir; and *inú* is the inside. Thus to *ronú* is to stir the inside of a person; and *irònú* is literally stirring the inside. But this does not make sense unless we identify the inside as the receptacle for the various organs and that therefore thought as an activity belongs to the totality of the organs. This runs against the Yoruba view of the matter, and it means that appeal to etymology will not help here. The question *Kíni èrò e?* means "What are your thoughts?", and this compares with *Kíni ó wà lókàn re?* which means, literally, "What is in your *okàn?*" or "What are your thoughts?" This seems to suggest that the seat [or source] of *èrò* [thought] is somewhere close to if not identical with *okàn*. But, as we have seen, *okàn* translates as physical heart; and in view of the Yoruba understanding of the heart as the organ for pumping and circulation of blood, they are not likely to see it as the seat of conscious thought. There would seem therefore to be some other source for such activities, though perhaps closely related to the heart. This is where the postulation of a double nature for the heart appears to make sense. For it appears, from an examination of the language, that while *okàn* [as physical heart] is recognized as responsible for blood circulation, it also has an invisible counterpart which is the seat of such conscious activities. It would seem that this invisible counterpart is the equivalent of the mind in English. This, of course raises a further problem. If *okàn* is thus taken as the seat of thought, what function is performed by *opolo* [brain]? *Erò*, as it occurs in *okàn* seems to refer to a wider range of processes than what the *opolo* does. These include willing, desiring, wishing, hoping, worrying, believing etc. When a person is described as an *aláèlókàn* [one with no *okàn*], it means that the person lacks the capacity for endurance. However, there is a class of activities which *opolo* seems to be particularly responsible for: ratiocinative activities. Thus a person who is incapable of simple logical reasoning is described as *aláèlópolo* [a person without a brain]. It is a misuse of language to refer to a hard-hearted person as *olópolo líle* [one with a hard brain], just as it is incorrect to describe a mentally sick person as *olókàn dídàrú* [one with a disturbed *okàn*]. Rather, the right description for such a person is *aláèlópolo*. In short, *opolo* seems to be recognized as the source of logical reasoning, while *okàn* is the source of all consciousness and emotional responses.

The fore-going has centered on *ara* and *okàn* as parts of the make-up of the person. *Ara* [body] is physical while *okàn* [heart] seems to have a dual nature with both physical and mentalistic functions. But even if *okàn* is given only a physical meaning, its combination with *ara* still does not exhaust the components of the person. There is *èmí* which is another element different from *ara* and is non-physical. *Èmí* has been variously translated as soul, spirit, etc., but I think such translations confuse more than they clarify. The way *èmí* is conceived in the language and by the thinkers is better approached by attending to how it comes into the body, and this cannot be separated from the religious aspect of Yoruba thought on the matter.

Enìyàn is made by the combined effort of *Olódùmarè*, the supreme deity, and some subordinates. The body is constructed by *Orìsà-nlá*, the arch-divinity. Then the deity supplies *èmí* which activates the lifeless body. *Emí* is thus construed as the active principle of life, the life-giving element put in place by the deity. It is also construed as part of the divine breath. But it is to be distinguished from *èémí* [breath] which is physically identifiable. *Eémí* is construed as a manifestation of the continued presence of *èmí*. In other words, once the body is supplied with *èmí* through divine action of the deity, *ara* [body] now has *èémí* [breath] and begins to *mí* [breathe]. The presence of *èmí* ensures that the human body, previously lifeless, now becomes a human being -- a being that exists. Since *èmí* is part of the divine breath, it will continue as the principle of life for a particular human being at the pleasure of the deity. When it is recalled, the human being ceases to exist. So èmí is more of the determinant and guarantor of existence. It is the breathing spirit put in a human body by the deity to turn it into a human being. Having èmí thus makes one a child of the deity and therefore as one worthy of protection from harm. Reference to one as an elèmí is an indirect warning against being maltreated. It is interesting that this usage is also extended to other creatures including insects, because they are believed to come into being by the creative activity of the deity.

Emí, as the active element of life, is thus a component common to all human beings. It not only activates the body by supplying the means of life and existence, it also guarantees such conscious existence as long as it remains in force. As an affirmation of life, it also brings hope and makes desires realizable. Two claims have been made about the nature of èmí: that it is spiritual and that it has an independent existence. Both claims are subject to philosophical dispute. First, it has been contested that èmí cannot be spiritual while it at the same time occupies space by being embodied. Second, the question of independent existence is disputed on the ground that it is not an entity but a force and as such cannot have an independent existence. So we must address the question whether èmí is conceived as spiritual by the Yoruba, and if so, whether such a conception is incoherent.

Frankly, attending to language alone by attempting to translate "spiritual" into Yoruba is not of much help to the objector. The Yoruba dictionary translates spirit as èmí, spiritual as ti èmí, matter as ohunkóhun tí a fi ojú rí, tí a sì fi owó kàn [i.e. whatever we see with our eyes and touch with our hands]., and material as nkan ti ara [that which pertains to the body]. Furthermore, however, it seems clear that the Yoruba understand èmí as the life wire of human existence. They understand it as a portion of Olódùmarè's divine breath. But since Olódùmarè is also understood as spiritual, that portion of this source of being which is given to the human being must also be spiritual. It is also recognized that it is the possession of èmí that makes humans children of Olódùmarè. It is the logic of the source of èmí, therefore, that suggests its nature as spiritual. Unless we deny the spirituality of *Olódùmarè*, we cannot deny, without inconsistency, the spiritual nature of *èmí*.

Now, we have to address the other question regarding the incoherence of the belief: how can a spirit occupy space and still remain a spirit? It must be remarked that this is not an issue which engaged the attention of the traditional thinker. Yet, I think there are two approaches to the issue. First, we may understand the reference to *èmí* as spiritual as in fact reference to an invisible entity and nothing more than that. The dictionary meanings cited above confirm this. On this showing, it may very well be that *èmí*, as a spiritual entity is only invisible to the ordinary eyes and may contain quasi-physical attributes which make the idea of its occupation of space coherent. Indeed, this is how people understand free spirit [*iwin, òrò*] that feature in fairy tales. Also, the *èmí* of a witch is understood in this way: it can fly away at night to attend meetings with fellow witches. For this to be an adequate resolution of the issue, however, it has to be the case that the spiritual nature of the supreme deity is also understood in such a quasi-physical sense since, as we have noted, *èmí* is a portion of *Olódùmarè*. A second approach is to brush off the apparent inconsistency. On this showing, one may just understand *èmí* as the spiritual entity which, in virtue of this, has the capacity to change forms, unlike a material entity. So it could assume a physical nature when there is need for it and revert to the spiritual nature thereafter. This would make it neither physical nor quasi-physical. It would just be that, in virtue of its spiritual nature [which presumably endows it with the power of changeability], it is capable of changing form. Again, this is how other free spirits are construed. And though *Olódùmarè* is sometimes presented as having transactions with human beings [in *Ifá* divination poetry], this is also understood in terms of the deity's spiritual nature. Indeed the traditionally acknowledged ability of some special human beings to 'see' and "communicate" with spirits does not suggest that such spirits have physical properties since they are supposed to operate beyond ordinary space.

Finally, there is the question of the independent existence of *èmí*. Thus it has been suggested that if *èmí* is like a force injected into the body by the deity, then it can have no independent existence and should be construed just as a principle or force which activates but which is not itself an entity.[5] I think this is too far-fetched. As I have remarked above, if we attend to the language, there is a difference between *èmí* and *èémí*. The latter is identifiable empirically. But when the Yoruba say *Emí wa* [there is *èmí*], they mean more than "there is breath." It is also important to constantly bear in mind the religious aspect of this conception of a person. If the deity is believed to be spiritual and to have an independent existence, what difficulty is there for conceiving the independent existence of an *èmí* outside the bodily frame? Further, if it is the *èmí* that is thought of as activating the human body, there also appears to be no problem conceiving its consciousness outside body. If we do not deny consciousness to the deity, construed as spiritual [and therefore not in bodily existence], then having no body cannot be a basis for denying the consciousness of *èmí* which, again, is just an aspect of the deity.

Orí is another element in the make-up of the human person. *Orí* has a dual character. On the one hand, it refers to the physical head and, given the acknowledged significance of the head vis-a-vis the rest of the body, *orí* is considered very vital even in its physical character. It is the seat of the brain and from what we have observed earlier on about this, its importance cannot be over-emphasized. The postulation of a spiritual *orí* beyond this physical *orí* is in recognition of this. In any case, there is the conception of an *orí* which is recognized as the bearer of the person's destiny as well as the determinant of personality. How does this element come into the picture? Earlier on, I referred to the creative process of the human being as a combined effort of the deity and some subordinates. I mentioned only *Orìsà-nlá* as the crafter of the body. The other is *Ajàlá*, the 'potter of *orí*.' The idea is that after *èmí* has been put in place, the newly created human being proceeds to the next stage -- the house of *Ajàlá* for the 'choice' of an *orí*. The *orí* is, as it were, the 'case' in which individual destinies are wound up. Each newly created being picks up her preferred 'case' without knowing what is stored there. But whatever is stored therein will determine the life-course of the individual in the world. It is thus the *orí* so chosen that, as the bearer of the individual's destiny, determines her personality.

There are conflicting accounts of the process of the choice of *orí* or, indeed, of its nature. Some accounts indicate that the *orí* itself, as a fully conscious personality-component of the person, kneels down to pick the destiny.[6] Others, however, suggest that *orí* is chosen by the individual after she is animated by the deity with the supply of *èmí*.[7] Both seem to be coherent accounts and may be made sense of by appeal to the language. Thus the latter account may be defended on the ground that it is derived from oral tradition as recorded in the Ifa divination poetry. Second, it appears to capture more clearly the idea behind the linguistic expression of the choice of destiny. For in the language, the process is described as the choice of *orí*, and *orí* is construed as an entity in which destiny is encased. That is, it is the *orí* that is chosen. The picture one gets from this latter account is that of numerous *orí*'s with different destinies or portions already wound up in them and the individuals [*ara* + *èmí*] going to make a choice of any *orí* that appeals to them without knowing the destiny wound up in them. The other account suggests that it is the *orí* itself, as a full personality that kneels down to make the choice of destiny. This does not take into consideration the fact that a personality is not determined before the choice of destiny. It is the destiny or portion that is chosen that forms a personality. On the other hand, one way of reconciling the two positions is to reconstruct the former position which claims that it is the *ara* + *èmí* that does the choice of *orí*. To do that one may allow that position to grant that what is meant by the choice of *orí* here is that the individual [*ara* + *èmí*] kneels down before *Olódùmarè* to *choose*, by verbal declaration, what he or she would be or do in the world. In other words, to choose one's *orí* just means choosing one's destiny. In this case, there is no entity in any form, physical, quasi-physical or spiritual which is picked up by the individual. He or she just speaks the words of destiny and these words are approved by the deity. This looks a lot more coherent. For one thing, it allows us to avoid the problem of how an *orí*, whether physically or quasi-physically construed, can enter into the physical structure of the person to become part of his/her component. But though it avoids this problem, it raises a number of others. First, it leaves no room for the deity that figures in the Yoruba account, namely *Ajàlá*, the potter of human *orí*. Second, it does not account for the fact that the Yoruba regard *orí* as a spiritual component of personality which is, in fact, raised to the level of a personal divinity. Finally, if *orí*, as understood by the Yoruba, just refers to the words of destiny as declared by individuals, then their constant reference to *orí* in supplications and the offering of sacrifices to it should be judged as a mistake. Yet, the fact remains that if it is a mistake, it is one which a typical Yoruba would rather make. The idea of *orí* as a spiritual component, chosen by the individual and having the power of a guardian and protector over them, seems too deep-rooted in their world-view to be given up.[8]

It is thus the *orí* so chosen, with the destiny wound up in it, that determines the personality of the individual. And though, the *orí* is symbolized by the physical head, it is not identical with it. For the *orí* is construed as the inner- or spiritual head [*orí-inú*]. And as Abimbola has pointed out "*Orí* is regarded as an individual's personal divinity who caters for their personal interests."[9] As such, sacrifices are offered unto it. This raises the question whether it is [or should be] regarded also as a component of the human person. I think it should be regarded as a spiritual component of the person. To regard *orí* as a personal divinity is to underscore its primacy vis-a-vis the divinities. This is already indicated by what it means. As the bearer of one's destiny, it has the key to one's future success or failure, in which case it is indeed more important than the divinities. The saying "*orí l'à bá bo, a bá f òrìsà sílè*" [we ought to offer sacrifices to our *orí*, laying aside the *òrìsà*'s] is indicative of the importance of a personality-determinant which means more to us than the divinities. Therefore, as the personality-determining element of the individual, *orí* is a spiritual component of her make-up. This way of putting the matter should take care of any puzzles that may arise from regarding the *orí* as a constituent of the human being. It may be urged, for instance, that if destiny is the pattern of events that will unfold in a person's life history, how can any constituent of that human personality be said to bear it?[10] The answer to this is that, as it has been mentioned above, though *orí* is construed as a component of the person, it is also construed as a divinity, in which capacity it is spiritual. It is in this respect that it is said to bear the destiny of the person. Indeed, this is also the meaning of its spiritual nature. If you perform an autopsy on a person, you are not going to be able to locate *orí* in addition to the physical head. So the *orí* that bears destiny is at once the personality component of the person, [in the sense that it determines that personality], as well as a divinity, in which capacity it is more or less the guardian spirit of the person. Another term for it in the language is *enìkejì* [the partner or double]. As we have seen above, this compares with the Kalabari concept of *teme*.

There are other problems with the concept. For instance, if the *ara* is physical body, how can it be available before birth to choose an *orí*? Or if the pre-natal *ara* is not the physical body, is it quasi-physical? Is the *èmí* that is involved in this combination of *ara* and *èmí* spiritual or physical? [11] First, the time frame here is pre-natal. These are activities going on in the spirit world where the divinities and prospective human beings are construed of as engaging in all kinds of relationships and exchanges. In that world, any thing is conceivable! Indeed, it will be recalled that a divinity [*òrìsà-nlá*] is postulated as responsible for moulding the human body. So it could be the physical body that is involved. Also there are images of physical activities presented: the newly formed *ara* with its associated deity-given *èmí* moves to the 'house' of *Ajàlá,* the 'potter of heads' who is responsible for the *orí*. It seems clear, however, that it is a combination of conceptualization and imagination that is brought into play here. On the one hand, there is a conception of a spirit world in which anything can happen. On the other hand, some of those things that can happen there are imagined on the bases of what is experienced in the physical world and are therefore endowed with its attributes. We may choose to impose the idea of a quasi-physical *ara* on this basis, and we may perhaps succeed in making the account look more coherent to us. However, we should note that such a reconstruction may fail to do full justice to the ideas as understood in the language.

We should next address the issue of the relationship between the so-far identified components of the person; *ara, okàn, èmí,* and *orí*. From what has been said thus far, the following seem clear. First, these components may be grouped into two: physico-material and mental-spiritual. *Ara* belongs to the first, *èmí* to the second, and *orí* and *okàn* have physical and mental aspects. Second, a mentalistic conception of *okàn* is postulated to account for the phenomenon of thought. Perhaps, there is no need for such a postulation but there is no doubt that it exists. We have seen also that it also exists in the ordinary use of the heart in English language. Third, *orí* is also postulated as a spiritual entity [in addition to its meaning as physical head] to account for the phenomenon of destiny. There is no parallel of this postulation in English language, and I consider it the distinctive aspect of the Yoruba concept of a person. Even when *okàn* is postulated to account for the phenomenon of thought, whatever it has to do with this and with the emotional state of a person cannot be separated from the *orí* as the bearer of her destiny. Therefore, *okàn*, as source of conscious thought and emotions, could be regarded as a subsequent [post-natal] expression of the destiny/portion encased prenatally in the *orí*. This may be cashed out as follows: *orí* determines the personality of the individual. The emotional states, on the other hand, are reflections and good indicators of the personality. *Okàn*, as the source of post-natal consciousness and emotions, therefore only reflects that which had been encased in the *ori* originally. In other words, *okàn* may be regarded as one of the avenues through which destiny unfolds in the post-natal existence of the person.

The symbolic representation of *orí* by the physical head is indeed indicative of how its importance is construed. As the location of *opolo* [brain], the physical head is the seat of intelligence. The introduction of *orí* [inner-head and bearer of destiny] as a spiritual element is to suggest that there is more to what is seen going on, and what is more is the spiritual direction of the *orí*. Hence the idea of currying its favor.

Orí is therefore the determinant of the personality of the individual. The *emi*, as the active life force supplied by the deity, is a common denominator. Though it guarantees existence and activates the lifeless body into consciousness, it cannot be the basis for identifying persons as individual selves because it is common to all. Further, that *èmí* activates the lifeless body does not make it the locus of conscious identity because an individual may have *èmí* [as an activating life principle] and still not be conscious of her existence as a self. On the other hand, *orí* is identified with each person; it is an essential component of human personality However, this does not make it the locus of conscious identity. Due to its spiritual dimension, *orí* functions as a remote controller of the person's fundamental activities including thinking; but it is not itself the center or seat of thought. The very thought of appealing to one's *orí* through sacrifice already presupposes the existence of the *orí* which is, in that case, the object of the thought. The subject of conscious identity responsible for the phenomenon of thinking, feeling, willing, desiring, from the Yoruba language is *okàn*, which would seem to correspond to the concept of the mind in English. The relationship, with directions of functional control may be represented as follows:

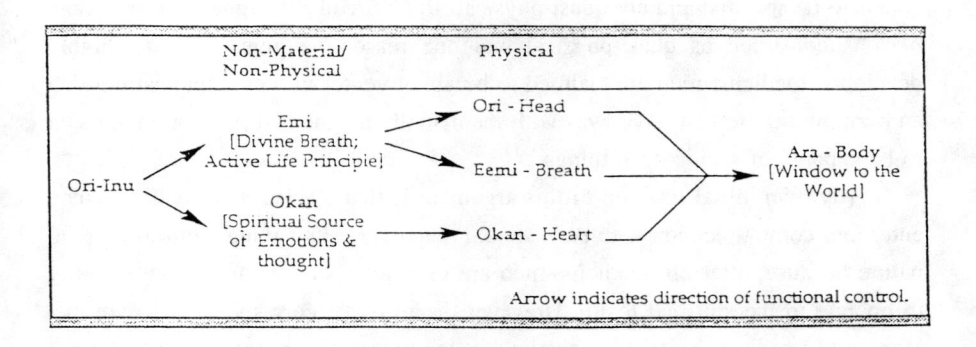

	Non-Material/Non-Physical	Physical	
Ori-Inu	Emi [Divine Breath; Active Life Principle]	Ori - Head	Ara - Body [Window to the World]
		Eemi - Breath	
	Okan [Spiritual Source of Emotions & thought]	Okan - Heart	

Arrow indicates direction of functional control.

Comparison with the Akan concept of the person.

The purpose of this comparison is to explore the similarities and differences between the Yoruba and Akan concepts of the person. For the most part, I adopt Kwame Gyekye's analysis of the Akan conception for this purpose with references to Kwasi Wiredu's as necessary.[12] I note also some major disagreements between the two Akan authors.

For the most part, there appears to be more similarities than differences in the two conceptions. The major difference is in the Akan conception of *okra* which is also regarded as the active life principle supplied by the deity, but which is also the bearer of destiny. It will be recalled that in the Yoruba conception *emi,* which is the equivalent of Akan *okra*, is not the bearer of destiny. Something else, *ori* is postulated for that. Furthermore, according to Gyekye, okra and *sunsum* [an immaterial entity responsible for thought] constitute a spiritual unity but they are not identical. There is a disagreement between Gyekye and Wiredu on the latter's account of the *okra* as "quasi-physical" and his denial that *okra* is postulated to account for thought. Gyekye's point, which seems to indicate a correspondence between the Yoruba and Akan thinking on the matter is that *okra* is believed by the Akans to be spiritual and not quasi-physical. But Wiredu has argued that the Akan *okra* is construed as quasi-physical and one reason he gives is that "highly developed medicine men are claimed to be able to enter into communication with an *okra*, and those that have eyes with medicinally heightened perception are said to be capable of seeing such things."[13]

My own initial reaction to this argument is that the fact that medicine-men enter into communication with *okra* should not suggest its having a quasi-physical nature because, after all, medicine-men are generally believed to have the ability to operate in the spiritual realm. However, in a private correspondence with me, Wiredu has further clarified his position on the matter. His point is this: "The eye is a sense organ and the concept of seeing is bound up with spatiality. However heightened the powers of an eye may become, if it *sees* something, that thing will have to be in space. In regard to any claim to see something, it must make sense to ask "Where is it?."[14] He takes this to be a conceptual point. While I understand this conceptual point, it seems to me to miss the crucial point of the dispute which is that the herbalists are, in such contexts, operating outside ordinary space and time and that even stories of para-physical sightings cannot be taken as evidence of a physical existence of the sighted beings. This is what the idea of extra-sensory perception is all about. If the concept of 'seeing' is involved, it is not ordinary seeing and is therefore not bound up with ordinary spatiality. Of course, scientists may deny the reality of such occurrences for the reason that there are no scientific proofs for them, but as Albert Mosley has observed, the "idea that each individual has an aspect of his being that defies description in terms of the classical concepts of space, time, and matter, which is non-physical, but which can nonetheless affect physical manifestations, is an essential metaphysical assumption underlying the beliefs and practices of traditional magic.[15]

On the other issue, it seems again that Wiredu's account of thought, which he uses to deny that *okra* is distinguishable from soul, needs to be broadened. While I grant that the concept of soul, as it features in christian and western philosophy is problematic in the context of African thought, it is not clear to me that, on the basis of the shared assumptions between Wiredu and Gyekye, they could not agree on the idea of an equivalence of *okra* and soul. For if thought refers to consciousness, and *okra* is the principle of consciousness, then it could be taken as the equivalent of soul. There seems to be a confusion, though, arising from Gyekye's account of a spiritual unity of *okra* and *sunsum*. On the one hand, *sunsum* is responsible for thought in the narrow sense [as ratiocination][16] and at the same time it is the "activating principle in the person."[17] On the other hand, however, Gyekye also says that *okra* "is the principle of life of a person."[18] What *sunsum* does as the "activating principle" becomes unclear since *okra* is also regarded as the "principle of life." In the Yoruba conception, *emi* as the activating principle brings the body to conscious existence and [as in the case of the *okra*] its departure from the human being is death. Again from the characterization of the *okra* as the bearer of destiny, it would appear that it [and not *sunsum*] should be regarded as the component on which "one's health, worldly power, position, influence, success, etc. would depend."[19] This is how *ori* (as bearer of destiny) is conceived in Yoruba thought. If *sunsum* is "that which thinks, desires, feels",[20] then it performs functions similar to that attributed to *okàn* by the Yoruba. But, again, the Yoruba do not regard *okàn* as the determinant of health, worldly power, position, etc. In so far as these various components go, then, the following seems to me to be the picture from this comparison:

1. *Okra* seems the equivalent of *Emí*, but while *okra* is postulated as the bearer of destiny, *èmí* is not.
2. *Sunsum* [as that which thinks, feels, etc.] seems the equivalent of Yoruba *okàn*, but while *sunsum* is postulated as the determinant of power, success, wealth, *okàn* is not.
3. *Okra* [in Akan] is postulated as responsible for activities for which the Yoruba postulate two parts [*Emí* and *Orí*].

I want to conclude this section with a few observations on Gyekye's argument to demonstrate the nature of *sunsum* as an immaterial element. To do this, Gyekye examines and attempts to debunk some anthropological accounts of *sunsum*. It is in this exercise that I find some of Gyekye's arguments unconvincing. It may very well be that the anthropologists are wrong in their accounts, but Gyekye's arguments fail to show this, at least in some cases.

The first position that Gyekye takes up is that which characterizes *sunsum* as "something that perishes with the body."[21] What is interesting here is that Gyekye does not conclude his argument against Danquah. He gives us only one premise in the form of a conditional: "Now, if the *sunsum* perishes along with the body, a physical object, then it follows that it is also something physical or material."[22] And he goes on to show that this seems to be Danquah's position. But he does nothing else to show the incorrectness of this position!

Next, Gyekye argues that:
1. The functions or activities attributed to the *sunsum* indicate that it is neither material nor mortal nor derived from the father.[23]
    1a. *Sunsum* moulds the child's personality [Busia]
    1b. *Sunsum* constitutes or determines personality and character of a person [Danquah], etc.
2. Personality involves such characteristics as courage, thoughts, feelings, actions, etc.
3. Such qualities [courage, jealousy, gentleness, forcefulness] are psychological, not sensible.

Therefore:

4. If *sunsum* is what constitutes the basis of an individual's personality, it cannot be a physical thing.

I sympathize with this argument, but it is not convincing to ground the position that a "material conception of *sunsum* is logically impossible." For suppose the function of *sunsum* is the development of personality, nothing prevents it from performing that function as a physical thing. Courage can be connected with a solid constitution of the physical *sunsum* which then strengthens the psyche. To press his point here, I think Gyekye has to rely on how religious concepts filter into the people's understanding of these relationships. Just as I argued in the case of the Yoruba *okàn*, it seems to me that a pure physical concept of *sunsum* is not logically inconceivable even on Gyekye's ground, unless it is argued that *sunsum*, like *okra*, is an aspect of the deity; and since the deity is spirit, *sunsum* must also be spirit. This may, in fact, be Gyekye's argument as the following seem to suggest:

1. Busia and others claim that *sunsum* derives from the father and that it is therefore mortal.
2. But *sunsum* derives from the supreme being.

Therefore:

3. It must be divine and immortal.
4. After all, trees, plants and other objects also have *sunsum*.
5. But if *sunsum* derives from the father these natural objects cannot have it.
6. Therefore *sunsum* does not derive from the father.

This argument could have nailed the point down at premise 3. Gyekye could have simply added that since *sunsum*, following its source, is divine and immortal and must therefore be spiritual too. But Gyekye goes on to premise 4 which suggests that since trees and animals have *sunsum*, it could not derive from the father, apparently because trees and plants do not have fathers. But must trees have human fathers for their *sunsum* to be passed on to them? One would think that the reproductive activities of trees and animals are sufficient to pass on their *sunsum* to their offsprings.

The concept of destiny

As we have seen, the belief in predestination, expressed in the concept of *ori*, seems to suggest that the Yoruba have some anxiety about human helplessness in certain situations. However, it also expresses the people's conviction that human existence has meaning. It suggests, for instance, that human beings are not on a purposeless mission in this world; that they have a mission to fulfill, a message to deliver -- which is the meaning of their existence -- and that this mission has been fully endorsed by the creator. Whatever is [or is not] done by them should therefore be explained by appeal to this original mission. The concept of *ori* expresses this idea.[24]

However, like most common cultural beliefs, there are a number of philosophical puzzles with this concept.[25] First, the relationship between *ori* and the concept of destiny has been variously conceived.[26] There is need for clarification. Second, there is a problem with regard to the relationship between the beliefs in predestination, immortality and reincarnation. Third, there is the problem of the apparent contradiction between the belief in predestination and the attribution of responsibility for actions to human beings. I shall take up these problems in turn.

Orí literally means head as has been seen above. Ordinarily, the physical head, in addition to its other functions, is used to carry things. It is the bearer of goods and commodities. Before the development of machines and vehicles, human portage was the mode of movement. Farm products were carried on heads to market centers or homes. The head therefore served an economic function. But more than this, the head is the location of important parts of the human body: the eyes, regarded by the Yoruba as *oba-ara* [king of the body] is there; so is the brain which controls intelligence and sanity. Perhaps, this special nature of the physical head, suggests to the Yoruba the idea that it must also have a spiritual dimension. Thus, the physical head is believed to symbolize or represent an inner head which is the bearer of a person's destiny and which therefore is the remote controller of one's endeavors in the world. It is this inner head which is referred to as *orí-inú*, or simply, *orí*. Therefore *orí* is not identical with destiny, though it is its bearer.[27]

Destiny refers to the pre-ordained portion of life wound and sealed up in an *orí*. Human beings have an allotment of this destiny which then determines what they will be in life -- whether a success or a failure. Destiny determines the general course of life, and since *orí* is the receptacle and bearer of destiny it is also regarded as its controller. Hence the idea of appealing to one's *orí* to lead one aright. But how does an actual destiny get affixed to a particular human being? The procedure has been variously conceived, giving rise to three models of destiny. First, there is the idea that the portion gets allocated to individuals as a result of their own "choice" or rather, the "choice" of their own *orí*. Hence the idea of destiny as *àkúnlèyàn* [that which one kneels down to choose]. Second, there is the conception of destiny as the position which is affixed to an individual, not necessarily by his/her own choice. In this model, the individual kneels to receive the pre-ordained portion from the creator. Hence the idea of destiny as *àkúnlègbà* [that which one kneels to receive]. Third, is the conception of destiny which seems to stand between the previous two. In this conception, though there is the idea of choice, the identity of the choice-maker is not clear -- whether it is the individual or some other being making the choice for him or her. In addition, there is the idea of a fixation of the portion on the individual. This is the idea of destiny as *àyànmó* [an affixed choice].

In all these conceptions, there is a common thread; namely, the fact that the individual is either the choice-maker or the passive receiver or the one for whom the choice is made and affixed. On the other hand, what is chosen -- the portion of life -- is wound up in the *orí* which is its bearer and therefore the object of choice or allocation. There is thus a close relationship between *orí*, the bearer, and *kádàrá* (destiny) the portion of life that is born. This has led to the idea of speaking of *orí* as if it were the portion itself, or as if it had a great deal of influence on shaping the course of the destiny it is supposed to bear. Thus appeals and supplications are made to *orí* to either help win a particular battle, or succeed in a particular endeavor. It is believed that if one's *orí* is against one, there is no question of success. Perhaps, there is a justification for this belief in the efficacy of *orí* to influence the course of destiny. After all, in the three variants of the conception of destiny discussed above, *orí* plays the role of bearer of destiny.

A word should be added here with regard to the question of the choice of destiny as explicitly conceived in one of the variants discussed above. A Yoruba song expresses the idea of choice of *orí* as bearer of destiny thus:

Emi 'ò mo ibi ol' órí nyan orí o
Mbá lò yan t' èmi
Ibì kan náà l' ati nyan orí o
Kádàrá kò papò ni

I do not know where people with good *orí* choose their *orí*,
I would have gone to choose mine there;
But no! We choose our *orí* from the same source;
It's only that our destinies are not identical.

Again, this is a song expressing anguish. But the point that I want to make now is in regard of the element of choice referred to in the song. It has been argued that, strictly speaking, an individual cannot be said to have chosen a destiny. This is because, for there to be a choice, there has to be adequate information and rational preference; and, as some have argued, none of this is present in the conceptualization of the choice of *orí*.[28]

Let us look at the problem more closely. The three procedures which have been identified as the manner in which ori and destiny get attached to a person are: [i] *àkúnlèyàn* [chosen while kneeling down] [ii] *àkúnlègbà* [received while kneeling down] [iii] *àyànmó* [affixed choice]. Of these, it is clearly the first that suggests the idea of an individual really making a choice. The second clearly does not; since it portrays the idea of an individual receiving the portion by receiving an ori [this is the version that agrees with the Akan concept of destiny]. The third also does not clearly represent the individual as making the choice; it may be made by someone else and then affixed to him/her.

If we focus on the first version -- *àkúnlèyàn* -- we may now raise the question whether indeed there is a genuine choice. First, let us have a picture of the individual who is to make the "choice." As we have observed before, the making of the human being is a collective effort of *Olódùmarè*, *Orìsà-nlá* and *Ajàlá*. *Orìsà-nlá* makes the body [complete], after which *Olódùmarè* supplies the *èmí* [active life principle - divine breath]. Then, this body plus life-principle, who is now a quasi-conscious individual, moves to the house of *Ajàlá* who is the maker of *orí*. The mission is to have his/her portion of life. The individual portions of life are wound up in the various *orí*'s in different shades and colors, some over-burnt, some not properly done. Some of the *orí* look beautiful outside, but inside are full of "worms"! Some of them look ugly, but inside are solid and neat.[29] The insides are not accessible to the individual, but the outsides are. So depending on the "taste" of each "body-life principle", that is the quasi conscious individual, one of the *orí*'s is picked up. After picking it up, the conscious individual is ready to proceed to the gate-keeper of heaven. There the *orí* just picked starts automatically to replay the wound-up information about what its owner will be; after which it is sealed again and the individual proceeds on his/her journey to the earth, on the way crossing the river of forgetfulness, which makes it impossible to remember what the *ori* had relayed at the gate.

We may now ask: is this a real choice? Obviously, if we are concerned with what is wound up inside the *orí*, the individual does not have an adequate information. However, the question may be raised as to why we should be so concerned with what is wound up inside the *orí* if we agree that in the choice of a particular *orí*, the individual makes a choice on the basis of his/her taste. That this turns out to be harboring a bad destiny, it may be urged, does not detract from the fact that *orí*, the bearer of this destiny, was chosen among others. To press this argument, we may be asked to consider the analogous case of a game of lottery. You are presented with fifty-four numbers out of which six will be the winning numbers. On your own, you pick six numbers that appeal to you. Of course, you have no idea which numbers will win. But you prefer the numbers you pick. If this is a blind choice, it remains your choice nonetheless. You did not choose to lose; you chose the numbers which you hoped would win. This may appear to be similar to what goes on in the choice of *orí*. A more similar situation of choice is that of a spouse! Let us assume that we all make our choices on the basis of our tastes, after some reflections. But it is also true that in most cases we do not reflect at all or at least not enough. Otherwise, the adage that love is blind may not make sense. Shall we say that in such cases we cannot be said to know every detail about our spouse and have therefore not made a choice in the real sense? Perhaps there are people like these. It may be argued then that the important criteria are consciousness of the alternatives [in the case of destiny, the various *orí*'s] and one's own judgment as to the preferable alternative.

This is an interesting argument, but I do not think that it succeeds without further assumptions. It is true that if one is conscious of what one is choosing, then one cannot complain. And in a sense, it may also be true that the individual at this point that the *èmí* has been implanted is conscious. However, there are problems. First, it is not clear that the concept of taste is applicable here since the personality of a person plays a crucial role in their taste. Yet it is the *orí* itself that determines the kind of personality a person can have. Therefore they cannot be expected to have a taste before they have made that 'choice' of *orí*. The choice is therefore blind in this respect. Second, it is not the *orí* in itself that is desired, if the concept of desire can even be applied here. Rather it is what is inside it. So, if what is inside is not known and there is no information about it, strictly there can be no choice. In other words, since the real object of choice is the destiny [life-portion] and not just the *orí* [as the carrier], we should expect more information on the former. Perhaps the important point about this concept is that the various destinies represent the various missions to be accomplished in the world, and the messages are to be born by different individuals. The most that can be done is to seal them up in various receptacles which may then be 'chosen' so that [i] there is no question of favoritism and [ii] all the messages get delivered. But if the receptacles -- *orí* as bearers of the destinies -- are 'chosen' on the basis of the 'tastes' of individuals who make the 'choice', whatever is inside should be construed as having been 'chosen'. As should be clear, this way of putting it does not remove the fact of the blindness of the choice of destiny. More important is the fact that the analogy with the game of lottery will not work for one obvious reason. With regard to lottery, an individual may choose not to choose, but this is not the case with destiny. You cannot refuse choosing an *orí* and this makes it a matter of forced choice in addition to its being a blind one.

The second problem I want to address is that of the relationship between beliefs in predestination, immortality and reincarnation. The Yoruba believe that earthly death is not the end of life and that a person who has reached maturity before death will reincarnate in a different form in a later life. This is why dead ancestors are not forgotten and why new born children may get named after a recently dead older member of the family. With respect to the belief in destiny, this raises the question whether the original destiny allotted to the individual governs his/her later life or whether a new portion has to be allotted each time the *emi* is about to reincarnate. There seems to be not much reflection on this problem in traditional thought. The problem is this. In addition to the belief in destiny and reincarnation, there is the belief in divine sanctions in after-life. Thus any individual who grossly misbehaved while on earth will be punished at death and the *èmí* of such a person may be made to inhabit the body of an animal to become a beast of burden in later life.[30] In such a situation, the question arises whether the reincarnated *èmí* will be expected to have a new portion (destiny) allotted to him/her or whether such a punishment will have been wound up in the original destiny. If the former is the case, it is quite possible that the new destiny so chosen may be a good one such that the reincarnated *èmí* escape the kind of punishment envisaged for such a wicked life, unless there is a way of teleguiding a reincarnated *emi* to pick the deserved destiny. Here, the idea of *àkúnlègbà* [that which is received while kneeling down] will seem to make sense. In other words, the second time around, it may have to be imposed as deserved. On the other hand, if the second alternative above is the case -- subsequent punishment or reward for the first life is wound up with the original destiny -- it follows that the individual has no chance of escaping the consequences of the original portion of his/her destiny. This may seem unfair; however, it is not even clear that we should consider it as punishment. For the suffering that the person now goes through in a subsequent life has already been included in the portion allotted to her/him originally and it is this original portion for the first life that is responsible for the behavior that warrants the subsequent life's suffering for him/her.

There is, in addition to the above, the problem of the apparent contradiction between a belief in destiny and the practice of attributing responsibility to human agents and the consequent apportioning of praise and blame. If a person is predestined to be a certain sort of person, can we at the same time hold him/her responsible for his/her actions along that direction? The problem is the subject of Ola Rotimi's *The Gods Are Not to Blame*, a Yoruba adaptation of Sophocle's *Oedipus Rex*. The main character of the play, *Odéwálé*, is predestined to kill his father [the King] and marry his mother [the Queen]. This was the voice of the oracle as the child was born and given names. To avoid this unspeakable tragedy, the parents were advised to get rid of the child. They did not disagree. He was handed over to the palace messenger to take to the forest and kill. The messenger, on his own initiative, decided against killing him. He gave him to a hunter from a far-away village where he could be raised without interacting with his real parents. However, the theme of an unchangeable destiny continued to sound as the boy grew. One day, he was informed by a soothsayer that he will kill his father and marry his mother. Thinking that he was living with his real parents, he voluntarily decided to leave home to avoid that kind of tragedy befalling him. On his way, he was confronted by a group of people from another village in what looked like a royal tour. They were rude to him to the point of ridiculing his parentage. He was annoyed, drew the sword, and killed the leader of the team, the king. He was his real father. He went on his way until he got to his real place of birth. Meanwhile, the town was thrown into mourning for the loss of their king. They were also troubled by some marauders who took advantage of their being without a king. *Odewale*, the 'stranger' helped them to get rid of the marauders and to get their lives together again. Indeed, he was a symbol of struggle, an optimistic human being who would not resign himself to fate. Hear him:

> Crossing seven waters
> I, a son of the tribe of
> *Ijèkùn Yemoja*,
> found my way,
> to this strange land
> of *Kútújè*. I came
> to see suffering,
> and I felt suffering.
> "Get up,
> Get up," I said
> to them; "not to do something
> is to be crippled fast. Up, up,
> all of you;
> to lie down resigned to fate
> is madness.
> Up, up, struggle: the world is
> struggle."[31]

He struggled against destiny. But did he succeed? For a while, it seemed he triumphed. As a reward for his help, he was made King of *Kútújè*. But he had to inherit the former king's widow, who was his real mother. In no time, things began to turn sour for the town. There was famine, pestilence and death. The oracle had to speak and it spoke the unspeakable: the king was married to his mother. Who is to blame? The boy, the parents or the gods? The title of the play gave the answer -- not the gods. Is it then the helpless victims of an unwanted destiny who tried their utmost to prevent it? This is the problem.

The tendency is for us to try to make sense of this belief by drawing a distinction between fatalism and predestination on the one hand, and between strong destiny and weak destiny on the other.[32] While fatalism [or strong destiny] presents the picture of a cut-and-dried portion of life, predestination (or weak destiny) leaves room for maneuvers within the context of a general allotment of destiny. Thus, an individual destined to be rich cannot fold his/her arms everyday and expect such a destiny to be fulfilled. Also, a person destined to be poor can turn things round by using her/his legs and brain, the symbols of industry and intellect. Again, there is the belief that the character of a person may influence the fulfillment of his/her destiny and if this happens, he/she is sure to be held responsible.

Though there is some sense in this reconciliation, it does not seem to me to solve the real problem. Indeed, one would have expected that such factors as character, industry or lack of it, mischief by others, can provide adequate explanation for significant events in a person's life thus diminishing the importance of predestination as an explanatory model.[33] But, apparently, the average Yoruba, like most Africans, is not satisfied with such explanations. After all, such factors may be present in other cases of other persons and different consequences may follow. It is especially in pathetic situations where a person cannot be wholly blamed for his/her misfortune that the Yoruba mind makes a final recourse to explanation in terms of destiny: what is the case is what has to be since it has been so predestined. The difference between fatalism and predestination does not seem to be noticed in practice in such situations.

But these are only grave situations in which a person is known to have tried his/her human best to avoid misfortune. Thus, the poverty of a lazy person is not blamed on destiny, nor is a notorious robber spared punishment on account of destiny. This is where the question "Why hold people responsible?" becomes legitimate. If a lazy person chose a destiny which makes him lazy, is it his/her fault? One way to make sense of this is to suggest that blame or punishment is not imposed by the community on their own; it is already included in the destiny chosen by the lazy person or the robber. That is, in the act of choosing the life of a robber, he/she must have chosen along with it, the punishment that goes with such a way of life. On the other hand, if we go back to the original choice of *ori* which bears the different destinies, and we come to terms with the argument that even if a choice of *orí* may be said to be made, the choice of a particular destiny has not been made, it would seem to follow that the individual cannot also be said to have made a choice of the punishment that goes along with their way of life.

A final problem with regard to this issue of destiny is the question of its changeability. Perhaps if destiny is changeable, then the responsibility belongs to individuals to make efforts to change a bad destiny. If he/she does not make such efforts, then s\he deserves to blame for any lapses. Is this the way the matter is expressed in the language? As we have discussed above, destiny is itself not easily appealed to. It gets into explanations when all else seem to have failed in spite of efforts. Thus a person avoids being killed in an automobile accident involving a mechanical fault only to be killed again when being conveyed to the hospital. How do we explain this but to say that he has been destined to die that way. It was, after all, not his fault. Could it have been changed? This is where the religious belief which feeds the concept of destiny creeps in. Before embarking on any important venture, a person is expected to consult with the god of divination to find out what will be the outcome. If the prediction is terrible, it will usually come with directions as to the kind of sacrifice to offer, and it is believed that a bad destiny may be changed if such a sacrifice is offered. If a person therefore refused to find out what is in store for him/her, or to perform the necessary sacrifice, he/she cannot blame everything on destiny. This is one way in which it is believed destiny may be changed.

Another means involves the character of the person. A good destiny may become bad as a result of a person's own character. It seems then that destiny expresses only a potentiality which may fail to be realized. This seems to account also for the belief in *esè* [leg] as an important element in human personality.³⁴ *Esè* is the symbol of movement. If a person has a good destiny but is not dynamic the destiny may not come to fruition. So individual destinies express the potentialities of becoming something, of accomplishing a task. If we look at the matter this way, the whole problem of responsibility and changeability appears to be resolved. But then the further question that emerges is this: What is the role of the concept of destiny? If character, industry, sacrifice, dynamism are essential to success, why may the concept of destiny not be eliminated? Again, this is the crux of the problem, but one that cannot be resolved easily. While this last point is understood by many Yoruba, they are not prepared to let go the concept of destiny. For, in the final analysis, neither good character nor dynamism nor industry guarantees a success that is not encased in one's destiny.

Comparison with the Akan Conception

The Akan conception of destiny, as presented by Gyekye, seems to avoid these problems, though it has its own. For in that conception, it is not the individual who chooses a destiny. Rather, it is *Onyame*, the Supreme deity, that imposes destiny and the deity always imposes good destiny which is unchangeable. If so, then there is no problem of apportioning blame or responsibility. But, as will be obvious, this hardly resolves the other problems. The following are the essentials of this concept:

1. God imposes destiny.
2. Destiny is always good.
3. Destiny is unchangeable.³⁵

Given these three facts, one then needs to have a way of accounting for the existence of wickedness in Akan society unless Gyekye is going to deny this exists. For if *Onyame* never imposes bad destiny, and destiny is unchangeable, from where do bad things come into the world? For Gyekye, there is no need for anyone to change their destiny since it is good, and "talk of changing destiny really refers to the attempt to better one's condition."[36] One may need to do this if one's path is "strewn with failures, either because of his or her own actions, desires, decisions, and intentions or because of the activities of some supposed evil forces."[37] What is crucial here is the recognition that [i] there may exist failures [which I suppose is bad, but not included in the message of destiny], and [ii] such failures may be caused by oneself [actions, intentions, desires, etc.] which seem to suggest that such things may cause a change in a good destiny, or [iii] they may be caused by some evil forces. Are these evil forces human or natural? If human, and their nature is to cause misfortune for others, can we say this is their own allotted destiny [in which case, there is bad destiny] or that their allotted good destiny has been thwarted [in which case destiny may be changed]. It appears to me that all three features that Gyekye attribute to the Akan conception of destiny can co-exist without tension only if there is no evil or wickedness in the society. And this appears to me to be contrary to the facts of life. It is also no use treating such evils as accidents, for this begs the question. If the premature death of a decent young man in the hands of a habitual hoodlum is an accident, which is not included in the destiny of either the young man or the hoodlum, the question of what the concept of destiny itself is supposed to account for is yet to be resolved, especially if we also believe in a good destiny which pertains to the key events of a person's life and is unchangeable. Obviously death is a key event just as murder on the part of the hoodlum is.

The Normative Meaning of Enìyàn

As can be seen from the foregoing, the concept of destiny is crucial in understanding the thought and practice of Africans in general. I have focused here on the Yoruba conception and it is clear that there is much in it that requires clarification and analysis. I would like to end this chapter with a brief note on the normative understanding of *èniyàn*.

As has been seen, destiny is construed as the meaning of a person -- the purpose for which the individual exists as chosen by the other self and sealed by the deity.[38] However, this purpose, though personal to him/her, cannot be separated from the social reality of which he/she is just a part. Here is the limit of individualism. The purpose of individual existence is intricately linked with the purpose of social existence, and cannot be adequately grasped outside it. Though destiny confirms the individual's personality, it also joins him to the community, and individuality and community thus become intertwined. Personality is rendered meaningful by appeal to destiny and community. This is because the individual is nurtured by the community, and the idea of destiny itself emanates from communal experience. It is a community-concept.

Persons are what they are in virtue of what they are destined to be, their character and the communal influence on them. It is a combination of these elements that constitute human personality. The "I" is just a "We" from another perspective, and persons are therefore not construed as atomic individuals. A person whose existence and personality is dependent on the community is expected in turn to contribute to the continued existence of the community. This is the normative dimension of the concept of *Eniyàn*. The crown of personal life is to be useful to one's community. The meaning of one's life is therefore measured by one's commitment to social ideals and communal existence. The question "What is your existence for?" [*Kíni o wà fún?*] is not always posed. It is posed when a person has been judged to be useless to his/her community. It is therefore a challenge, a call to serve. It presupposes a conception of human existence which sees it as purposeful, and the purpose is to contribute to the totality of the good in the universe. This is achieved by a life of selfless devotion and service to the communal welfare. Here selfishness and individualism are abhorred and are expected to be superseded by a developed sense of community. But does this mean that the individual is therefore crushed under the heavy weight of the community and its moral order? This is the subject of the next chapter.

3

INDIVIDUALITY, COMMUNITY AND THE MORAL ORDER

The issues of interest to us in this chapter are mainly two: What is the relationship between individuality and the community in traditional African thought system? Included in this are the value placed on individuality vis-a-vis community, the expectations of the community on its members and the humanist foundations of communalism. Second, the philosophical basis of traditional moral values will be explored. There have been controversies over the alleged religious basis of morality in Africa and this needs to be clarified. In the process we will discuss some of the moral values in the hope that they will throw some light on their foundation.

To better understand the meaning of the individual in relationship to the community, it is worthwhile to trace our steps back to the coming-to-being of the new member of the family and community. The new baby arrives into the waiting hands of the elders of the household. Experienced elderly wives in the household serve as mid-wives, they see that the new baby is delivered safely and the mother is in no danger after delivery. They introduce the baby into the family with cheerfulness, joy and prayers: *"Ayò abara tíntín"* [This is a little thing of great joy]. From then on, the new mother may not touch the child except for breast feeding. The baby is safe in the hands of others: co-wives, husband's mother and step-mothers and a whole lot of others, including senior sisters, nieces and cousins.

On the seventh or eighth day, the baby gets his/her names, a ceremony performed by the adult members of the household. Before the actual naming ceremony, the most elderly male member - usually the baby's grandfather - consults the *Ifá* divination oracle to find out the child's portion, the chosen profession and òrìsà. The appropriate names that will be given to the baby are then decided upon by looking at a combination of factors, including the household profession [e.g., hunting family will give a name reflecting this - Odéwálé], the household òrìsà [e.g., Sàngó devotees will give a name after Sàngó - Sàngófúnmiké]; the day of birth [Bósèdé]; the significance of the birth [e.g., a reincarnation or a symbol of a recently dead member of the family - Babáwálé or Iyábòdé-or a symbol of victory over a recent crisis - Olúségun]. In all these, the importance of the new arrival as a unique individual is reconciled with his or her belonging to an existing family which not only decides his or her name but also have a duty to see his or her birth as a significant episode in its existence. The Yoruba say "Ilé ni à nwò, kí á tó so omo lórúko" -[We look back at the family traditions before we give names to a new baby]. The meaning of this is that the child, as an extension of the family tree, should be given a name that reflects his/her membership therein, and it is expected that the name so given will guide and control the child by being a constant reminder for him/her of his/her membership in the family and the circumstance of his/her birth.

The process of socialization begins right from birth. The mother constantly communicates with the baby by tracing the family tree from the beginning, reminding him/her of the nobility of his/her birth and the uniqueness of the family. Co-wives [step-mothers] are on hand to tease the growing child, chanting the family praise-names and demanding gratifications in return. All these raise the consciousness of the child as a member of a family and he/she begins to internalize its norms.

The structure of the family compound makes the process easy. Members of the extended household of several related extended family belonging to a common ancestor occupy a large compound called *agbo-ilé*. The compound is usually in the form of a circle with one or two main entrances. The various extended families have their own houses joined together [to form the compound or household] and each family member has apartments within the house, with each wife having a room. There is a large covered corridor into which all the wives' rooms lead and there they all sit, play and eat in the daytime with their children, and at night they retire to their rooms. Inside each apartment, the children of co-wives and other elderly members play together and are overseen by the elders. A child who misbehaves is corrected immediately and may be punished by any of the elders. This is the first exposure to socialization. Then in the larger compound, all the children play together and, again, any of them may be punished by any older member of the household for misbehaving. Where there is a misunderstanding among the co-wives, the elderly male or female members intervene, or if they do not succeed, the matter is taken to the head of the compound - *Baálé*, assisted by other male members. In this kind of environment, growing children are able to see themselves as a part of a household and not as atoms. They see their intrinsic relation to others and see the interdependent existence of their lives with others. Here is the limit of individualism. Not that the community forces itself on an unyielding individual; rather the individual, through socialization and the love and concern which the household and community have extended to him/her *cannot* now see himself or herself as anything apart from his/her community. Interest in his/her success is shown by members of the extended family who regard him/her as their "blood" and the community are also able to trace their origin to a common even if mythical ancestor. There is therefore a feeling of solidarity among its members and this is neither forced nor solicited. It develops naturally as a result of the experience of love and concern which the growing child has been exposed to.

The process of socialization that begins in the family apartment and the household compound finally gets into the larger community where the child is further exposed to the virtues of communal life. Here children of the community are exposed to the display of selfless efforts by others to uplift the community. They have a first-hand experience of how adults are contributing to the welfare of children, how women and men work on the farms and how the warriors risk their lives to save the community. Building on the initial exposure in the family compound they now see themselves as one of those who should carry the banner and, having been prepared for the task, they, severally and collectively, cannot but shun individualism. This is the meaning of the common reference to the typical

African as saying "I am because we are; I exist because the community exists." From what we have discussed above, there is the simple truth.

It follows that the usual rendering of this to the effect that the individual in traditional African societies is crushed by the almighty presence of the community is not the whole truth. Of course, individuals are valued in themselves and as potential contributors to communal survival. For why should the new baby be so immersed in love and affection? Further, it is known that many individuals have the wisdom to guide the community and such people are well respected. Emphasis is placed on usefulness for self and community and not on wealth or strength. If individual uniqueness were not recognized, how could we have such powerful figures as *Kúrunmí, Látóòsà, Obòkun, Móremí* becoming charismatic leaders?

The example of *Moremi* is worth recounting here. A native of Ile-Ife, *Móremí* was a woman of great strength, power and communal feeling. At a time when *Igbo* invaders were troubling the Ife kingdom, *Móremí* decided to do something. She went to ask for permission from the *Oòni*, the king of Ife, to be allowed to pursue the invaders. After some hesitation occasioned by surprise, the king allowed her. She then sought help from the *Ifá* oracle about how she can accomplish the task. She was advised to perform some sacrifice to the Esinminrin river. She did this and a spirit appeared to her with information on the *Igbo* and how to capture them. Specifically she was informed that they disguised themselves in grass-made costumes which made them look like spirits and she should prepare fire to burn them down. Armed with this information she went back and prepared the warriors against the invaders. They came as usual and they were routed.

Now, before this information was given to *Móremí*, she had promised the spirit of *Esìnmìrìn* river anything it would take if she could succeed in her mission. The spirit demanded the sacrifice of her only son, *Olúorogbo*, in return for the favor. *Móremí* could not go back on her words. She sacrificed her only son for the sake of her community. This is an example par excellence of the spirit of community, the voluntary submission of individual happiness to the community. There are common examples like this in African social history as elsewhere. Such cases exemplify the possibility of individuals foregoing their own interests when the interest of the community is at stake, and so the idea of individual right does not, for traditional people, defeat the claim of the community. A high premium is placed on the practical demonstration of oneness and solidarity among the members of a community. Every member is expected to consider him/herself as an integral part of the whole and to play an appropriate role towards the good of all. Cooperation is voluntarily given and is institutionalized in several ways. Wives of the family [co-wives, wives of brothers, wives of cousins, etc.] know that they are expected to cooperate in raising their children as full members of the family. They are free to borrow household items from one another, they feel free to baby-sit for one another, they advise one another and settle any dispute between themselves and their children. A person who watches while children fight or when tension mounts between two adults is not a good person. Also, properties left outside are taken care of by other members around in case there is rain or storm. Everyone is expected to be the keeper and protector of the interests of others which are, by extension, their own too.

All the above point to the value that traditional Yoruba place on community and communal existence with all its emphasis on fellow-feeling, solidarity and selflessness. This leads directly to the social order of communalism. The structure of traditional African society is communal. This means that the organization of socio-economic life is based on the principle of common ownership of land, which is the major means of production in a non-industrial, agrarian subsistence economy. Ownership of land is vested in the community which gives out portions for individual use as required from time to time. Such land reverts to the community when it is no longer needed by the individual. Some scholars have identified this social practice as an outgrowth of the principles of solidarity and selflessness which pervades the traditional society. This is only partially so. More important is the fact that in traditional society a man is not able to accumulate and appropriate a large area of land because he does not have the machinery and technique to operate it. So the reasonable thing is to have some portion earmarked for each adult. This is with respect to the distribution of land and its communal ownership.

On the other hand, however, the indigenous values of fellow-feeling, solidarity and cooperation feature prominently in the economic activities of individuals. Thus there is the system of *òwè*, a cooperative endeavor in which people help one another on a specific task; for instance, building a new house or clearing a forest for farmland requires help from others. Such is freely given on the basis of reciprocity. Sometimes a male adult with married female children may seize this opportunity to call on his sons-in-law to help with the task. They are only too willing to do this. There is another kind of mutual cooperation known as *àró* in the form of a standing cooperative association. A member may call upon the group to help him harvest or plant or clear the weeds. He only has to feed the participants and later on he may also be called upon to help.[1] In this kind of situation, where commercial labor is not available and not encouraged, it becomes clear that individuality is helped by communality. "I am because we are" becomes an understandable and reasonable expression of dependence which does not thereby mean suppression. For even here the sky is the limit for an enterprising person.

The picture presented thus far should not be interpreted as meaning that there were no conflicts at all in traditional Yoruba societies. Any human society is bound to have cases of conflicts involving individuals who either refuse to conform or who feel offended somehow. Even in such occasions of conflict, there are avenues for resolution in the traditional system. Elders intervene, to reconcile the disputing parties on the basis of the community's accepted moral principles. For instance, a man may be blamed for mistreating his wife and for not considering her interests as a human being. The point here is that appeals are made in such cases to some moral principles or standards which also occur in Western societies. However, in the case in which survival of the community is pitched against an individual's will, it is clear that the community's welfare is more emphasized. The reason for this is not far-fetched. As has been observed earlier, the individual involved also understands and appreciates the meaning of community: "I am because we are." From this it follows that there need not be any tension between individuality and community since it is possible for an individual to freely give up his/her own perceived interest for the survival of the community.[2] But in giving up one's interest thus, one is also sure that the community will not disown one and that one's well-being will be its concern. It is a life of give and take. The idea of individual rights, based on a conception of individuals as atoms, is therefore bound to be foreign to this system. For the community is founded on notions of an intrinsic and enduring relationship among its members.

This same theme of individuality-in-community is prominent in other African social thoughts. For instance, K. A. Busia says of the Akan that

> There is, everywhere, the heavy accent on family -- the blood relatives, the group of kinsfolk held together by a common origin and a common obligation to its members, to those who are living and those who are dead .... The individual is brought up to think of himself in relation to this group and to behave always in such a way as to bring honor and not disgrace to its members. The ideal set before him is that of mutual helpfulness and cooperation within the group of kinsfolk.[3]

Furthermore:

> Cooperation and mutual helpfulness are virtues enjoined as essential; without them, the kingroup cannot long endure. Its survival depends on its solidarity.[4]

And Gyekye recalls an Akan proverb on the same theme:

> The prosperity [or well-being] of man depends upon his fellow-man.[5]

Such proverbs are numerous in African social thought and they help to point up the wisdom of traditional thinkers concerning matters pertaining to the good of the community.

Foundations of Morality

What is the basis of morality in traditional African thought? There are two opposing views on this question. On the one hand there is the view held by Mbiti and Idowu that religion is the source and foundation of morality. On the other hand, Wiredu is in the forefront of those who oppose this view with his claim that at least for the Akan of Ghana, the moral outlook is "logically independent of religion."[6] The same position [modified in a sense] is held by Gyekye.[7]

Idowu starts off by questioning the positions of two schools of thought regarding the foundation of morality: the social school and the common sense school. The first traces morality to society: "it is essentially a social phenomenon. Society must keep itself alive and its machinery smooth-running, and to this end it evolves a system of self-preservation."[8] Conscience on this hypothesis is nothing more than "a complex of residual habits", which society implants in him as if it brings him up..."[9] The second school of thought sees morality as "a product of common sense. In order to live, man must adapt himself to his environment. Experience soon taught him what could be done and what must be avoided. A steady accumulation of this experience over a long period has resulted in a very strong sense of what has come to be popularly known as 'right' and 'wrong'."[10]

Idowu rejected both hypotheses on the ground that they are partial explanations. They "have conveniently overlooked two vital questions. The first school still has to make it explicit why this 'mass' which is called society should be so keen on its own preservation."[11] Idowu's point is that were society a soulless machine, it would not bother about its own breakdown. So someone must be responsible for giving society its sense of its own value. Obviously, God is needed as a basis for society's concern for morality. On the other hand, the second school of thought has not made its case. For it remains to tell us, Idowu argues, "what it is that puts so much 'common sense' in man. Why is it that, like the candle-drawn moth, he does not fly into the flame and be burnt."[12]

I find these arguments interesting but not convincing. But before raising my objection, let us note that Idowu has not here given an account of the Yoruba view of morality. Thus far, it is his own view about the foundation of morality. This view may or may not agree with the Yoruba account; and one may disagree with the view without thereby denying that it is one held by the Yoruba.

Now, the problem with this view is simply that the way Idowu puts it does not help his case. If one says that society creates morality to avoid its own self-destruction, why is that not enough as a reason? Why must we assume that there is some other being responsible for putting the soul in man to think of his survival? This would seem to deny the independent rationality of human beings. The second objection is even less helpful. The denial of the sufficiency of common sense experience as a basis for correction is something I find rather interesting. So we are being asked to agree with the view that if a child puts his finger in the fire a first time, he cannot on the basis of this experience, refrain from fire next time unless we assume that something other than the pain of the first experience intervenes to convince him to so refrain. Then what prevents a wicked person from claiming that God has not intervened to guide him in his actions?

Idowu's view is that "morality is basically the fruit of religion and that, to begin with, it was dependent upon it. Man's concept of the Deity has everything to do with what is taken to be the norm of morality. God made man, and it is He who implants in him the sense of right and wrong. This is a fact the validity of which does not depend upon whether man realizes and acknowledges it or not."[13] Perhaps one point may be granted here -- that human beings are created by the Deity and that the creature endows them with reasoning ability as well as the conscience as source of moral reasoning. However, it does not then follow that given this reasoning ability, human beings cannot, on their own, make moral choices, and determine their ideas of moral rightness and wrongness. The Euthyphro Question is pertinent here.

But as I have observed, this is Idowu's view and we are concerned here with traditional Yoruba account of moral values. On this too, however, Idowu has argued that:

> With the Yoruba, morality is certainly the fruit of religion. They do not make any attempt to separate the two; and it is impossible for them to do so without disastrous consequences.[14]

Idowu then goes on to observe that:

(i) The Yoruba belief in taboo [èèwò -- what ought not to be done] took its origin from the people's discernment of certain things that were morally approved or disapproved by the Deity.

(ii) Some scholars have misunderstood Yoruba religion and morality in their assessment of the cruelty of certain Yoruba practices as emanating from their religion.

(iii) But they are wrong because such practices they attack, e.g., human sacrifice, do not originate from religion but rather from the desire of the Yoruba to fulfil an imperative, what they understand as a sacred duty.

(iv) But they [i.e the Yoruba who sacrifice human beings] are wrong because the Deity's demand is not for physical sacrifice but for one's heart and his demands are purely ethical and spiritual

What is interesting here is that one would expect Idowu to follow through his original claim that as God is the source of our conscience and therefore of notions of right and wrong, everything is traceable to him. But if, in fact, humans can discern on their own, what is good [even to please God] then the identification of morality with religion is not as tight as first assumed. In other words, since the people are credited with discerning what is good or bad [as in the concept of *eewo*] they should also be credited with an independent arrival at notions of right and wrong using their reasoning ability which is granted to be God-given. This is clear especially if we examine Idowu's claims (iii) and (iv) above.

Again this seems to be borne out more clearly in Idowu's treatment of covenants in Yoruba ethics. "Person-to-person, and divinity-to-person relations," Idowu observes, "have their basis in covenants."[15] In person-to-person covenants, the parties bind themselves to each other by bilateral obligations. It is like a contract. But while the divinities are called in as witness to the covenant in most cases [e.g., the Earth or *Ogún* divinities] to give it more force, the essence and purpose of a covenant is to assure the parties of the sincerity of each other. And as Idowu goes on to suggest [rightly, I think]:

> Although every covenant has a ritualistic basis, nevertheless, the obligations which are its outcome are ethical. It would seem that the

Yoruba have found it necessary in an imperfect society to introduce this element of subtle "coercion" in order to strengthen their weak will in the performance of ethical duties.[16]

This suggests that we have a distinction between rituals and ethics and that therefore the Yoruba may have an independent basis for their ethical duties but bring in the Deity for enforcing such duties in the minds of the not-so-trusted fellow human beings.

Theologians are not the only ones defending the idea of a religious foundation for morality in Africa; philosophers are also into it. Thus Moses Makinde has recently attempted "to defend the religious foundation of an African system of morality and to show that this position is reasonably defensible, in spite of the views of some contemporary Africans to the contrary."[17] His position is that "whatever else anybody may say, religion is surely a competing foundational theory of morals in African societies."[18] In defence of this position, which appears to be a modest one, he gives some arguments and appealed to the authorities of Kant, Mill and Awolowo. I must say, however, unfortunately, that the defence does not succeed because the considerations brought in its support are too weak for the realization of the objective. I would like to examine here six arguments which I have been able to dig out from the clusters of considerations that Makinde has urged us to accept.

The first argument is based on the authority of Mbiti who has asserted that Africans live in a religious universe. Makinde's argument, based on this, may be reconstructed as follows:

1. Africans live in a religious universe [as confirmed by Mbiti and others].
2. Religion plays a great role in the lives of African peoples [another way of putting the first premise].
3. All their activities must be influenced by one religion or the other [yet another way of putting the first premise].
4. Therefore an African system of morality , based on African cultural beliefs, **must** have a religious foundation.[19]

Spread out in this way, it seems obvious that the conclusion does not follow. Even if we grant that premise 1 is true, and that premises 2 and 3 are just other ways of stating premise 1, premise 4 still does not follow. Religion may influence peoples' activities and play a great role in their lives. This is still a long way from the conclusion that therefore morality must have a religious foundation. At best, we may conclude that religion may [even must] have influence on their morality. But from this, it does not still follow that it is the foundation. To say it is the foundation or must be the foundation is to suggest that without religion, the people cannot have any conception of what is good or bad. Perhaps this is what Makinde wants to establish, but this argument is too weak to accomplish that task.

2. In his second argument, it seems to me that Makinde's purpose is to establish the meaning of the claim that Africans live in a religious universe by connecting it with their belief in God's existence. However, the argument here even seems to me to be less successful. Makinde notes that:

[a]. Some religions are based on a belief in God, Jesus Christ, Prophet Mohammed and in lesser deities.....

[b]. The existence of God cannot be established empirically, neither can it be established by *a priori* reasoning.

[c]. Nonetheless, Africans, like the rest of the universe, do believe in the existence of God and do attempt to establish His existence *a priori* [does this include traditional priests too?]

[d]. But the existence of God can be established *a priori* only if that existence is completely independent of experience.

[e]. If African systems of morality depend on the existence of the deity, then perhaps morality can be established *a priori* too, since it will be completely independent of what is.

[f]. African morality is prescriptive and *a priori*, not descriptive or empirical.

[g]. Therefore, because African system of morality is prescriptive and *a priori*, the idea of [the will] of God [which is also established *a priori*] comes in as a ready foundation for it.[20]

The problem with this argument seems easy to identify. To establish that an African system of morality can be established *a priori*, he ties it with the existence of the Deity in premise [e]. But premise [g] now uses the same premise that African morality is *a priori* to conclude that therefore it has a religious foundation. In other words, Makinde is urging on us the following:

i. If African system of morality depends on the existence of the Deity, then morality can be established *a priori*.
ii. African system of morality can be established *a priori*.
iii. Therefore, because it is *a priori* and prescriptive, it depends on the existence of the deity. [This can be the only meaning of "the will of God comes in as a ready foundation" in this context].

Spelled out in this way, the probem with the argument seems obvious.

3. The third argument is an appeal to the authority of Idowu and others.[21] If my argument against Idowu's position is sound, Makinde's appeal to it falls with that position. Besides, it is important to note that the idea of taboo among a people is not an adequate proof of their having a religious foundation for their moral system. The wise people of a community have their own well-tried ways of motivating their less cooperative members to perform. If there is an appeal to God or religion, as in some taboos, it is only to influence behavior. But surely the concept of support should not be confused with that of foundation. Consider this. A building has a foundation. When, however, the foundation becomes weak, there is the danger of its collapse. Then the owner is advised either to demolish it and rebuild or provide a support for it. In our traditional villages, it is a common practice to prop up buildings with columns or beams. Furthermore, it cannot be true that the idea of "things not to be eaten" [taboo] is never understood except in connection with religion.[22] And even if it is, it is not quite clear how that could help the case of a religious foundation for morality. *Obàtálá*, the Yoruba deity of creativity, hates palm wine. His devotees are therefore forbidden to take it-perhaps a clear case of a taboo from religion. But *Orúnmìlà*, the deity of wisdom has no such taboo for his devotees. From Makinde's showing, drinking palm wine [against *Obàtálá*'s injunction] must also be an offence against *Olódùmarè* since any offence

against the lesser deities is also an offence against the supreme deity. But are the devotees of *Orúnmìlà* who drink palm wine also committing an offence against *Olódùmarè*? Perhaps not. For we may say that since they are devotees of different deities, what is morally wrong for one [*Obàtálá*] is just not so for the other [*Orúnmìlà*]. What is not clear is how this helps the case of a religious foundation for morality. For we now have a relativity of morals in which what is right is determined by particular *òrìsà*'s. Since people serve different gods, how they are expected to organize their social life from a moral perspective is not clear if we deny them an independent source of morality.

4. There is, next, an appeal to the authority of Kant which may be reconstructed as follows:

1. Though Kant argues against our need for God in a moral law, he nevertheless based his moral law on the Golden rule [do unto others as you would wish them do unto you]
2. This is a corollary of the biblical injunction: love thy neighbor as thyself.
3. Since Kant's statement is in every sense similar to that of the Bible, there is the possibility that he actually derived his categorical imperative from the same source and later claimed that morality did not depend or not based on religion.[23]

There seems to me to be a problem with this argument. Kant insists that the categorical imperative is a principle of reason. Even if there is reference to the golden rule in Kant's theory, does this make it the foundation of the theory? Is there no difference between the golden rule and the categorical imperative even in terms of their logic? Notice that the golden rule takes its cue from what "you would wish others do unto you." Thus if you would wish other people to steal from you, you would presumably be free to steal from them, following the golden rule. But the categorical imperative does not depend on any prior desire, at least in Kant's various formulations of it. It is a formula of reason. Kant's theory, of course, has its problems. But a motive of basing that theory on religion or God is hardly an adequate criticism of it.

Makinde also takes Mill's reference to the golden rule as an evidence that he thereby derives it from the Bible. Mill's point is that *even* Jesus of Nazareth lived by and preached the ideas that make up the content of the utilitarian morality. In other words, Mill would say that more than anything else, Jesus was a utilitarian! Which is to say that the utilitarian ethics was the *basis* of Jesus' injunction as contained in the golden rule. Since there was an historical Jesus, Mill's point is that he [Jesus] understood and utilized the insights that inform the utilitarian theory. Recall here, again, the Euthyphro question. We may well ask why Jesus recommended the golden rule. The answer, for Mill, is that because he knows that the general consequence of following that principle is good. And regarding the appeal to the authority of Chief Awolowo who, according to Makinde "is convinced that virtually all systems of good morality spring from the Bible"[24], we can only infer that, contrary to what Makinde has deduced from this claim, it must be Awolowo's view that traditional Yoruba, as other Africans, had no [good] morality until the Bible was introduced to them. I am not sure that this view could be attributed to Awolowo. But assume that it is a view that Awolowo may in fact be willing to have attributed to himself. This fact alone does not make the view correct. For there are a number of other people who hold quite contrary views, and we need to weigh the reasons for each of the views. Tai Solarin, for instance, comes from the same home town as Awolowo and he would certainly deny that view. I am sure that if we look close enough there would be at least a few Tai Solarins in the traditional society. Are we to say that such people cannot behave in a morally responsible way? Or that in the traditional society, they are not given due respect if they so behave?

5. A fifth argument is supposedly derived from the Yoruba understanding of the dialectics of good and evil as necessary for a meaningful experience of reality. The following is a reconstruction of a very obscure passage.

1. Moral principles only make sense when we can distinguish between moral and immoral acts, between good and evil.

2. The concept of good and evil [*ire* and *ibi*] are necessary for our understanding of moral concepts and moral principles.
3. God's will is the source of good and evil in man's behavior without which we would never have had the concept of morality.
4. Therefore God must be the source of our concept of morality.
5. Therefore God is the source of our moral ideas.[25]

This reconstruction of the argument should reveal the problem with it: premise 3, which seems to be the crucial one for the conclusion is asserted without any argument.

Finally, I would like to comment briefly on Makinde's use of the *Ifá* literary corpus. Put simply, I do not think that it helps his case. It is true that the most important religious and moral ideas of the Yoruba are contained in the *Ifá* corpus. But, as is clear to even the traditionalists, *Ifá* is not only a religion. It is, as Abimbola puts it, also "a literary and philosophical system." Furthermore, it is "the store-house of Yoruba culture inside which the Yoruba comprehension of their own historical experiences and understanding of their environment can always be found."[26] Makinde himself refers to it as "the ancient wisdom" of the Yoruba.[27] The *Odù*'s make use of parables to teach moral ideas, in most cases, without reference to Olodumare or the other deities. Makinde also provides a clear illustration of such cases in his first example which deals with the ethic of respect for elders and the consequences of breaking it as a moral law: "Don't you know that prosperity ever eludes those who assault a *Babaláwo* of high repute, long life will not be within the reach of those who beat up reputable herbalists. Surely a young man who physically assaults a Mallam at his prayer is courting premature death."[28] The point of this *Odù* is to emphasize the undesirable consequence [in this world] of disrespect for elders, not just for experts. Besides, Yoruba proverbs, regarded as signposts in Yoruba ethics, also feature numerous cautionary notes of good behavior and respect for elders. Thus, they say "*omo tó mó ìyá rè lójú, òsì ni yóó ta omo náà pa* [a child who makes an abusive face at his mother will die in abject penury]. Or *omo tí kò gbó ti ìyá, tí kò gbó ti baba, òde níí lé'mo wálé* [a child who habitually disobeys his mother and pays no heed to his father's admonitions, will need to seek refuge with the same parents, when chased [from outside] by malevolent strangers."[29] These make no reference to oracles or religion. It is clear, from the foregoing, that Makinde has not succeeded in making a case for the idea of a religious foundation for morality in Yoruba thought.

It is one thing to claim that religion influences peoples' approach to moral behavior; but another thing entirely to argue that religion *must* be the foundation of their morality. To say that religion is the foundation of a people's morality is to say that without it they could not behave in a morally responsible manner. But the questions remain: which comes first, religion or morality? Indeed, is it not plausible to suggest that it is the concern that people have about their moral and social relationships that force religious concerns on them? Second, is it really the case that we do not have people who are not bothered about spiritual issues among the traditional Yoruba? I have myself argued elsewhere[30] that there are evidences for the view that some moral values have a religious *influence* for virtually all Nigerian traditional thinkers, but that this does not mean that morality is founded on religion or that a further ultimate source cannot be found for their moral ideas. I referred to the belief common among the Yoruba that a person who is morally good, who is generous in giving, or respectful to elders, or chaste in words and deeds would find favor with the gods and, barring the evil machinations of the people of the world, he or she would prosper. I then observed that from this last point, it appears that "morality is also justified by reference to its consequences for the individual. It seems now the answer to the question "Why be morally good?" is the prudential one: "It will pay you." This appears to be the ultimate appeal for moral goodness in traditional Nigerian world-views.[31] As a Yoruba saying puts it: *Enití ó se oore, ó seé fún ara rè, enití ó se ìkà, ó seé fún ara rè. Ati oore àti ìkà, òkan kìí gbé. Ojó àtisùn l'ó sòro.* [The person who perform good deeds does so for him/herself. The person who performs wicked acts does so for him/herself. Neither good deeds nor wicked acts will go unrewarded. The time of death is the hard fact that should be born in mind]. Of course, this is not to say that the Yoruba therefore emphasize selfish considerations in moral matters. The question why should I be morally good is not posed by everyone. It is posed by those who have inclinations to do otherwise. They are the selfish ones who need to be motivated for reasons that appeal to themselves. The point, therefore, is that, for those who may, for selfish reasons, not be motivated to do what is right, there are considerations in the system to help them. The important thing is to get people to do what is right. There are several evidences for this contention.[32] In Yoruba world-view, a person is expected to show hospitality and generosity to others since s/he may sometimes be in a position in which s/he would need the hospitality of others, and if s/he has denied it to others sometimes, s/he cannot expect to have it from anyone. For "the calabash which contains poison does not break easily" [*Igbá oró kì í fó*], meaning whatever one sows, one would reap; or on the positive side, "kindness begets kindness" [*oore loore í wó tò*]. Even when it cannot be guaranteed that one would reap the fruits of one's character in one's life-time, moral goodness is still enjoined by appeal to one's moment of death -- so that it may be a peaceful one.

A wealthy and powerful person who thinks he or she may afford to be selfish and arrogant should think twice then. On the one hand, no one knows what tomorrow may bring. Today's powerful human being may be the most underprivileged tomorrow. A wise person would therefore be open handed and respectful of others, however poor and wretched they may be. Even when people are sure that they cannot themselves need help from anyone; they should think of their children's fate. For their own seeds of selfishness or, indeed, real wickedness, the Yoruba believe, would be reaped by their children. On the other hand, one of the most valued things in life is a peaceful moment of death. For this is generally regarded as an indication of a pleasant life in the land of the dead. A wicked person, it is believed, would start paying for his or her deeds on the death-bed by an unusual agony that would be their lot. Far from having a religious foundation, then, we have here a system of morality which, while it makes use of religion as a motivating factor, is clearly pragmatic and this-worldly to the core.

Iwà: The Primacy of Existence and Character

Iwà is, for the Yoruba, perhaps the most important moral concept. A person is morally evaluated according to his/her *iwà* - whether good or bad. A miser [*ahun*] is an *oníwà-burúkú*; a generous person [*òlàwó*] is an *oníwà-rere*. A gentle person is an *oníwà- pèlé*; a short-tempered aggressive person [*onínú fùfù*] is an *oníwà-líle*. It is interesting, though, that each of these evaluations has an adjective attached, suggesting that *iwà* may be good or bad, gentle or tough, generous or stingy. *Iwà* as character needs further elaboration.

That elaboration has been provided by Wande Abimbola and Roland Abiodun in two original contributions to the issue. According to Abimbola, the original meaning of *iwà* is "the fact of being, living or existing." So *iwà* means existence. *Iwà* as character is therefore a derivative from this original. In its original meaning, the perfect ideal of *iwà* is *àikú* (immortality). Hence the saying "*Aikú parí iwà*" [immortality completes existence or immortality is perfect existence].[33] However, *iwà* [as character] and *iwà* [as existence] do not just have a homophonous relationship; they are also related by etymology and one appears to be a derivation of the other.[34]

Iwà as existence has a strong connection with *iwà* as character. According to a myth recorded in the Ifa Literary Corpus, *Iwà*, the daughter of *Sùúrù* -- the first child of *Olódùmarè*, was married to *Orúnmìlà*. *Iwà* was extremely beautiful, but lacked good behavior and character. When *Orúnmìlà* can no longer accommodate her bad dispositions, he sent her packing. However, he later discovered a terrible plunge in his fortunes which had been made possible by *Iwà*'s presence. He therefore decided to seek out for *Iwà* again, even if it meant selling all his property. He eventually went out looking for *Iwà*, singing the praise names of *Iwà* along the way : "*Iwà, Iwà l'à nwá, Iwà. Kámúrágbá tarágbá, Iwà; Iwà, l'à nwá, Iwà*" etc. He got her back finally; but he [not *Iwà* and her misbehavior] was blamed. The moral is that he is expected to be tolerant; to understand *Iwà* for what she is: "*Mo iwà fún oníwà.*"

As Abiodun rightly noted, it is noteworthy that *Iwà* [as the one with bad character] is not blamed, but *Orúnmìlà* [who cannot tolerate her] is blamed.[35] This should point to another element in the emphasis on individuality in the tradition. *Iwà* is the handiwork of the deity; the originator of existence; and her beauty as well as her character are expressions of her existence as an individual being. The fact of existence which *Iwà* illustrates is an endowment of the deity. Her beauty is consistent with that endowment and so *Orúnmìlà* is expected to treat her as an individual expression of *Olódùmarè*'s creativity. Existence is primary, then, and character is derivative, based as it is, on human ideas of morality. Each creature of *Olódùmarè* is thought of as having its beauty [*Iwà l'ewà*] by the fact of its existence, and it is not to be undermined by human valuation. Thus among the Yoruba there are admirers and devotees of such historical figures and deities as *Sàngó* [inspite of his recognition as a strict disciplinarian], *Èsù* [trickster god, in spite of his unpredictability], *Sònpònná* [god of smallpox]. All these manifest characters which may be inadequate in human terms.[36] And physically deformed persons are also expected to be appreciated and respected in virtue of their special relationship to *Orìsà-nlá*, the creation divinity who is supposed to have made them specially as his devotees. Thus they deserve special protection: *òwò òrìsà làá fíí wo àfin*.

Yet *iwà* as character is given its own place too. Individuality is symbolized by the appeal to *Iwà* [as existence], the wife of *Orúnmìlà*. On the other hand, paradoxically, it is *Sùúrù*, [the father of *Iwà*] that symbolizes the idea of *iwà* as character. *Sùúrù* means patience. Patience is therefore symbolically the father [we may say master] of *Iwà* [in both senses]. *Iwà* [as existence], wife of *Orúnmìlà* who lacks good character needs patience to understand her, deal with her and, if possible, transform her. On the other hand, *iwà* [as character] is a child of *Sùúrù* [patience] in the sense that patience is the overall embodiment of good character.-- *Agbà t'ó ní sùúrù, ohun gbogbo l'óní*.-- [The elder who has *Sùúrù* has everything]. *Sùúrù* is the source of gentle character [or *iwà pèlé*] and good character [*iwà rere*]. A demonstration of *iwà pèlé* is to be mindful of the individuality of others, to treat them gently, to be tolerant and accommodating of the peculiarity of others' existence. The Yoruba expression *"Iwà l'ewà"* depicts their understanding of existence itself as constituting beauty, while the cognate expression *"Iwà rere l'èsó èniyàn"* [Good character - good existence - is the adornment of a human being] depicts the significance attached to good character. An existence, in virtue of its source in the deity, is good and to be appreciated. It is good to exist. Existence itself is beautiful. But however beautiful a thing is, there is always room for improvement. There are degrees of beauty. Thus an original beauty of existence could be improved upon by adorning it with character. The difference between one form of existence and another would then be located in the quality of its adornment, that is, the quality of its character. This is the meaning of *ìwà rere l'èsó èniyàn*. But *èsó* [cosmetic] is fleeting; it could fade. Does this mean that *ìwà* [character] could fade too? It would appear so. It is not unusual to find a person who has been known to be a very good model of excellent character [*omolúwàbí*] suddenly turn bad. This may be due to several factors: downturn in fortunes, sudden and shocking loss of a loved one, etc. The case of *Efúnsetán Aníwúrà, Iyálóde Ibadan* comes readily to mind here. In the play written by Akinwumi Isola, Efunsetan is presented as a very cheerful and generous woman. Then something happened. Her only daughter died during childbirth and suddenly Efunsetan turned monstrous, committing all kinds of atrocities. The point that needs to be noted in this is that even in such cases, when the cosmetic of existence suddenly disappears, there still remains the core of existence and its original beauty. The moral that appears to come out of this, therefore, is that to avoid this sudden degeneration of *ìwà* [character], there is need for character training from the beginning so that the cosmetic of *ìwà* [character] may have time to sink into the core of *ìwà* [existence] very early in life. This is what the socialization process is all about, though the limits on how far it can go are also very well appreciated in the pragmatic approach of the people to moral education. Both concepts of *ìwà* are therefore important for our understanding Yoruba moral ideas and attention is normally paid to them in traditional patterns of moral education.

Children are appreciated for what they are. Though they are encouraged to be the best they could be, when, for some reason, they do not conform, they are not thrown out because, as they say,"*a kì í fi omo burúkú fún ekùn pa je*" [we do not throw a child to the tiger just because he/she is bad]. Indeed, it is recognized, in various idioms, that a child cannot be altogether bad; he/she must have certain traits of goodness or virtues and even if all bad, he/she must have certain useful features even in his/her badness:"*omo burúkú ní ojó tirè*" [a bad child has his/her day of usefulness], and also "*nítorí wèrè ti ìta làá fií ní wèrè ti ilé*" [since there are rascals outside, we should not mind the rascality of our own kids - because they can stand up to defend us if the rascals from outside should attempt to attack us]. These sayings show that the Yoruba have a more or less pragmatic approach to the moral upbringing of children and an attitude of tolerance to adult behavior. While they do not encourage immoral behavior, they know that once a while people may behave immorally when they are out of sight. [*Kò sí enití kìí hu ìwà ìbàjé bí ilè bá dá tán; enití Olódùmarè pa tirè mó ní èniyàn rere.*]

It may be argued, by advocates of the claim that religion is the foundation for Yoruba morality that the foregoing reference to *Iwà* as the primacy of existence and character supports their position and contradicts the point I have made concerning the pragmatic nature of Yoruba ethics. However, it would be a misconception of the whole point. As I have observed above, *Ifá* is not just a religion. It is a source of Yoruba collective wisdom. It is generally acknowledged that *Orúnmìlà* speaks in parables and when traditional thinkers need to drive home a point, they make easy recourse to what appears to be the age-old tradition of speaking in parables. Notice also that in the story, *Orúnmìlà*, the oracle himself is *blamed* for maltreating his wife. This should strike a note: that even the oracle is not spared as far as the moral judgment of actions is concerned. And for a devotee of the *Ifa* oracle, the morality of the society appears to provide a yardstick for even judging the conduct of the oracle. It follows therefore that the Yoruba are very pragmatic in their approach to morality, and though, religion may serve them as a motivating force, it is not the ultimate appeal in moral matters.

4

TRADITIONAL AFRICAN RELIGIOSITY: MYTH OR REALITY?

In contemporary philosophical debates on African traditional religion, two issues are raised: [i] are traditional Africans notoriously religious? [ii] is there a conception of a supreme God identifiable with the Christian God among traditional Africans? To manage the discussion, I will not here go into the issue of whether it now makes sense to talk of traditional Africans. I will assume that we understand by *traditional* Africans, those Africans who have either not been unredeemably exposed to Western world-views, or whose indigenous world-views have not been irreversibly affected with atrophy in the face of decades of forced exposure to foreign ideas, and who therefore still remain loyal to the age-old ideas, beliefs and values. My main interest is to answer the above questions by focusing on these ideas, beliefs and values as they are preserved in the oral traditions. I also assume that there is no serious doubt concerning the place of oral traditions as preserved in myths, oral literature, music, poetry and proverbs as sources of information about the beliefs and values of a people. I will argue that, in an original sense of religion, the idea that traditional Africans are *deeply* religious may be pressed without any problem, though I am myself not comfortable with the idea of being *notoriously* religious which seem to suggest that Africans do not have non-religious perspectives to issues. Perhaps this is the point that those who have denied the idea of African religiosity are making, in which case I share their concerns. I suspect, however, that they have operated with a different, but perhaps, non-representative notion of religion. With regard to the second question, I will maintain that while many traditional African societies have the concept of a supreme deity, there is no evidence for us to conclude that such supreme beings are identical with the

Christian God. I conclude that this should not be a drawback to African traditional religion because, apart from the fact that its practitioners consider it as an effective means for the satisfaction of their spiritual and material needs, it also contributes significantly to the promotion of social peace in a way that other great religions cannot boast of.

Are Traditional Africans in all things Religious?

Scholars are divided in their answers to the two questions listed above. On the one hand, Mbiti and Idowu present arguments to support the view, not only that Africans are in all things religious and that they live in a religious universe, but also that throughout traditional African societies, there is knowledge of the one supreme God universally acknowledged as Lord of the universe[1]. On the other hand, scholars such as Okot p'Bitek argue that there is no conception of a supreme God in Africa, talk less of *the* one supreme God; though he does not appear to deny the religiosity of traditional Africans[2]. In this group is Kwasi Wiredu who, while granting that traditional Africans have some religion, and that the Akans at least have an idea of a supreme God, nonetheless questions the claim that they are religious in all things [3]. How are these questions to be settled? I propose to address both questions by examining the oral traditions carefully. For obvious reasons, again, I will focus mostly on the traditional Yoruba world-view without pretending that what I find there may be generalized for the whole of Africa. The point that I will make is that if traditional Yoruba are a deeply religious people, then there is at least one African people that satisfy that description. But first, there is need for a basic agreement on the meaning of the basic terms: religion and religious.

First let us look at Religion. Among the entries listed in *Webster's International Dictionary* on Religion, the following are relevant:

> [i] the service and adoration of God or a god as expressed in forms of worship, obedience to divine commands, especially as found in accepted sacred writings or as declared by recognized teachers and in pursuit of a way of life regarded as incumbent on true believers.

[ii] An apprehension, awareness, or conviction of the existence of a supreme being, or more widely, of supernatural powers or influences controlling one's own humanity's or nature's destiny.

Following from these, the following is offered as a definition of
Religious: manifesting devotion to, or the influence of religion; pious; godly.

This seems to me to be as close as we can get to an adequate and non-technical sense of the words 'religion' and 'religious.' They represent the common meanings of the words. This is especially true of the second meaning under religion. The central idea in religion is the conviction that there exists some superior being[s] capable of affecting one's existence and therefore deserving to be worshipped and pleased. This conviction naturally goes with the desire to be in the favor of such a being. But while the first definition above emphasizes 'service and adoration' and refers to the sacred writings as sources of divine commands regarding worship and service, the second focuses on the awareness or conviction regarding the existence of supernatural powers. Since there are no sacred writings as part of the paraphernalia of African traditional religion, we should focus on the second definition which is equally valid as a common meaning of the term. When, therefore, we desire to address the question of the religiosity of traditional Africans, what we are asking for resolves itself to the following: do Africans manifest devotion to or show the influence of religion in their lives? In other words, following from our definition of religion, do Africans manifest an awareness of, or manifest devotion to, or show the influence of a supreme being or of supernatural powers or other influences controlling their destiny? To address this question, we need to review some of the cosmological ideas from oral traditions. I will focus here on the Yoruba world-view.

The Theme of Religion in Yoruba World-view

In the Yoruba world-view, as found in oral traditions, the universe is made up of two planes of existence: visible and invisible. The visible plane is further divided into two levels. First is the level of direct experience- the earth- which is the abode of humans, animals and plants. The other is the level below this which has a significance for them as will be seen below. On the other hand, the invisible plane is the abode of non-human beings of various kind who are the object of sacrifice and devotion. But of course, it is important not to regard these divisions as exclusive. The visible plane simply refers to a plane of existence occupied by beings having material nature and therefore capable of being directly experienced by all human beings. The earth belongs to the visible plane insofar as it is inhabited by beings having material nature. On the other hand, there are beings of a different kind, who are believed to have powers that falsify the laws of nature. They can change their nature at will, affect others physically even from a distance, and thus change their destinies. These beings are conceived as inhabiting the invisible plane which is also thought of as either having an identical spatial location with the visible plane or, at least, not too far away from it. There is, in any case, the belief that inhabitants of the two planes have constant communication with one another. Generally, because the inhabitants of the invisible plane are credited with such extra-ordinary powers and they are not visible to the ordinary eyes, they are referred to in the literature as spiritual beings. Their essential nature, again, is that they are believed to be not susceptible to the ordinary laws of nature. And though, they are sometimes described in physical terms and endowed with spatial location, the fact that they have powers which are beyond the ordinary suggest that they are a different and superior being whose favor should be courted for security. Thus, though the earth is said to be the abode of human beings and other material natures, spiritual beings also exist in their own invisible plane. Within the universe, therefore, there is a world of humans and a world of spirits existing for the Yoruba in a relation of complementarity. To say that there are spiritual beings in this sense is to say that there are beings whose existence is invisible to the ordinary eyes. It cannot therefore be a serious objection to this postulation [of spiritual beings] to suggest, as Wiredu does, that " the beings in question can be seen by those who have suitably medicated eyes."[4] If by that is meant the eyes of strong herbalists endowed with extra-ordinary powers, there is no contradiction in saying that such beings are 'seen' by them, and the super-human nature of those beings is not thereby compromised. I have evidence that Wiredu is probably not disputing the attribution of belief in extra-human forces to traditional Africans.[5] His quarrel seems to be with the term spiritual to designate such forces because the term is, in his view, incoherent, even in its English-language sense, popularized by Descartes. What he understands by extra-human forces is what is, in the literature, referred to as spiritual forces.

Beside the earth as level of direct experience, there is the level below the land which is the source of sustenance as well as the final resting place for human beings. For this reason, this level has a great significance for them. For instance, the land is an important symbol as source of life and it is forbidden for anyone to desecrate it in any way. Indeed as a general practice, people swear by the land to demonstrate their sincerity and fidelity. In spite of its importance, however, the land is still part of the earth and belongs to the material plane. As a resting place, too, the part of human beings that go into it is the body, the spirit having left for the land of the dead.

The invisible plane, as noted above, is the world of extra-human forces and the deities. Though it has no definite location in view of the ethereal nature of its inhabitants, the part of it which is postulated as the seat of *Olódùmarè*, the Supreme deity is normally identified with the space above the sky.[6] And as if they are not aware of the apparent contradiction in postulating a spatial location for a spiritual being, they also postulate an original physical interaction between *Olódùmarè*, the divinities and human beings. In one of the Yoruba myths, *Olódùmarè* used to be so close to the earth that human beings could reach the deity and the divinities directly at any time. Then something happened which annoyed the Supreme deity and he decided to move farther up in the sky. In spite of this, however, and in spite of the fact that their characterization of the Supreme deity is often in anthropomorphic terms, the Yoruba have no doubts about the purely spiritual nature of the deity. The divinities are conceived in the same light and are regarded as the link between human beings and the deity. They [*òrìsà*'s] thus become the direct contacts of humans. Sacrifices are offered to them for good fortune and for protection against disasters and to ward off the forces of evil [*ajogun*] such as death [*ikú*], disease [*àrùn*], loss [*òfò*], trouble [*òràn*], paralysis [*ègbà*], curse [*èpè*], imprisonment [*èwòn*], and afflictions [*èse*] which are all conceived as extra-human forces[7]. Humans are unable to detect these forces when they approach because they do not belong to the same plane. The divinities, in virtue of their character, are in a stronger position to do battle with them and save their human clients from destruction.

Olódùmarè, as the topmost in the hierarchy of beings in the spiritual realm, is supposedly endowed with certain qualities. He is the source of being [*orísè*], the owner and giver of life breath [*elèmí*] and the most perfect and just. He is the controller of events in both the spirit and human worlds, and without his consent nothing worthwhile can be accomplished. The divinities act with his authority, though sometimes they are rebellious. As we will see later, however, though the deity is conceived as having these attributes, he sometimes depends on the divinities too. This suggests that he lacks omnipotence.

Apart from the supreme deity and the divinities, there is a third group of spirit-beings: the ancestors. Though they were once human beings residing on the material plane of the universe, the Yoruba believe that once an adult has died, he has changed his material being for a spiritual being and has thereby become a divinity. As Abimbola rightly claimed, death "is viewed as a medium for the transformation of human beings from one level of existence in *aiyé* to another level of existence in *òrun*. When a man moves from one plane to the other, he automatically acquires greater authority and becomes an *òrìsà* to his own family or lineage."[8]

Thus the protective relationship which exists between parents and their children here on earth is not terminated at death. The ancestors continue to protect their offsprings from all misfortunes, including disease, trouble and death. But their human nature is not totally transformed; hence they could be angry, and they need to be remembered from time to time to avoid their anger and slackness in pleading the cause of their descendants. The Yoruba have specific ways of doing this.

Sacrifices are made to the ancestors from time to time and at a special season of the year. The latter is usually a colorful ceremony in each Yoruba community. The most widespread is probably the *egúngún* festival when it is believed that the ancestors come down in spirit to participate in and receive the sacrifices offered to them, and to assure their descendants of their continued protection.

From the foregoing account of the Yoruba conception of the universe, some questions may be raised: First, how true of the Yoruba cosmological idea is this account? Second, in view of these ideas, is it correct to describe the Yoruba as a deeply religious people? Third, from a philosophical perspective, is this Yoruba conception of the universe a defensible one? The rationale for the first question is simple. Issues have been raised about the authenticity of similar accounts of cosmological ideas on the allegation that they smack of an imposition of foreign ideas. Some writers argue that scholars who have urged this kind of interpretation have been influenced by Christian ideas of God and the universe, which they have turned around to present as the Yoruba's. Specifically, issues have been raised about the place of *Olódùmarè* in the hierarchy of beings. To resolve this kind of issue and answer the objection, we have to address a further question: is there any evidence from the Yoruba world-view in support of this account?

In the absence of written history, all we have are oral traditions as indications of Yoruba traditional beliefs about the universe and human beings. Among these are myths, folktale, and the *Odù-Ifá*. It is from these sources that we can have a knowledge of any relevant Yoruba beliefs; and if we search carefully, the evidence found would support the picture of the universe presented here. The aim of myths is to explain the world and the place of human beings in it. They are inspired by the existence of that objective reality which otherwise appears mysterious, and the inevitable confrontation between human beings and this reality. Myths are the conscious responses of the human mind to the brute facts of experience, especially those which impinge on their sense of security and survival needs. As such, myths are veritable sources of knowledge about the beliefs of a people in the absence of a written literature. As purported explanations of reality, myths presuppose some level of knowledge; but of course, this may, to the scientific mind, be grossly inadequate. This possibility is always there, but it is not the issue for now. Our concern in this section is to show that if we need to know about the beliefs of a people in the absence of written records, their myths are a dependable source of information.

In the particular case of the Yoruba, there are mythical stories about the structure of the universe, the nature of the supreme being and divinities and the relation between them, as well as between both on the one hand and human beings on the other. For instance, the Yoruba have a myth to explain the distance between the sky and the earth, and the apparent physical remoteness of the deity from human abode. In this myth, *Olódùmarè* used to be very close, in his skyey abode, to the earth. But one day, a woman was pounding yam in a mortal and mistakenly hit the seat of *Olódùmarè* with her pestle. This annoyed him and he decided to move farther up beyond human reach. Another myth attempts to explain and defend the belief in the superiority of *Olódùmarè* over the other divinities. In the myth, the earth, which is a divinity on its own, is reported to have contested the superiority of the deity by refusing to let him have a greater proportion of their joint catch after a hunting expedition. *Olódùmarè* annoyingly went back to heaven with a vow to teach earth a bitter lesson. Thereafter, he shut the gates of heaven so that neither rain nor sun was able to penetrate to the earth. This adversely affected human beings and the earth was forced to make propitiation to *Olódùmarè* for forgiveness. The myth underscores the fact that in spite of the Yoruba belief in the closeness, and therefore stronger presence of the divinities, they also acknowledge the supremacy of *Olódùmarè*[9].

There are further evidences for the veracity of the account of Yoruba cosmology presented here in the *Odù-Ifá*. For instance, there is the story of how the one thousand and seven hundred divinities known to the Yoruba conspired against *Olódùmarè*. They contested his absolute authority over the universe and demanded that he should withdraw from the governance of the earth so that they too may try their hands at it. Not being in the mood for argument, *Olódùmarè* suggested that they should first try their hands on the governance of the earth for sixteen days instead of the sixteen years which they had asked for. They agreed and went away rejoicing on their newly won position of responsibility. However, *Olódùmarè* had decided to expose their folly before their very eyes. He withdrew his attention completely and with it went the benefits of life including rain, sun etc. The divinities tried unsuccessfully to control the situation as life became terrible for them. They were forced to go back to *Olódùmarè*, they "confessed their folly, acknowledging his absolute sovereignty and supremacy over all, and pleading for mercy."[10] This story, found in the *Odù* corpus, again shows that the Yoruba belief in a hierarchical structure of the universe with *Olódùmarè* at the apex.

Finally, in the matter of evidence, there is also a support from ordinary language as expressed in proverbs, wise sayings and common expressions, many of which suggest a common agreement on the dual nature of the universe and the superiority of *Olódùmarè* in the hierarchy of beings. Of course, there is no doubt that ordinary language has been affected by exposure to foreign ideas and beliefs. Yet, there always remains a core which may serve as a basis for authenticating the kind of claim that is made here. In the language, there is *isálaiyé* [earth] and *isálòrun* [heaven], and there are traditional incantations which make use of the ontological relationship between these as well as the real nature of specific beings. The following is an example:

Mo júbà Eégún aiyé, Esìbà òrun
Atiyo ojó; àtiwò-oòrùn, ìkóríta-méta ìpàdé òrun
Otàlénírinwó irúnmalè tó j'átàrí ònà òrun gbangba.[11]

I salute the powers of the earth, and the controller of heaven.
The coming of the day, the setting of the sun; the junction of heaven.
Four hundred and sixty invisible forces at the gates of heaven.

This also shows, I think, that the Yoruba have a fundamental belief in the existence of a deity, divinities and invisible forces. The Yoruba word for extra human beings referred to here as invisible forces is *imalè*. More than this, the above incantation is a salute to these powers and forces of the universe, and this should lead us to the question whether the Yoruba adopt a religious attitude to these powers that they acknowledge in their world-view. In other words, given this conception of the structure of the universe and the hierarchy of beings acknowledged by the Yoruba, we may raise the question whether they are a deeply religious people.

Perhaps we should first note that, by itself, this conception of the universe does not make a people religious. Instead one should see it as an explanatory device born out of a sense of curiosity regarding the universe in which human beings finds themselves. Cosmological and cosmogonic myths are human devices-at the level of mythical consciousness- to explain events which confront them as extraordinary and, as such, they are analogous to such devices at the level of scientific reasoning. However, the kind of attitude that is shown toward the entities postulated in such devices is what determines their religious import as well as the degree of the people's religiosity. For instance, scientists are not described as religious persons just on account of their discovery or affirmation of the existence of atoms. Neither are they described as agnostic just on account of their defence of the theory of gravity. Human beings are described as religious on the ground of [i.] their attitude to the entities which they postulate in their account of ultimate reality; and [ii.] their perception of the connection between their flourishing and these entities and their reactions to this perception. Thus if I postulate an entity as part of the fabric of the universe and I attach no significance to it in terms of its consequence for my well-being, and my attitude to its existence is one of indifference since it has no special importance for me, such an attitude cannot be described as religious. But if it means so much for me that I believe that my life depends on its being pleased with me, then I would make efforts to satisfy it in appropriate ways, whatever it is. Of course, my perception may be wrong [from a scientific point of view], but the veracity of my perception is not the determining factor in my attitude. Even when it is pointed out to me that I am wrong, I may not accept the corrections of others, because in my situation, my own perception has a stronger force on me than the scientific theory of others [cf. the effect of the theory of evolution on fundamentalists].

In the matter of the attitude of the indigenous Yoruba to the entities they postulate in their accounts of reality, I do not think we need long arguments to sustain the claim that they adopt a religious attitude. It seems to me that those scholars who have thought otherwise have not examined the matter carefully enough. For it only requires an unbiased investigation to discover that the traditional Yoruba express their dependence on the unseen powers they believe to be governing the universe in a variety of ways. They ensure that before they embark on any important journey, they consult with the divination oracle for its probable outcome. They may be asked to offer sacrifices to *Ogún*, the god of iron, for protection. A typical Yoruba will not leave his or her house until that sacrifice has been offered. They also offer various kinds of sacrifices to all the recognized gods for protection and provision of needs. For bumper harvests they appease *Orìsà oko*, the deity of agriculture; and for successful hunting expedition they offer sacrifice to *Ogún*. Each significant aspect of life has an assigned deity. It is a general knowledge that the Yoruba recognize more than four hundred deities, beside *Olódùmarè*. Ile-Ife, the spiritual home of the Yoruba, has only one day in the year when no deity is worshipped. The question that needs to be addressed by those who deny the religiosity of the Yoruba, therefore, is this: what purpose do these deities serve and why are they recognized? If being religious means paying regard to such unseen powers that may influence people's situation, it seems to me that we cannot deny the fact that this definition is applicable to the traditional Yoruba as a people.

This claim may be valid for some other African culture-groups, though I am not here generalizing. It is true, however, that similar claims have been forcefully made in respect of the Akan of Ghana. Thus, according to Kwame Gyekye, the Akan universe "is conceived as a hierarchy of beings with *Onyame* at the apex, then the deities, ancestors. humans, and the world of natural objects and phenomena, in that order."[12] He disagreed with the position of Parrinder who had conceived the order of the universe in pyramidal terms and placed the nature gods [deities] and ancestors on the same footing. The reason this is wrong is that "the deities are considered more powerful than the ancestors who are considered to be nearer to man- for they were once human, whereas the deities were never human."[13] Gyekye concludes, therefore, that "a vertical line would be a more appropriate figure to use in displaying the ordered relation between the different entities in Akan ontology."[14]

There is recognized a power structure between the various entities in the hierarchy: "an entity can destroy or affect any other below it. Thus *Onyame* can destroy the deities [hence the obeisance made to him by the priest who serves a deity] as well as the other spiritual beings, humans, and the whole world."[15] From these remarks, it would seem to follow that the Akans have an awareness of some powers capable of influencing their existence and to avoid negative influence or to solicit favor, they adopt an attitude which may not be incorrectly described as religious. If Gyekye's account is correct, this deduction should also be correct.

Beside Gyekye, other scholars of Akan cultural philosophy have given similar accounts. Thus, W. E. Abraham, noting "the proliferation of minor deities which the Akans claimed to be an avenue to God's munificence and bountiful protection" concludes that "the correct and proper derivation of *Onyame* is *Nya*: to get, or *Onya*: fortunate possession, and *Mee*: be satisfied, want nothing" To confirm this derivation, he appealed to the "assiduity and frequency with which the Akans appealed for all sorts of help to minor deities whom they conceived as lieutenants of the Supreme Being, almost even the expression of his omnipotence."[16] Abraham also rejected the idea that *Onyame*, conceived as supreme God is a European importation: "Onyame is too central to the speech and thought of the Akans, he figures in the immemorial prologue to Akan ceremonial drumming, and he was well known in the deepest fastness of the forest where missionary zeal had not been."[17] It is true that Abraham, in the following page, says also that "the proliferation of Gods that one finds among the Akans is in fact among the Akans themselves superstitious."[18] The question is what do we make of this? As long as their attitude to the deities is still that of reverence, such a perception may not mean much. But even if their attitude to the minor deities is thus adversely affected, the question still remains what their attitude is to the Supreme deity. But it cannot be denied that it is one of reference and veneration as long as they still regard *Onyame* as the source of bountiful protection.

Busia also shares this view with respect to the hierarchical ordering of the Akan universe and the religious attitude of the Akan. According to him, "the contemporary problems of Africa must be seen in the context of Africa's own cultural heritage-that heritage is intensely and pervasively religious."[19] He further maintains that all African communities "postulate God as a Supreme Deity who created all things"[20] and that "it was not possible to distinguish between religious and non-religious areas of life. All life was religious."[21] Though Wiredu has taken issue with this last statement, arguing that it makes no sense to still talk about Africans being religious if no distinction can be made between their religious and non-religious life[22], I do not see any incoherence in Busia's claim, which is simply that a typically religious attitude can be discerned in the people's approach to matters in all areas of their lives. They see the influence of the gods in all that they do or need for survival, and this naturally calls for appropriate response from them.

There is, however, a sense in which Wiredu's point may be understood. Religion, as it is now understood especially in contemporary western societies, is an institution distinct from such other institutions as the economy, politics, law, etc. It has its own identity and distinctive set of practices and apparatus which need not filter into other areas of life. Thus a civil servant may attend the church on Sunday, and have devotional hours with the family at night or before leaving for work in the morning, but he or she is not expected to be controlled by her or his religious beliefs at work. A fundamental principle of social life in most modern industrial societies is the separation of church and state. However, in traditional African societies, religion does not stand apart from other sectors of life. This is the meaning of the statements of Busia and Mbiti. Life is not compartmentalized in traditional Africa, and religious devotion [in the sense of a feeling of submission to the supreme powers acknowledged as having power over one], permeates all areas of life. In this case, if the conception [of religion in Africa] is different,

Wiredu may argue, we may not apply the same term to it as we apply to the idea as it features in the west. I do not think that the observations warrant the conclusion. For it may very well be the case that the idea of religion that now dominates the west is itself a corruption of the original meaning, a development made possible and necessary by the rational outlook that feeds the structures of industrial capitalism. The idea of religion as something separate from all other areas of life is alien to traditional Africa. All festivals are occasions for celebration and joy and sacrifice. There are no separate worship hours, no temples or houses of worship. It may even very well be that there is no special term for religion as it is practiced by traditional Africans.[23] The king is both political head and the deputy to the gods. All religious festivals must be fixed by him, and he is responsible for the success of the rituals. This concept of religion as something that is inseparable from the other areas of life may appear strange to a contemporary westerner, but I do not think that this is a sufficient warrant for denying the religiosity of the traditional African, especially if the meaning of religion offered by *Webster* is accepted.

There is another position, which while not denying the religiosity of the Yoruba, offers a model which may lead to a similar conclusion. In a lucid and well-argued article, Karin Barber offers what may be termed the "Big Man Model" of religion.[24] The essential point made by Barber is that "[t]he *orisa* [gods] are, according to Yoruba traditional thought, maintained and kept in existence by the attention of humans. Without the collaboration of their devotees, the *orisa* would be betrayed, exposed and reduced to nothing. This notion seems to have been intrinsic to the religion since the earliest times."[25] Her explanation of this belief makes use of a social relations model. According to her, "[r]elations between humans and *orisa* are in some sense a projection of relations between people in society." Her suggestion then is that "if the Yoruba see the *orisa*'s power as being maintained and augmented by human attention, this is because they live in a kind of society where it is very clear that the human individual's power depends in the long run on the attention and acknowledgement of his fellow-men."[26]

One problem with this Big Man model of religion is that it seems more of an interpreter's account than the devotee's, and it is obviously based on very recent history. It appears that Barber's informants were unable to go beyond the 19th century since the town of Okuku where she conducted her research itself does not appear to have an earlier history. But we know that by this time in the history of Yoruba societies, there have been exposures to foreign ideas and beliefs. Thus the influence of Christianity and Islam with their denigration of traditional religion is clear in some of the chants to the orisas, as when a devotee threatens to defect to Christianity if *Sàngó* did not bless her. This was a time when Christians came up with many choruses depicting the emptiness of traditional religions: *ènìyàn leégún, orò n'igi; à fi bí a ba mpa'ró* [The masquerade is nothing but man, the *orò* [the cult used for keeping women indoors for seven or more days] is nothing but a plank, unless we want to lie]. Thus this kind of development and its influence on the people's attitude has to be put in proper perspective. The question why people got converted is a different one entirely and cannot be tied up with this attitude which cannot also be said to be original. I have a suspicion that Barber seems to believe that if the kind of attitude she has highlighted were not there originally, the conversion of the people would not have been possible. For instance, she thinks that it was the "willingness to try something new that conditioned the way Islam and Christianity were received, rather than Islam and Christianity which introduced a new attitude of skepticism."[27] I think this is too simplistic as an approach to the issue of conversion.

Barber herself seems to recognize the limitation of her model and constantly struggles to correct a wrong impression. Hence her cautious remarks that "an *orisa* cannot just be abandoned if it fails to respond to a devotee's needs- or it might get its revenge by inflicting further misfortunes."[28] Yet, the theme of the choice of *òrìsà* and the ease of defection runs through the paper. But it is not really true that devotees just shop around for *òrìsà*. Usually, the *òrìsà*'s are thought of as having specialties and people with problems get to know which *òrìsà* to approach through the priests of *Orúnmìlà*. *Ifá* may advise an individual with a problem to approach one or more òrìsà, depending on the nature of the problem. Thus, as a result of the different specialties of the various òrìsà's, it is not impossible for the same person to become a devotee of more than one òrìsà. As Barber also rightly noted, the òrìsà do not compete among themselves. This may be one of the reasons for the ease of conversion among the Yoruba. There was no bias against any òrìsà as long as the human problems are solved. They are all thought of as workers in the service of Olódùmarè and humankind.

It may be true that some òrìsà's are objectively human-made. This may be true of those that are not recognized as belonging to the original pantheon. But from this, it cannot be concluded that all are therefore human-made. It is also true that there is now a general decline in the following of traditional religion and devotees may be genuinely concerned about the loss and may also, like the contemporary Big Man, try to do something about it. But the question that needs to be addressed about the usefulness of this model is whether what goes on in contemporary society provides an adequate grounding for understanding the traditional ideas of religion. Barber derives her conception of the òrìsà and their relationship with their devotees from the model of contemporary society. It seems to me that such a model cannot adequately account for the reality of the people's perception of their relationship with the òrìsà. For, central to this perception is the reality of the existence of the òrìsà for the devotee. It is interesting that even with her model, Barber does not deny this.

The concept of a Supreme God

The second question: is there a conception of a Supreme God identifiable with the Christian God is more difficult than our first question. It may be approached by resolving it into the following: [i] do Africans have conceptions of the Supreme Deity? [ii] if so, are such conceptions identical with the conception of the Supreme Being by Christians? For instance, is Olódùmarè identical with God in Christian conception?

Again, addressing the first of these questions first, if we attend to oral traditions, there seems to be little doubt about the conception of a supreme deity in African thought in general, and especially in Yoruba thought. With regard to the Yoruba, the *Ifá* divination poetry which cannot be said to have been influenced by Christianity is explicit on this. *Olódùmarè* is recognized as the supreme being. Thus *Orúnmìlà* is recorded to have exclaimed in poetic language: "You who travel by sea, you who travel by land, surely you perceive that the works of *Olódùmarè* are incomparable."[29] And as we have seen earlier, there is a similar concept among the Akans. Other parts of Africa have their own conceptions of a supreme being. In Botswana, there is *Modimo*; among the Mende of Sierra Leone, there is *Ngewo*; for the Nupe of Nigeria, there is *Soko*; for the Igbo there is *Chukwu*; for the Edo, there is *Osanobwa*; and for the Teme, there is *Kuru*. All these are additional to the varieties of deities which are, in many cases, more directly consulted by the people.

If these accounts are correct, and oral tradition is a reliable source of information, then we may conclude that there is the conception of at least, a supreme deity in African traditional religion. The further question is however not that easy. This is the question whether the supreme deity in the African context is identical with the christian God. There are also two opposing views on this:

[a] there is only one God; and while there may be various concepts of God according to each people's spiritual perception, it is wrong to limit God with an adjective formed from the name of any race.[30]

[b] The interpretation of African deities in terms of the Christian God does not help us to understand the nature of the African deities as African peoples conceive them.[31]

Which of these views is right? It seems to me we cannot avoid going back to oral tradition. We have to inquire whether the Yoruba conception of *Olódùmarè* suggests any identity between the deity and the christian God.

In the literature on African traditional religion, especially by scholars-clergymen, this question is answered in the affirmative.[32] Thus *Olódùmarè* is described by Idowu as All-wise, All-knowing, All-seeing, Omnipotent, Creator, Holy, etc. Interestingly, while Wiredu agrees that the Akan have a notion of a Supreme Being, he does not include the attribute of a creator in his list of attributes for such a being because, according to him, the conception of the Supreme Being among the Akan is one of a cosmic architect.[33] This makes the Akan Supreme Being logically different from the Christian God. The problem is that Idowu's account, which suggests that the characteristics of the Yoruba *Olódùmarè* are identical with those of the Christian God appears to conflict with some other characterizations of the deity in the oral tradition. For instance, an *Odù Ifá* relates the story of how *Olódùmarè* had to consult an Ifa priest on the possibility of immortality for himself. The Ifa priest then instructed *Olódùmarè* on what to do. He did it and thus became immortal. This seems to suggest that *Olódùmarè* is not All-knowing. Even the story of how the earth was formed suggests that *Olódùmarè* lacks the power of absolute knowledge. Thus he had to send someone to go and see what was happening to *Orìsà-nlá*, the arch-divinity who had been charged with the responsibility of populating the earth. Finally, *Esù*, the trickster god, is often portrayed in many Yoruba myths as sometimes having more power than *Olódùmarè* himself in view of the fact that he can do what he wants with the scepter of *Olódùmarè*'s authority which he keeps. Thus *Esù* can use the *àse* to help a favored client change an unfavorable destiny. All these seem to suggest that one should be cautious in interpreting the supreme Gods in African beliefs in terms of the Christian God. The circumstances that lead people to discover their Gods differ from place to place, and people from different historical backgrounds need not discover the same ideas of God.

There seems to be no doubt that in their finding an identity between the African supreme deities and the Christian God, Mbiti and Idowu are not only influenced by Christian theology, but they are also concerned about furthering the notion of the universality of the Christian God. If the Christian God is truly and objectively real, and no other deity can be compared with Him, then attributing a different supreme being to Africans would amount to underestimating their ability to discover the 'true God.' This seems to be the reasoning of the advocates of a universal God. But the 'if' above is crucial, and until it is adequately accounted for, the reality and universality of the Christian God cannot be a yardstick for judging the reality of other people's Gods. It seems to me therefore that traditional Africans have nothing to worry about concerning the differences between their conceptions of their supreme God and that of the Christian. Indeed it seems to me that there is a lot to lose by forcing the kind of identity that African Christian theologians are forcing. First, there is the danger of the loss of identity. Of all the factors that make for an authentic cultural identity, language and religion are the most important. Africans stand the risk of losing both at this point in time. The growth of fundamentalism in both christian and islamic religions among African youths is an indication of this danger. It also poses a grave danger to social peace, and this is an area in which African traditional religion can be instructive. Indeed, in the light of the distinctive contributions of African traditional religion to social peace, one may say that the practitioners of the religion have a lot to be proud of.

Tenets of African Traditional Religion

The main teachings of all variants of African traditional religion seem to coincide. Thus, they all take interest in the interpersonal relationships among their devotees who are enjoined to take themselves as one body. Co-worshippers receive their instructions from and enter into covenants with the divinities to be of good behavior. These covenants oblige them to enter into good relationships, not only with one another, but also with their fellow community members who belong to different òrìsà's. For instance, Orìsà-nlá, the Yoruba arch- divinity, is believed to be the god of purity. His devotees are therefore expected to be clear in thought and upright in action. They are prohibited from drinking wine to avoid intoxication which may lead to misbehavior. The priests of *Orúnmìlà* are expected to assist in the fight against the *Ajogun*'s- the forces of evil which afflict unprotected human beings. These priests are not expected to use their positions to enrich themselves; they are to be disciplined and helpful to others. In so doing, they are contributing to the promotion of social peace. It is important to note that an important emphasis of these religions is the improvement of the earthly condition of their devotees. Indeed, appeals are made to extra-human powers with the primary objective of having people do their share in maintaining social harmony.

Another area in which the traditional religions of the Yoruba contribute to both personal and social peace is in the emphasis on the need to curb desires. Human expectations from life, and the desires they expect to fulfil, are subject to the limitation of two forces: destiny and the social reality of existence. Predestination suggests that there is a purpose to human existence and that each person is in the world to achieve a purpose or to deliver a message. Their desires are therefore limited by the nature of that message. Furthermore, the aim of human existence, from the point of view of *Olódùmarè*, is the promotion of the good for the totality of existence. This means that *Olódùmarè* wills the good for all and of course the good includes adequate peace of mind for each and communal peace for all. But there is evil! This is what *Orúnmìlà*, the god of wisdom is introduced to remove. He is sent to the world to neutralize the power of malevolent forces and that of wicked persons so that the good may prevail.[34]

The difference between other world religions and Yoruba traditional religions in terms of their contribution to peace may now be located. While the other world religions place a great deal of emphasis on evangelization, the Yoruba traditional religions do not. In the process of spreading the "good news", there is bound to be conflict between the devotees and the non-believers. The history of the world is littered with numerous examples of such conflicts. On the other hand, however, it is an historical fact that Yoruba societies did not experience any kind of religion-inspired conflicts until the infiltration of the proselytizing religions- Christianity and

Islam. Both of these religions insisted that the indigenous religions they met on arrival should be abandoned. It is significant that the devotees of Yoruba religion were willing to accommodate these new religions; but the new-comers were not ready to accommodate the hosts! This is what led to several violent clashes between the religions. It is the same attitude of intolerance on the part of the native evangelists of these proselytizing religions that is creating religious crises in Nigeria today.

In other words, it is in the process of evangelization that those religions normally betray their tendency to promote conflict and violence in spite of their teachings. While they may be able to contribute to peace in religiously homogenous societies in virtue of their teachings, they are most unlikely to succeed in doing so in heterogenous societies in virtue of their proselytizing activities. It thus appears that in a plural society, it is only a religion that is non-evangelical that can effectively promote both personal and social peace. Such is the nature of Yoruba traditional religion in particular, and African traditional religion in general. Maintaining this distinction seems to me more important in virtue of its lesson and hope for a peaceful world than the efforts of African theologians to force an identity between African Gods and the Christian God.

Summary

Let me now summarize. In this chapter, I looked at the question whether traditional Africans may be truly said to live in a religious universe. With the support of oral tradition, I answer the question in the affirmative. Second, addressing the question whether there is any notion of a Supreme being in African traditional religion, I also answer in the affirmative, again with the support of oral tradition. Finally, regarding the question whether the Supreme beings in the variants of African traditional religion can be identified with the Christian God, I answer in the negative, again utilizing oral tradition. My focus in all these is the Yoruba oral tradition with which I am familiar, though in a few cases, I refer to the Akan world view using the available literature. I have, however, not attempted any generalization for the whole of Africa because I agree with Bolaji Idowu's apt remark that "African traditional religion with reference to the whole of Africa, as a subject of study, is an impossible proposition, where detailed study and thoroughness are concerned."[35] The fact remains, though, that from available literature, it is easy to discern certain common elements in the various world views which suggest common religious beliefs and practices. As Idowu also notes "[t]here is a common Africanness about the total culture and religious beliefs and practices of Africa. This common factor may be due either to the fact of diffusion or to the fact that most Africans share common origins with regard to race and customs and religious practices."[36] This probably accounts for the common practice of having African traditional religion identified as a separate branch of academic study ; but it does not justify a generalization for the whole of Africa from the study of a particular group.

5

CAUSALITY AND THE CONCEPT OF HEALTH AND ILLNESS

In a useful essay on the concept of cause, R. J. Collingwood identifies three senses of the term 'cause' as follows:

Sense 1: That which is caused is the free and deliberate act of a conscious and responsible agent. Such agents may be non-human provided that they are believed to act in the same conscious ways attributed to human agents.[1] Here, 'causing' an agent to do something means affording him or her a motive for doing it; and 'causing' is synonymous with compelling, inducing, forcing, persuading etc. Thus, "Ojo's death is caused by Ade"; "Ancestral wrath is caused by the neglect of the offspring" are good examples of this usage.

Sense 2: That which is caused, X, is an event in nature, and it is caused by another event or state of affairs, Y, which can be produced or prevented by a human agent, as a means to producing or preventing X. Here, Y, as the cause of X is within the power of the agent to bring about or prevent.[2] Thus, "The accident was caused by brake failure"; "Mosquito bite is the cause of malaria"; "Aina's dullness is caused by witchcraft" are good examples of this usage.

Sense 3: That which is caused is an event or state of affairs, X, and its cause is another event or state of affairs, Y, which stands in a one-one relation of causal priority to it such that [a] if Y, then X necessarily follows; and [b] X occurs only if Y occurs. Here causation designates the dependence of events in nature on one another, but not necessarily on humans.[3] Thus, "climatic change is caused by the movement of the earth''; ''rainfall is caused by the presence of sufficient amount of moisture in the atmosphere'' are good examples of this usage.

In Collingwood's categorization, sense 1 is historical sense; sense 2, practical sense; and sense 3, theoretical sense. Senses 1 and 2 are relevant to my interest here and I shall elaborate more on them before moving on to the question of the nature of causality from an African perspective. In sense 1, both humans and non-humans can be causal agents, provided that they are conceived to have motives, capacity for deliberations and choice. To say that one is caused to do something is to say that one has a motive for doing it. And, as Collingwood remarks, this is probably the original sense of the term; the other senses may have derived from it.[4]

Sense 2 is however the most common usage in the practical sciences. Here, cause also has a tight relation with human conduct in the sense that we identify as ''cause'' something that we are able to control, produce or prevent. Here, therefore, we may talk of the relativity of cause. What causes X from the point of view of A is what is under the control of A and A's identifying that thing as cause is the first step towards controlling it. To speak of cause is to speak of what we can [i.e. have power to] control at will. In this sense then, cause refers to ''an event or state of things which it is in our power to produce or prevent and by producing or preventing which we can produce or prevent that whose cause it is said to be.''[5] ''X is the cause of Y'', uttered by me, means X can be controlled or prevented by me to get a desired result with respect to Y. For instance, to say ''mosquito bite is the cause of malaria'' is to suggest that I can control malaria by controlling mosquitoes. This is the reason for identifying this sense of cause with the practical sciences like medicine, mechanical engineering, etc. What people identify as cause in a matter of interest to them is what they are capable of producing or preventing at will with respect to that state of affairs. Yet cause is not an arbitrarily selected matter, since anything so selected arbitrarily cannot be trusted to produce or prevent the end in which we are interested. The idea is that, for any state of affairs, there may be a number of causes, but a practical person, interested controlling such a state, will be concerned with identifying that which s/he is in a position to control as cause. To say that X is the cause of Y, *in a practical science*, but I am not able to control X is, on this perspective, to misidentify a cause. Thus if I witness a car accident, and I am neither the driver, nor a car designer, nor a road surveyor, I may not be in a position to identify the cause of the accident for practical purposes. As an innocent on-looker, I may still speculate about the cause from a theoretical angle, but not from a practical angle, the end of which is the prevention of accidents in the future.

When one is concerned with practical matters, the identification of cause comes along with the intention of doing something. What is identified as such is what one is capable of realizing for controlling the state of affairs. In medicine, cause must be something which a human being who identifies it is capable of controlling to produce an event [cure, healing] or prevent an event [disease, illness].

Collingwood sums up his account of this sense of the term "cause" with some suggestions as to its foundation which he traces to two different ideas about the relation between humans and nature:

> First, there is the anthropocentric idea that human beings look at nature from their own point of view as practical agents, anxious to find out how they can manipulate nature to achieve their own ends.[6] Second, there is the anthropomorphic idea that the manipulation of nature by human beings resembles one person's manipulation of another person, because natural things are alive in much the same way in which humans are alive, and have therefore to be similarly handled.[7]

Collingwood traces the first idea to what the educated European people nowadays think about their relation to nature; and the second to what they used to think about that relation. As I will show, the second is very much alive among many African peoples, educated, and non-educated [whatever that categorization stands for]. The question we will eventually raise is whether it is now to be considered anachronistic or irrational to build ideas of causality on such a conceptual framework. Before this, however, I would like to put the issue in the perspective of the debate currently going on among African scholars. For it appears to me that the debate is itself motivated by considerations of what it is rational to attribute to Africans as part of their conceptual scheme.

Causality, Naturalism and Supernaturalism

There is a division among scholars on what are the correct views of African thinkers on the question of causality and the concepts of the natural and the supernatural. On the one hand, J. O. Sodipo maintains that "the gods take over too soon in the explanations of most African societies" and that "the reason for this is that the preoccupation of explanation in Yoruba traditional thought is religious; because it is religious, it must satisfy emotional and aesthetic needs, and because of this, its explanations *must be given* in terms of persons or entities that are like persons in significant respects."[8] It is not certain, however, whether Sodipo will be willing to extend these remarks to cover other traditional African groups.

On the other hand, there have been denials of this claim. It has been suggested, for instance, that the attribution of the concept of the supernatural to traditional thought is inadequate and needs rethinking because no distinction is drawn by the thinkers between nature and supernature. Thus, Kwasi Wiredu, writing about the traditional Akans of Ghana, has maintained that "the distinction between the natural and the supernatural does not exist for them."[9] What is interesting about Wiredu's position is that while he seeks support for this claim in Busia's 1962 remark that in Akan world-view, there is an "apparent absence of a conceptual cleavage between the natural and the supernatural"[10], he also concedes that in a later book [11], Busia wrote about "the belief held among African communities that the supernatural powers and deities operate in every sphere and activity of life."[12] The interesting point in this is that Busia's two claims do not appear to be as contradictory as Wiredu seems to suggest, and neither claim can be used to support Wiredu's position that the Akans do not have a concept of the supernatural. Indeed, in the same passage which contains Busia's 1962 remark to which Wiredu refers, the former goes on to say that "In the search for the causes of an illness, we observed that connections were conceived both in natural and in supernatural terms; physical and magical linkages were involved."[13] If this was a contradiction on the part of Busia, the contradiction may be taken to have occurred in the same passage, and Wiredu should not have sought for the contradiction in a book published by the author five years later. I do not think that such a contradiction would have escaped Busia's attention, but I cannot be too sure about this.

The relevant question, however is this: what exactly does Busia mean by the claim that there is an absence of a conceptual cleavage between the natural and the supernatural while he at the same time claims that the people conceive causes of illness in natural and supernatural terms. I think there are two ways we may try to understand this. First, to say that there is an absence of conceptual cleavage could mean that the people do not observe any such cleavage in their thought system. This would mean that they have no concept of the supernatural because only ideas of the natural feature in their conceptual scheme. They conceive of illness only in natural terms and their category of causes does not move beyond nature. I do not think that this is an accurate description of what goes on in the conceptualization of the people, though I concede that what goes on in their conceptualization may not capture accurately what goes on in reality. A second way to understand the claim of an absence of conceptual cleavage is to see it as a claim that, in their thinking about causality, people move from one realm [of nature] to the other [supernature] without acknowledging that there is any cleavage between the two. In other words, for the same illness, they postulate a cure which is natural in the sense that it makes use of natural substances while, at the same time, they see a supernatural influence behind its effectiveness. Though I think this aptly describes part of what goes on, I do not think it does full justice to the claim that there is absence of conceptual cleavage. To say that there is absence of cleavage is not to say that ideas that make up the concept of the supernatural do not occur at all in the conceptual scheme of the people. For that seems too obvious to deny. What I think it means, rather, is that there is no unbridgeable division between the two in the conceptual scheme of the people. It is to suggest that there is no total split which could prevent moving from one to the other. It is to suggest that what is referred to as the supernatural is, in fact conceivable, as an extension of the natural; that is, as the natural viewed from another perspective.

Consider the familiar scenario of claims about the power of charms, amulets and incantation. It is believed that the medicineman who has access to such powers can act at a distance to affect the fortunes of others who are less knowledgeable. But the power still belongs to someone existing in nature. He probably makes use of ingredients from nature even though the incantations he uses seem to make reference to forces unseen. Yet these forces, though unseen, are part of the forces in nature. But the power he uses is regarded as extraordinary because it seems to falsify the known laws of nature and it is not everyone that has access to knowledge of it. This is what people mean when they refer to such powers as supernatural: that they exceed normal or expected capability of human beings. Perhaps the term does not quite represent the whole range of things that go on. The fact remains, though, that it is such category of factors that people refer to as the supernatural. In Yoruba language, the person with such a power or knowledge is said to have *agbára* [power] and is described as *alágbára* [a powerful person]. The *agbára* is, of course, built up from the resources of nature and to that extent may be said to be natural. On the other hand, partly because not everyone can claim such powers, and because the *agbára* yields results which appear to falsify the known laws of nature [as in the case of action from a distance], it is considered extra-human and supernatural. To say then that there is no conceptual cleavage between the natural and the supernatural in the conceptual scheme of the people is to suggest that [i] the people understand that, were everyone to have the kind of knowledge of the web of nature that the medicine man has, they could prepare similar charms and get similar results; yet [ii] the results thus derived is still understood to belie the claims of the known laws of nature and is to that extent, supernatural. There is therefore no sharp division, no unbridgeable gulf between the natural and the supernatural in the thought system.

Since this point has been raised by others, it is perhaps necessary to focus more on it. What I intend to do, therefore, is to investigate the matter, focusing on the following questions:

(1) Is there a concept of the supernatural in traditional African thoughts?
(2) Does such a concept [of the supernatural] feature in the causal explanations of traditional Africans?
(3) Does the concept have any religious connection?
(4) Is causal explanation in traditional thought religious in motive?

Causal Explanation

These questions cannot be answered adequately without some overview of the features of causal explanation in traditional thought. I will therefore start with this. Fortunately, it is an area in which people can commonly agree since it involves only a descriptive report of the world-views. The interpretive and critical aspects can thereafter proceed smoothly focusing on the questions just raised.

Take the following case as typical:

> Ojo and Aina are half-brothers. Ojo is the son of the first wife; Aina is the son of the second wife who is also the favorite of the husband/father. Aina is, however, sickly and dull in school. His parents have spent a lot on him without improvement. The mother begins to worry and therefore goes to a herbalist who prescribes some medicine, to no avail. In the end, as a hypothesis, the mother attributes his son's predicament to the second wife's jealousy. She must be a witch. Another herbalist is consulted who confirms that Aina's problem is the handiwork of an evil force.

Such forces are, of course, numerous in the conceptual field of traditional thinkers. These include the supreme deity as the ultimate cause, the deities, forces in nature which can be tapped by human beings, and human beings with innate abilities which are, for the most part, inexplicable. The question is, what do we make of this account? First, there is little doubt that it is an attempt to explain a puzzling situation. The predicament of Aina worries the parents and needs to be understood in terms of the *cause*. Second, there is an effort to find an explanation within the regular order of nature and thus be in a position to control it. Hence, the first consultation with the herbalist -- as the traditional medical practitioner who can diagnose and prescribe. But third, when this fails, and no explanations in terms of the regular order of nature -- as it occurs to them -- is forthcoming, recourse is made to explanation in terms of *forces* seemingly outside the regular order of nature.

Why is it believed that such forces are causally efficacious? This goes back to the issue of the universe of the people and their understanding of its ordering. The universe is conceived as an orderly one "in which all significant events are caused and are potentially explicable."[14] If this is true, then any particular occurrence must have a causal explanation. Secondly, though human beings are in the center of the universe, there are other forces which operate on them as well as those which they operate on to effect changes in their world. Such operations are based on the principle that "the higher a force is, the more causally efficacious it is." Thus the supreme being is the most causally efficacious, followed by the divinities, the deified forces including the ancestral spirits and other extra-human forces which can be conjured by humans. In all, it is still to be recognized that some human beings have such powers to control nature.

But why is causal efficacy attributed to these forces in the first place? Why do traditional thinkers feel the need to postulate any forces for accounting for such changes outside and independent of the regular order of nature? This is the heart of the problem. But before this is even addressed, there is a prior question arising from what the former question seems to presuppose, namely, that the forces thus postulated are non-empirically determined. Since this is the assumption that underlies most accounts of causality in traditional Africa, but rejected by Wiredu, it seems we need to address the problem.

Are the various causal agents, Supreme deity, divinities, extra human forces, humans with special powers, non-natural or supernatural? Let us say, again, as a

Causality and the Concept of Health and Illness

first approximation, that a supernatural entity (being) is one whose conception goes beyond natural limitation; an entity which, in people's conception, is not bound by the laws of nature. This is in keeping, again, with the dictionary definition of the term. Webster, for instance, defines the word as follows:

(1) belonging or having reference to, or proceeding from an order of existence beyond nature, or the visible and observable universe;

(2) divine as opposed to human or spiritual as opposed to material;

(3) ascribed to agencies or powers above or beyond nature or based upon such an ascription;

(4) beyond the powers of the laws of nature.

All these are quite consistent. The question, then, is whether the various causal agents referred to above are conceived as supernatural by African traditional thinkers. The best way to approach this is to review the features normally attributed to such agents. The Supreme deity, in the various African world-views, though called by different names as a result of tongue differences, seems to be conceived in similar terms, having similar features or attributes. Thus in Akan language, *Onyame* is, among other things, *Odomankoma* [Infinite, Boundless, Absolute], *Obiannyew* [Uncreated], *Atoapem* [Ultimate, Final], and *Onyankopon* [Supreme Being].[15] The Yoruba conceive *Olódùmarè* as immortal. According to a verse of *Ogbè Yèkú*:

Kòròfo, Awo Ajà-llè   Kòròfo, the Cult of Underground,
L'ó d'ífá fún Olódùmarè   Is the one which Consulted
Tó so wípé   the oracle about Olódùmarè
Nwon kò ní gbó ikú rè láéláé.   And declare that Olódùmarè will never die.[16]

Olódùmarè is also conceived as *Elèdá* [Creator], *Asèdá* [Maker], and *Elèmi* [Owner of divine breath]. These are attributes which go beyond nature, that objects or persons bound by the laws of nature cannot lay claim to. This makes them supernatural or at least extra-human. Nothing more is implied in the concept of the supernatural; and so, if it is agreed that the various attributes identified above are found in the references of traditional thinkers to any being, it follows that they construe such a being as supernatural, or at least as having supernatural attributes.

How about the divinities? These, as it has been noted in our discussion of the religiosity of Africans, fall into two or more categories: primordial gods [believed to be associates of *Olódùmarè* or the Supreme being] and deified communal priests and ancestors. The primordial beings are supposed to also have non-natural attributes derived from their association with the supreme being. Thus, for instance, *Esù*, the Yoruba trickster god, is believed to be the messenger of *Olódùmarè*, having the power of invisibility. *Esù* also has the scepter of authority from *Olódùmarè* and can effect anything or change the course of something even without the blessing of *Olódùmarè*, and in defiance of the laws of nature. That is a supernatural attribute. *Orúnmìlà*, the god of divination was believed to be present with *Olódùmarè* at the choice of destiny by every individual coming into the world. This is why the priests of *Orúnmìlà* are normally consulted when a new child is born in order to know what is the preappointed portion of the child. This is also framed in supernatural terms.

The deified communal priests and ancestors are once members of the community. At death, they become deified because of the extraordinary power they wielded while alive and if such powers are believed to be beyond natural or human means. For instance, *Sàngó*, the Yoruba god of thunder was a former king of the old Oyo Empire. A powerful and effective ruler, he commanded fear and respect while alive. He had extraordinary powers with ability to tap the forces of the universe. With time, he had numerous enemies, but also friends and loyalists. As a result of a conspiracy for which he was partly responsible, he had to abdicate the throne and to go into exile. Along the way, he and his wife parted company; thereafter, he decided to hang. Some people returning from a journey saw his body hanging on a tree and broke the news at home. But his loyalists had gone quickly to remove the body and came back to refute the story with the words: *Oba kò so* [The king did not hang]. This became a praise-song for *Sàngó* devotees and he became an object of worship. It is therefore correct to say that *Sàngó* is a human-made god. But this does not detract from the fact that before he became a god, he was seen as manifesting superior powers. His powers went beyond the natural and the concept of *Sàngó* therefore assumed a divine dimension. This is true of the other divinities in the Yoruba pantheon and this is why they feature in causal explanations of significant events. The rationale seems to be that if such beings, while in this world, could manifest "beyond-natural" powers, then when they exchange earthly life for the abode of the dead, they acquire more powers and are therefore able to influence the course of events. It does not really matter whether or not their earthly life was kind or wicked. *Esù* is appeased because of the potentials he has for causing misery for others; but *Obàtálá* is worshipped and adored because of his goodness. Enough has been said, I think, to press home the point that what people mean when they refer to such forces as supernatural is simply that the people conceive of them as having powers and attributes beyond the ordinary; beyond nature; and so causal explanations in which they feature appeal to the level of the supernatural to explain events on the level of the natural. This answers our first question: the concept of the supernatural features in traditional African [Yoruba] thought.

The next question to address is whether the concept of the supernatural features in the causal explanations of traditional thinkers. I have provided a hint towards an answer to this in the preceding paragraph as well as in the illustration above regarding the case of Aina which presents a puzzle and therefore requires explanation. As I also mentioned, the first level of explanation [Level I] is to look for appropriate natural events that could be responsible. Why is Aina not doing well? Is it hunger? Is it fear? Is it ill-health? The consultant herbalist/diviner tries all available concoctions to deal with such problems plus advice to the mother. However, if after all these, there is still no improvement, he starts asking questions regarding the mother's relationship with others around her or with the *orisa*'s. And, of course, consultation with the divination god may confirm that the second wife is, indeed, a witch having supernatural powers with which she has "crippled" Aina's brain. Such powers are, however, invisible because they are not bound by the laws of nature. They are spiritual or at least non-natural. This, then, is a different level of explanation (Level II). While Level I appeals to nature, Level II appeals to supernature. This is how the supernatural features in the causal explanation of events: ordinary natural powers are necessary and sufficient for the explanation of ordinary events: an attack of fever that leaves in the normal time; a general bad harvest for lack of rain; the financial ruin of an extravagant person. Extraordinary events are explained by appeal to powers beyond nature, also as necessary and sufficient causes: fever attack that refused to go in spite of all medication; long period of drought -- the community gets worried about the intervention of a god; a son's recklessness and extravagance bothers the parents and it gets explained, thanks to the diviner, by appeal to witchcraft power or as a last resort, an uncooperative destiny.

Even with regard to such matters which can be explained by appeal to natural laws as, for example, a fatal accident resulting from brake failure during a heavy downpour, the question is still raised, "Why should it be my son's car?" The significance of such a question is the belief that it presupposes; namely, that there is something more in most occurrences than a mere fortuitous combination of events. It is not as if there is no belief in the regularity of nature. Indeed, this belief is also partly presupposed in any quest for explanation. We seek explanations for events which seem to belie the idea of regularity of nature; and such are of the kind which disrupt the regular flow of life. So when such events occur, adequate explanations cannot be cast in terms of some natural laws, because they are too general to be useful and satisfactory.[17] Of course, it is also objectively true, perhaps, that such a search for further explanations beyond that which is provided by natural laws may be due to ignorance about the laws of nature and the constitution of objects of nature. It is however true that for the person asking the question "why?", the need is for an explanation that answers that question in a way that makes sense to him/her. Such is the answer provided by appeal to the supernatural powers.

There is something also more fundamental in this. D. R. Price-Williams has noted that one of the fundamental beliefs of the Tiv is that "good life, good health, and good luck proceed in an unbroken straight line if not disturbed by evil influences, such as *Mbatsav*." Given this belief, it follows that illness will need to be explained by appeal to witchcraft power which goes beyond nature and which therefore has the power to disrupt its regularity. Thus, for the Tiv, none of the causes of illness is natural; they are either the *Mbatsav* [witches], or *akombo* [non-human forces] invoked by the *Mbatsav* to harm others.[18]

The further question is whether the concept of the supernatural has any religious connotation. This question should really not arise in view of the definition of religion which we worked with in the last chapter. If we may recall, religion is defined as "an apprehension, awareness or conviction of the existence of a supreme being, or more widely, of supernatural powers or influences controlling one's own humanity's or nature's destiny." From this, it should be clear that not only does the concept of supernatural involve religion, the two seem to be inseparable. But beside, there is also involved, some subtle reference to causality since the supernatural power is believed to control one's destiny. But the point of the question is not so much in itself, but in the bearing of the answers to it for the final question we have to address: Is causal explanation in African thought religious in nature? Again, the answer seems to be obvious in a certain sense. If, as we have shown, causal explanation in African thought make reference to supernatural entities, and if the concept of supernatural powers has religious bearing, then causal explanation in African thought would appear to have some religious bearing. It is the fundamental belief in the existence of religious objects and supernatural powers which underlie the search for causes in the realm of supernature. To put it in another way, following the Tiv belief referred to earlier, it is the belief in an ordained universe in which life is expected to flow without any hitch unless disrupted by evil forces, that suggests where and how to look for causes of disruption when it occurs. If there is such a fundamental belief which can be described as religious and it is the foundation of the search for causes of events which take people to the realm beyond nature, then such explanations have religious bearing, if not religious motives.

One reason that has been given for rejecting this interpretation of African notion of causality in quasi-religious terms is that in African thought there is no conceptual cleavage between the natural and the supernatural, and that nature is an integral whole. At the same time, Wiredu agrees that the people believe that "everything is ultimately explicable in both the animate and inanimate realm." This is supposed to be a unitary conception of the universe in which no distinction is made between the natural and the supernatural. This seems a bit puzzling. From the discussion thus far, it seems to me a bit far-fetched to say, for instance, that the Yoruba do not mark a distinction in their thinking, between the natural and the supernatural when the whole structure of their cosmology rests on this distinction. There are terms in the Yoruba language which name beings whose existence is considered supernatural. These are beings whose activities are believed to be not subject to the laws of nature. Pioneer literary figures such as late D.O. Fagunwa made extensive use of characters illustrating this belief. His *Ogbójú Odé Nínú Igbó Irúnmalè* is classic example. The world of such beings is certainly not conceived as identical with the world of human beings and other natural objects.

The idea that there is no conceptual cleavage between the two worlds only suggests, as we have noted above, that the results of the activities and use of power that go on apparently in the natural world with materials apparently taken from nature have results which by no means appear natural. This makes it intelligible to couch causal explanations in terms of both natural and supernatural linkages. This is the meaning of Busia's views, and this is confirmed by his further observation that: "In the search for the causes of an illness, we observed that the connections were *conceived* both in natural and in supernatural terms, physical and magical linkages were involved."[19] I do not see how this can be interpreted as meaning that the people have no concept of the supernatural.

In further support of his position, Wiredu goes on to observe that "the beings in question [i.e., supernatural or spiritual beings] can be *seen* by those who have suitably medicated eyes";[20] and he thinks that this disqualifies them from being spiritual. Again, as I have argued in the last chapter, the qualification "suitably medicated eyes" is important here. For it is not just anyone that can see these beings. Otherwise they will be just as natural as anyone. That Wiredu concedes this qualification is important and it should have helped to clarify the apparent confusion in the first instance. Of course, Wiredu is also not suggesting that "the gods or ancestors are conceived of as material or physical",[21] he is apparently worried about the appropriateness of the spiritual-material dichotomy which is a Western philosophical category. This worry is legitimate, but should not lead us to the extreme of denying that the people have this kind of conception. Instead, we should look carefully into our different languages and oral traditions to find out the appropriate terms. In Yoruba tradition, for instance, the òrìsà are construed as having powers which are not bound by natural laws. So are the *ebora* and *imalè*. Of course, Wiredu is right in maintaining that these beings are not conceived to be spiritual in a Cartesian sense. But they are also not construed in physical sense. They belong to a special class of non-human forces with extra-human powers. This is the important fact about them, whatever description we are inclined to give them. People who *know how* to control such powers can appropriate them and use them for good or ill, and in so doing they become causal agents. To such class of humans belong witches, sorcerers, herbalists and medicinemen. Even when people explain events of human significance in empirical terms, it does not stop there. A death of a human being caused by a snake bite in the bedroom is not fully explained by reference to the poisonous venom of the snake. Of course, the people are aware of this. But a snake in a bedroom must have something more to it, than just the ordinary appearance of a snake!

The question, of course, is what more and how can this 'more' be demonstrated? Is this not a case of postulating unnecessary agents of causality? Unless there is a principle that can be demonstrated as underlying the working of such agencies, the traditional thinker will not convince the skeptic and this is where the problem is, as the contributors to the special issue of *Second Order* on the rationality of witchcraft clearly showed.[22] When the question of the rationality of belief in the 'activity' of supernatural forces is raised, the request that is usually addressed to the believers is for them to show why they are justified in holding the belief. Defenders of such beliefs have sometimes objected to such demands on the ground that the rationality of a belief must be seen as relative to its context. In a sense, they are right, but this should not be mistaken as an excuse for not providing the principles underlying such a belief even if they are not shared by the objector. In what follows, I attempt to explore the principles underlying the belief in one aspect of causal agency by the Yoruba: the causal efficacy of the spoken word.

Ayajó: The Nature and Principle of Incantation

The Yoruba have a strong belief in the causal efficacy of a category of the spoken word: incantation. There are several kinds of this including *ofò, èpè, àpèta, àse, àwúre, ayajó*. What they have in common is that they are verbal utterances with particular tasks of changing the circumstances of life of a group or an individual for better or for worse. There is actually little or no difference in the principles underlying the working of *prayers* and the workings of incantation. A prayer, in the Christian faith, is directed at God to perform a particular task; that is, if it is a prayer of request or supplication. Prayers in this category vary according to their force which is also a function of the strength of the supplicants' faith and how much the request means to them. Prayers are verbal utterances which make use of analogical reasoning, reminding God of certain things which He had accomplished in the past under similar circumstances; or just simply asking the particular request to be answered for the reasons given. It is not unusual for people to have an instant answer to their prayers. Years ago, at the height of a serious drought, there was a prayer session for rain at 1st Baptist Church, Okeho, Nigeria. The prayer leader, late Pa Joseph Gbadegesin, prayed for one hour, reminding God about similar situations recorded in the Bible when God's people prayed for rain. Before the church session closed that day, there was a heavy downpour. It became the talk of the town. The agnostic will, of course, not be impressed by this. After all, it may just be a coincidence. To the believer, however, it is a perfect evidence that God answers prayers.

The point here is this. The universe is full of forces. Human beings participate in the activities of such forces because they also combine spirituality with material nature. Part of the function of the spoken word is to name things and to communicate with fellow humans as well as with spiritual forces. Ability to make words perform such causal functions depends on how much of the essence of the forces in the universe is known; including the names and essential nature of particular human beings.

Ayajó is one of the several kinds of incantations listed above. It is connected with *Orúnmìlà*, the Yoruba God of wisdom and divination. *Orúnmìlà* is believed to be one of the primordial divinities who co-existed with *Olódùmarè* in primordial times. It is believed that both *Orúnmìlà* and *Esù* -- the trickster god -- were not created, they were more of *Olódùmarè*'s associates than creatures, albeit occupying a less than equal position with him. The creative work of *Olódùmarè* is performed in the presence of *Orúnmìlà* who was the only witness to every being's choice of destiny as well as to their departure to the earth. According to the myth, *Orúnmìlà* stood on the junction of heaven and earth to see to the departure of all earth-bound creatures including normal humans, witches, sorcerers, and even animals and birds. He gave names to everything and they made a departing pledge to him to the effect that they will not harm or disturb the peace of any one of *Orúnmìlà*'s belongings, including his devotees and those who depend on them. *Ayajó* is the term that refers to this parting pledge.[23]

After this parting, it is not unusual to discover that either through ignorance, forgetfulness, or sheer mischief, some of the creatures who make this pledge came to disturb or attempt to harm *Orúnmìlà*'s own children. When such happens, they are quickly reminded by the priests of *Orúnmìlà* of this pledge as the latter recall the names and real nature of such offending creatures. Thus a scorpion which stings a human being is reminded of the name given to it by *Orúnmìlà* and how it had promised the latter to avoid harming his children. The scorpion is then asked to keep its promise by withdrawing or neutralizing the poison it had injected into the system of its victim.

Ayajó is thus an incantation which makes use of the real name or essence of particular beings - humans or animals - to make them perform or refrain them from performing a task. They may or may not be present at the scene of the command; so long as their true name is used; they are expected to perform. In a private correspondence with me, Professor Wande Abimbola has compared the underlying principle at work in *Ayajó* with the principle of acoustic physics. The idea here is the feature of resonance in certain systems. Any system that can resonate is capable of activating other similar systems when its frequency is the same (or nearly the same) as the natural vibration frequency of the source, even when they are not located in the same room. It is the same principle that underlies the working of *Ayajó*. The real nature of a being is activated once its name, which describes its essence, is correctly invoked. For this to work, therefore, one has to have a good understanding of the nature or essence of beings or objects. Witchcraft-doctors are able to control witches because they know their names and operate on the same frequency with them; witches are able to injure their victims because they know their real names as well as the real names or active principles of the mediating forces they use for this purpose. Herbalists know the real nature of herbs and what they are made to achieve for human well-being. But this is not all; there are other requirements, the most crucial of which is honesty. Thus a Yoruba saying goes thus: "*Bí o lópò oògùn, bí o bá nsèké kò ní jé*" -- "Even if you have a houseful of incantations and medicine, if you are dishonest, your medicine will not work." Therefore specialists in the use of incantations must be honest. They must also not be the rash or quick-tempered type. They are not expected to pronounce curses arbitrarily or at will. This is also why younger people are not let into the secret of traditional medicine.

The following is an example of Ayajo, from Chief M. A. Fabunmi, which makes use of the real name/nature of its object, in this case *àkeekèé* (scorpion). This is an incantation for the soothing of the pain from the scorpion's poison:

Akéré-soro-omo-Ogún, A-fì-rù-soro-omo-Osanyìn
Ijà Ogèdè l'o jà l'o ò mórí dé'lé,
Oró mérìndínlógún l'Olúfè fún o nígbànáà
Eranko-igbó l'óní kó o máa fi ta
Omo Olúfè ná à lo mà wá fi ta yi i o!
Yára wá so oró ná à di èjè
Bí oo bá wá so oró ná à di èjè
Olúfè yío mà gba oró ná à lówó re o.[24]

Akéré-soro-omo-ogún, (The real name of the scorpion)
A-fì-rù-soro-omo-Osanyìn, (Another real name of the scorpion)
You fought over a plantain and never got home,
Olúfè (the creator) gave you sixteen poisonous stings;
But you were to use them on beasts of the forest,
Now you have used one of them on a child of *Olúfè*,
Come quickly and change the poison to blood,
If you don't, all the poisonous stings will be withdrawn from you.

Note that this *Ayajó* makes use of the real name, nature and characteristics of the scorpion to command it to perform the task of neutralizing its poison. In the same way, human beings can be commanded to do things even when they are not physically present. Chief Ajayi Fabunmi has this to say:

Lóotó ni 'kò si ohun tuntun lábé òrun'. Lati ààrò ojó ni awon Yoruba ti mo wipe bi gbólóhùn òrò kan bá ti jade lenu enìyàn, ibi ti atégùn le gbe iró òrò naa de ko lopin rárá ni. Nwon mo wipe awon èdá Olorun miran wa pupo ti a ko le fi oju lásán ri, ati onikaluku gbogbo awon eda Olorun wonyi ni o ni oruko tire, titi kan'ra awon eranko ati eiye ati koriko ati bee bee lo. Gbogbo wa naa la si mo wipe bi a ba pe enikeni ni oruko abiso re, Oluware yio dahun ni. Wayi o, awon Yoruba atijo mo oruko ti nwon maa fi npe òpòlopò awon èdá Olorun ni à-pè-dáhùn.[25]

Truly, 'there is nothing new under the sun'. From the beginning of times, the Yoruba know that a word that is spoken out can travel miles in the wind. They also know that there are invisible beings and that every creature of *Olodumare* has their own real names, including animals, birds and even plants. And we all know that if a person is called by his/her given name, they will respond. Now, the traditional Yoruba of ancient times know the real name of all the creatures of Olodumare and they know how to call them and make them answer and perform desired tasks.

We may now raise the issue of the rationality of the belief in [i] non-physical entities and [ii] the causal efficacy of such agents as the spoken word. The skeptical theoretical scientist and philosopher maintains that only physical forms of matter exist and act as causal agents. So s/he is not likely to be impressed by the effort of the traditional thinker to provide the principle of *Ayajo*. The traditional thinker, on the other hand, concerned with practical matters, acts on the conviction that non-physical entities exist and act as causal agents. How do we settle the question of the rationality of belief here? Indeed, which account of rationality do we appeal to here? Consider the following as a candidate:

1. S's belief is an irrational belief if and only if S has the belief and realizes [or at least should realize, given his intelligence, information and experience] that there are little or no grounds for the truth of the belief but overwhelming grounds for the falsity of the belief;
2. S's belief is a rational belief if and only if S's belief is not irrational;
3. S's action is an irrational action if and only if S's action is based at least in part on S's irrational beliefs;
4. S's action is a rational action if and only if S's action is not irrational.[26]

On the basis of this definition, Hans Penner argues that "traditional religious thought and action are as rational as modern scientific thought and action."[27] I am not myself sure that this is the case. For one major problem even from this definition is the question of the determination of truth. What would be the ground for the truth of a belief in this context? What determines whether a belief is true or false? Is it correspondence with reality? But whose reality are we talking about?

Indeed, the point that Penner seems to be making is that, to identify a belief as rational is to identify it as based on another belief concerning its truth. If that belief is reasonably held, given the information available to the agent, including those which s/he *ought to be apprised of-* then the first belief is rational, even if mistaken [in the sense that it is not true]. But this seems to take the ground off the concession. If a person ought to realize that there is little or no ground for his beliefs [from whose perspective?], and he does not, then it is irrational. From this, there is little basis for characterizing a belief that is mistaken as rational unless we want to suggest that those who hold it have some ground, given their [limited] intelligence, for holding it. This then seems to be another rabbit from the hat of the good old paternalist.

It appears to me that we can use the insight from Collingwood's account of cause to settle this issue. If the identification of cause is with a view to controlling events, and there is therefore a relativity of cause, because out of the several conditions, an individual may choose to highlight the one that she can control or produce, then each of the empirical scientist and traditional priest/thinker has a choice which cannot be faulted as long as the end is achieved. The traditional herbalist identifies the machination of the witch as the cause of Aina's poor performance in school. The main question will be whether he is able to control the witch in such a way that Aina's performance is improved. Who is to answer to this but Aina's mother on the basis of her evaluation of Aina after the herbalist has done his job? But suppose we are now told that the herbalist, even after pointing to his achievement in getting Aina's performance improved, should *demonstrate* empirically how he did it and that if he cannot, then his approach is not rational.[28] But how should we expect the herbalist to respond to this kind of request? We are, in effect, requesting him to cross a gulf which it has not been his responsibility to create in the first place. We are telling him that though he had identified a cause which he has been able to control, he should also identify the one that does not lie within his area of control.

Take again the example of the automobile accident. The road engineer identifies the condition of the road as cause. That is what he is able to control. He cannot be asked to also identify the driver's speed, for that lies outside his area of control. If the interest for identifying cause is to control events, then the idea of division of labor based on competence in dealing with specific causes is in place. This is the situation with respect to practical sciences. If this is true, then the principle of relativity of causes is also applicable. According to this principle, for any person, the cause of a thing is that one out of several possible conditions, which she is able to produce or prevent. In medicine, this means that one disease may have more than one cause as seen by two or more doctors with inclinations toward bio-chemical causation, psychological causation or supernatural causation.[29] The test of the adequacy of the identified cause will then be in the success of the cause to prevent or cure the disease. This will, ultimately, also be the test of the rationality of the belief in the causal efficacy of non-physical entities.

From the discussion of *Ayajó*, it is clear that people are held to cause events to happen just by the spoken word. The causal efficacy of this is not in doubt. Obviously, there is a lot that we do not know about how this is done; but that it is done, at least in the minds of the people, is beyond dispute. Even now there are people who act at a distance to produce effects. This is, of course, not peculiar to the Yoruba as has been demonstrated by parapsychology. It is therefore no use denying the causal efficacy of the spoken word just because we do not know how it works. Indeed, the best answer to the question: "does it work?" may well be "dare it". What we really need, however, is more effort to find out more about the principles underlying the belief. For, it is crucial even for our understanding of some aspects of traditional medicine.

Conceptions of Health, Disease and the Ethics of Health Care

In this section, our objective is to explore the foundations of traditional health care system, including (i) traditional conceptions of health and disease and their metaphysical presuppositions (ii) the components of traditional medical practice, including herbal medicine and divination and (iii) the prospects of integrating traditional and modern medicine.

Traditional Conceptions of Health and Disease

Conceptions of health and disease constitute important components of the world-view of traditional Africans. The Yoruba, like most other African culture groups, have a holistic conception of health and disease. To be well or healthy is to be in a position to do one's daily task; it is to have a strong body and mind. The common greeting asks after the strength of the body: Is the body strong? But though this asks after the body, the Yoruba word for health, *àlàáfíà*, means more than physical health. It refers to a person's physical, social, psychological and spiritual well-being.[30] If any of these aspects of a human's life is in a state of dis-ease, then she cannot claim to have *àlàáfíà*. Indeed, though to be healthy is to have *ìlera* [strong body] and to be unhealthy is to have *àilera* [weak body]; reference to *ara* [body] here should be understood in a broad sense to include soul, spirit and psyche.

A person who is not healthy or who is ill is in a state of dis-ease and needs to be reinstated wholly. The meaning of this state is that there is an imbalance in the order of nature regarding the person's existence and this imbalance needs to be corrected. It could be natural or supernatural. The task of the healer is to identify the cause of this imbalance and set it right. A healthy person, they say, is a wealthy person, and so the Yoruba will do anything to avoid illness and if it occurs, to reinstate themselves to a healthy state because nothing compares with health [*Kíní tó àlàáfíà?*].

The Hausa conception of health is similar to the Yoruba. Indeed, the Yoruba word for health [*àlàáfíà*] is a variant of the Hausa word. It is perhaps originally an Arabic word incorporated into Hausa vocabulary. Thus the phrase *Lafiya jiki* means "well-being of the body" [physical health] and the Hausa proverb "*Lafiya ta fi kudi*" meaning "Health is better than money" compares with the Yoruba phrase "*Alàáfíà l'ójù, ìlera l'orò*" [Health is the most important thing, bodily strength is wealth].

The Hausa have another word '*Karfi*' which means 'strength', and the term '*karfin jiki*' [bodily strength] compares with '*lafiya jiki*' [bodily health]. This is the positive state of existence. Illness occurs when this positive state no longer exists. So illness is negative, it is the absence of health:

> Within the purview of Hausa medicine, *lafiya* refers to the correct, balanced, properly ordered state of the body. When that balance is upset *lafiya* is no longer present and a state of illness results. One is either healthy and has lafiya, or not healthy, and lacking lafiya -- the absence of *lafiya* is a pathological state to be corrected by the application of an appropriate remedy.[31]

This holistic conception of health is common among all African cultures. With this in mind, it is appropriate to raise the question what is conceived as the cause(s) of the disruption in the balance: What causes illness? First, it is important to note that the notion of disease is not commonly used. A person is said to be ill (or unwell) not to have a disease. Disease in terms of the background to illness is not before the observer or the sick. The picture that appears to the observer is that of a person who is not well, who lacks àlàáfíà and the question is what is the cause of this imbalance. As Wolfgang Bichmann rightly observes "African medicine does not primarily treat diseases, but sick people. One cannot therefore understand African medicine by regarding its pathogenetical concepts and its nosology, but rather from its cosmology, i.e, the hierarchy of forces which are thought to belong to every being, whether alive or dead."[32] This should not, however, be misconstrued as suggesting that Africans do not have an idea of natural causes of illness; for the cosmology allows for the incorporation of such an idea.

Contrary to common misconceptions, and in spite of the appeal to supernature in causal explanation, neither the Yoruba nor the Hausa (nor other African cultures) make an immediate appeal to the supernatural to explain illness. Indeed, there are two major categories in the causal explanation of illness:

Non-supernatural (Natural) Causes -
   Germs
   Psychological Disturbance
Supernatural Causes -
   God(s), Ancestors, Spirit beings
   Powerful medicinemen, witches, sorcerers

Causal Agents

Non-supernatural causes of illness are sought when a case of illness is first presented. Any adult person knows for instance that fever is caused by certain germs (*kòkòrò*) and that to get rid of it one should do something about the germs. Such diagnosis is natural and empirical. The cause of illness is traced to nature. Of course, this may be only an immediate cause. A further question may be raised as to why the person is bitten by the mosquito which caused the malaria. But this is not generally raised. The traditional herbalist knows the immediate causes of some illness and how they come about.

Apart from the category of germs, however, another non-supernatural cause is a person's psychological make-up or state of mind. The reason this is considered non-supernatural is that it does not make reference to any cause beyond nature. In other words, an illness that is caused by psychological disturbance can be cured by a process which includes psychotherapy: talking to. Here then we have another category of immediate cause.

When a case of illness attributable to natural causes persists in spite of medical care, then there is fear that there is something more to it. Questions are then raised about the possible involvement of some supernatural beings or at least human beings with power. We then have to move beyond immediate to ultimate causes which include witchcraft, sorcery, spirit-being, etc. In some cases, a combination of supernatural and empirical causes is appealed to, as when, for instance, it is feared that a person's illness is as a result of poison which has been effected by action at a distance. This also applies when an illness is due to the piercing of the flesh by a small thorn which, otherwise considered insignificant, has now produced infection of the blood. The natural occurrence providing immediate cause of illness, has now led to an explanation in terms of "why?" which appeals to supernature.

It is here that a misunderstanding by the Western thinker sets in. On the one hand, some would say that traditional Africans are incurably superstitious because they make quick recourse to the gods. This is not true, from what has been said above. On the other hand, however, it is also claimed, following Levy-Bruhl, that the African mind is pre-logical and pre-rational and that this explains the supernatural explanations of illness. Levy-Bruhl has been refuted by scores of anthropologists after him, especially Evans-Pritchard and Robin Horton. The point made by these two scholars bothers on the cultural dimensions of rationality and logic. The western conception of rationality makes sense within the western culture and world-view. But this cannot be imposed on others. Beside, there is a basis for a rational explanation of witchcraft-belief within the African world-view. As Gluckman puts it:

> Witchcraft is a theory of causation, but it is a theory which explains causal links which modern scientists do not attempt, cannot attempt to explain......The belief in witchcraft provides explanation for the particularity of misfortune. It does not, for the African, provide the whole interpretation of the misfortune.[33]

Horton, on the other hand, attempts to explain supernatural explanations as a *kind* of theoretical explanation in which spiritual entities function as theoretical entities in science:

> The situation is not very different from that in which a puzzled American layman, seeing a large mushroom cloud on the horizon consults a friend who happens to be a physicist. On the one hand, the physicist may refer him to theoretical entities: 'Why this cloud? Well, a massive fusion of hydrogen nuclei has just taken place.' Pushed further, however, the physicist is likely to refer to the assemblage and

dropping of a bomb containing special substances. Substitute 'disease' for 'mushroom cloud', spirit 'anger' for 'massive fusion of hydrogen nuclei' and we are back again with the diviner. In both cases reference to theoretical entities is used to link events in the visible tangible world [natural effects] to their antecedents in the same world [natural causes].[34]

According to Horton, then, witchcraft belief emphasizes the disturbance of personal relations in its explanation of illness, whereas modern medicine emphasizes the germ theory. Yet it is true that there are now aspects of modern medicine [psychosomatic] which also emphasize disturbed social relation in its diagnosis. Indeed, both the western industrial man and the traditional African may be in a similar situation with regard to their understanding of the language of modern medicine. But the traditional man is in a better position because he is not too far removed from the language of the healer/diviner. Medical cure is a socio-cultural phenomena. As Peter Morley puts it: "In traditional societies, medical knowledge is far more closely integrated with the institutions and all-encompassing cosmology of the society as a whole than is the case in more differentiated societies."[35]

The importance of the world-view of patients in any effective program of therapeutic care cannot be too stressed. Human nature differs historically and spatially and we cannot therefore rely on an abstract concept of human behavior as a basis for therapeutic healing. People's assumptive frame of reference need to be taken into consideration.

Traditional Healers

Herbalist

The herbalist deals with herbs and herbal medicine. He is versed in the knowledge of leaves, roots, barks of trees and other plant physiognomies. He uses such medicinal properties to cure the ailment -- the natural cause. As a specialist in names and application of herbs, he is expected to know the true nature of plants. He cannot afford not to because he is relied upon by clients to distinguish poisonous from efficacious plants.

A metaphysical presupposition of this, as observed in the previous section, is that plants have their own essences and real names. A herbalist goes out in the morning to collect plants for medicine. If he prepares himself well and is close to nature as he is expected to be, it is believed that he will see through the appearance of the plants with a clear knowledge of their uses. The herbalist is, for this knowledge, subordinate to the priests of Ifa, since as was noted above, Orunmila is regarded as the only witness to the nature given each creature and the purpose it is expected to achieve. Of course, this is the metaphysical foundation of the belief: each creature has its nature and purpose; the universe is expected to be a harmonious balance in which the totality of all contributions achieve the good for humankind. Thus, in collecting plants, leaves and roots as herbs, a herbalist approaches these objects of nature with respect, in the understanding that they are (i) inhabited by powerful forces which pass on powers to them and (ii) made for the purpose of contributing to the totality of good in the universe.

The impression should not be given that traditional healers only operate on the basis of such metaphysical assumptions. Indeed, they also have an empirical understanding of the composition of herbs and an acute knowledge of diseases and their symptoms. This is due to the fact that many of them have long family traditions as healers and new generations get introduced to the intricacies early in life. It is not unusual for a child to start learning at the age of seven. In such a situation, by the time he becomes an adult he must have an encyclopedic knowledge of herbal medicine. This aspect of the training and exposure of traditional healers is not usually emphasized because it has been identified as purely magical.

The psychotherapeutic aspect of traditional healing is equally, if not more important. We know, for instance, that many illnesses have psychological causes and traditional healers have the best resources for dealing with such. They, as elder members of the community, know that a social disorder may create psychological disorder of disproportionate dimensions. They are familiar with the family history of their clients. They can therefore provide adequate counseling to cushion the effects of sudden shocks. Some psychiatric problems are indeed best handled by traditional healing procedures as the Aro (Nigeria) experiment clearly showed.

There are, of course, problems that need to be addressed if the traditional healer is going to be a continuous effective participant in the health care system. First, the problem of mistrust has always been there. Many traditional healers are reluctant to allow their formulae to be put on record or tested. There is a sort of secrecy surrounding the practice, and this is a serious handicap. Without records, many of the formulae that could be useful have died with their discoverers! Of course, Western trained medical practitioners, who should encourage such records, do not help matters by their own attitudes which also border on mistrust and lack of respect for the traditional healers. One expects them to know better that even modern Western knowledge of medicine is cumulative, having been built on the trials and errors of traditional medical practice. Second, the majority of traditional healers, especially in the rural areas, do not understand the importance of measurement in the dispersing of drugs. This is a small problem which can be remedied once there is collaboration between western and traditional healers. So is the problem of cleanliness.

The most serious problem, however, is that of method of diagnosis and symptomatology. Without precise instruments for diagnosing the cause of illness, a healer can only continue to adopt trial and error method which may prove costly in real emergency situations. It is not unusual for a patient to die under such circumstances. Yet one may hold that, where there is readiness on the part of traditional healers to improve on their diagnostic methods, there will always be a way. The question is whether this would indicate an abandonment of "traditional" healing as we know it for "scientific" healing. I do not personally think so. To maintain otherwise is again to think of a static tradition of doing things. The real obstacle to improvement is the attitude of those involved. Many traditional healers, for instance, have no problem identifying the genuine causes of certain minor illnesses, e.g., mosquito bite as the cause of malaria fever. But as Buckley's confrontation with his informant shows, there are some for whom malaria is caused by too much exposure to the heat of the sun. Even here, however, one cannot be too sure that we are dealing with the same concept of malaria. What is also interesting is that, even the herbalist here will identify the correct herbal medicine for malaria.[36]

The Diviner

This is the spiritual-medical personnel who knows the secret of the divine-being as well as the knowledge of the various plants. As has been explained above, *Orúnmìlà*, the god of divination, is the Yoruba god of wisdom. He was present with *Olódùmarè* on creation and therefore has unfathomable knowledge about the universe. The diviner is a priest of *Orúnmìlà* to whom he has passed on knowledge of the secret of the universe.[37] The diviner's role in health-care becomes important in view of the metaphysical conception of health, disease and existence in general. Central to this is the belief in predestination. A sick person wants to know, for instance, whether the illness is in his destiny or it is caused by malevolent forces, whether he will survive or die. In a sense, access to the diviner makes a lot of difference since he is in a position to psychoanalyze the problem and offer some hope. Of course, hardly does a diviner say that a person is going to die. Even if he sees death in the horizon, he assumes that sacrifice can prevent it.

The world-view of a people is their assumptive frame of reference. But a tension arises in case the assumptive frame of reference is clearly incompatible with the expectations and goals of action. In medical practice, the goal is to heal or cure. Is reference to supernatural causes of illness compatible with this goal? Or should we condemn such appeals on grounds of irrationality? This is obviously a difficult question. Orthodox medicine is based on the cannons of scientific method. Diagnosis is an empirical matter deriving from years of experience. But it is also true that what is now reliable experience is a child of trial and error. That is not the issue. Rather the issue of interest is whether the goal of medical practice -- healing -- is unrealizable by attending to people's metaphysical ideas.

To address this question it has to be kept in mind that the matter of curing and healing is not a matter of objectivity independent of people's feeling. There is a lot of subjectivity surrounding it. If a person believes seriously that he is tormented by witches or other powers, that is enough to make him/her sick even to the point of death. A doctor may diagnose malaria and give treatment appropriate to that diagnosis and s/he may not succeed in curing the patient, simply because the problem is more psychic than medical. The effectiveness of drug is a function of the beliefs of the sick. If this is true, then to achieve the goal of medical practice, a people's belief system cannot be discounted and it follows therefore that both supernatural and natural causes have to be taken into account. Can modern medicine accept this? Is it going to be of any real benefit?

The question of acceptance has to be decided by appeal to our goal again. If we have the objective of providing healing, we cannot avoid the integration of traditional approach with modern approach. The question whether it will help will be determined by experience. But there have been worthwhile experiments in this area especially in the field of psychiatry.

Professor T. A. Lambo, a pioneer psychiatrist in Nigeria launched a project of treatment at Aro, Abeokuta which integrated traditional and modern approaches to mental illness. Traditional medical men were brought in as partners. Indeed, for Lambo, the traditional healer should be in charge, with the western trained psychiatrist just helping, because the emphasis should be on a holistic socio-cultural approach which looks at the totality of man.[38]

The point is that in many cases, mental illness represents problems in living, manifestations of disorganization in the social context; and the traditional healer, familiar with such contexts, is in a position to help. With such an approach, sacrificing to a god will not be an irrational thing to do. If a mentally sick person comes from a locality in which the belief in witchcraft power prevails, that will probably dominate their thought and have an effect on the therapeutic procedure. In such a situation, it makes sense to use both traditional healing procedure and orthodox medicine. This point is supported most clearly by the result of an investigation carried out on the pattern of utilization of health services in the Ibarapa division of Western Nigeria by Dr. Z. A. Ademuwagun of the University College Hospital Ibadan. The study shows, among other things, that:

[1] there was no evidence of association of a particular ailment with either orthodox or traditional practitioners preventing a patient consulting both for psychological reasons, or to reassure himself;

[2] degree of education did not appear significantly to affect the pattern of utilization of health services among majority of consumers;

[3] most people with traditional, cultural, religious, and psychologically related health problems, such as excessive worries over matters of life and death affairs and sleeplessness, consulted traditional healers;

[4] there is some indication that traditional practitioners are more competent at dealing with some health problems 'native' to the locality [e.g. malaria and yellow fever] than those which are 'foreign' [e.g. tuberculosis and measles/chicken pox].[39]

The findings from this study aptly confirm of the position we have maintained on this issue. What it calls for is a commitment on the part of the authorities to recognize and encourage traditional healers as partners in the effort to provide health care for the people.

Part II Contemporary African Realities

6

THE CONCEPT OF ULTIMATE REALITY AND MEANING AND CONTEMPORARY AFRICAN REALITIES: THE RELIGIOUS VIEW

Certain realities stare contemporary Africans in the face, whether they have any view(s) on Ultimate Reality and Meaning (URAM) or not. I shall refer to these as Contemporary African Realities (CAR). These are not conceptions; they belong to the class of experienced reality, which in a sense, give meaning to conceptions and, therefore, seem to be prior. These CAR may be explained by appeal to certain principles, according to particular views of URAM. Such fundamental principles may then be taken or conceived as the ultimate reality that underlie the contemporary reality and provide its explanation. It seems to me that three such views can be identified in contemporary Africa. These may, for convenience sake, be referred to as the Religious view, the Cultural view and the Ideological view. The consequence that is normally drawn from such analysis, then, is that any adequate approach to understanding CAR must come to terms with the nature of their ultimate ground already identified. In what follows, I attempt an analysis of CAR and the various principles that have been appealed to for understanding them. These CAR may, for the sake of discussion, be grouped into three: economic, political and social. It is obvious that this division is artificial - there is no clear dividing line between them. But again, it does not really matter as long as we take this division as dictated by our analytical objectives. Finally, in my discussion of CAR in the following brief remarks in this chapter, I am only presenting a picture of the situation that I refer to as CAR. An elaborate analysis, together with views on the causes and solution, is the focus of my attention in the remaining part of this book.

Contemporary Economic Realities

Under contemporary African Economic realities, we have poverty and hunger, low productivity in the midst of wealth and natural abundance and economic exploitation of individuals and nations. Contemporary Africa is blessed with natural resources in an enviable proportion vis-a-vis the rest of the world. Yet there is nothing to show for it. David Attah's observation in 1972 aptly summarizes the situation: Africa is a paradox which typifies poverty in the midst of plenty. In terms of development potential and natural resources, Africa is about the richest continent in the world and yet in real terms the poorest and the most underdeveloped.[1] The average person cannot feed his/her family on a balanced diet. Children are particularly worse hit by the phenomenon of hunger. Famine has become almost uncontrollable in many parts of the continent. Food aid has become the only hope of life for millions. A situation in which the next plate of rice is very uncertain because it depends on the goodwill of foreigners and the frame of mind of leaders [to accept or not to accept aid] is, to say the least, an undesirable one. But that is the reality for many Africans today. This must sound inexplicable at least to those familiar with its natural wealth. While others have as few as five months of the year for cultivation, Africa is blessed with a wonderful climate which supports all-year round farming. Where others have to worry about alternative sources of energy to cut down on bills, Africans are blessed with natural energy which only wait anxiously to be tapped. This is beside the unfathomable wealth of potential energy that lies under the surface of the land. Indeed, the green pastures upon which Africans are made to lie seem greener than Biblical David's. The contemporary reality, though, is that all these resources and wealth of nature have not helped to alleviate the suffering, hunger and the poverty of the common African. It would appear that the problems are soaring beyond reach. To compound this is the scourge of disease which has proved almost insurmountable. Of course, it seems a logical consequence of the aforementioned reality of hunger and poverty. Poverty is the father of hunger, while disease is its grandchild.

Finally, there is the reality of economic exploitation at the individual and national levels. On the one hand, our economic system gives room for the exploitation of individual workers who have no choice but to sell their labor and/or products at prices dictated by the buyers due to a variety of reasons. Agricultural workers, are for instance, subjected to the vagaries of the seasons and, in a situation where proper attention has not been paid to the need for mechanization and storage, bumper harvests normally mean low returns to the farmers. In most cases, therefore, these class of workers are objects of exploitation; with its telling effect on their morale and therefore on the prospects of a solid agro-based development for the continent. It is a hard-learned lesson now that farming is no longer attractive to anybody precisely because of this kind of neglect that entrenches exploitation.

Just as individuals suffer exploitation, African nations are not saved, precisely because of their inability to develop their natural resources as a way to industrialization. African nations either depend on a single-commodity [e.g. petroleum] as a means of earning foreign exchange or they export raw materials [e.g. cocoa, timber] at prices dictated by the industrial West which later export the finished product to Africa again at prices determined in the West. It is a case of double exploitation. As Obafemi Awolowo once noted with regret: "In international trade and finance, and in the supply of export management and technical know-how, the terms are consistently loaded heavily against Africa which is terribly short of expertise in many vital areas of development."[2] It is indeed more regrettable that in many cases the shortage of expertise is more artificial than natural, because many African experts have been forced to seek greener pastures outside Africa as a result of intolerable political or economic conditions.[3]

Social Realities

These realities of economic nature have created social problems in large dimensions. In the 'good old days', as thinkers like Nyerere would say, unarmed robbery was uncommon and armed robbery unthinkable. Members of society saw themselves as their brothers' keeper. There was poverty on the social plane. But it was not privatized. No one individual felt the scourge of poverty in an unbearable way. This was prevented by a web of social relations in which extended family members were accommodated and taken care of. In Nyerere's words, "In tribal society, the individuals or the families within a tribe were 'rich' or 'poor' according to whether the whole tribe was rich or poor. If the tribe prospered all the members of the tribe shared in its prosperity."[4] But the contemporary reality is that each individual has to solely bear the brunt of the burden. Those who cannot, have resorted to all sorts of devices including robbery with violence, drug pushing, suicide and other kinds of anti-social behavior. And these have all become part and parcel of CAR. Society, on its part has responded, not by a sympathetic look at the probable cause of such behaviors, but by institutionalizing the most inhuman punishments to deal with them. Such reactions only have aggravated the situation by breeding a cabal of hardened criminals.

Political Realities

In addition to the aforementioned, there is another group of realities not fundamentally different from them. These are the realities of the political climate of African societies. These include political violence, election rigging, political intolerance and racial discrimination. The phenomenon of political intolerance has particularly become a living reality in the majority of African states. 'Democratically' elected leaders detest opposition while dictators hate criticisms. Leaders seem now to be the only patriots as critics are declared saboteurs and are liable to indefinite incarceration.

Racial prejudice and segregation is mounting high, in spite of the various campaigns against it. Killings, maiming, arson, all politically motivated, are the unfortunate realities of contemporary African societies. Majorities are oppressed by minorities with superior power of terror and support from powerful allies. The color of the skin is still a portent factor in the determination of who gets what in some African nations.

All these have succeeded in bringing to the fore the depth of alienation and despair among the peoples of Africa. Alienation is the crux of contemporary African realities. In all aspects of human life, it can be sensed: Cultural, Economic, Political. A people barred from open criticism of government policies and actions cannot consider themselves an integral part of the nation. Criticism is an essential lubricant for the smooth functioning of governmental machine. It is part of human nature to talk even if one is not listened to. It is bad enough if you decide to shut your ears to avoid or ignore a person. It is worse when you decide to silence him/her. For then you are denying his/her personhood. This is what happens in most African societies. Hence the sense of alienation and despair among those who genuinely want to contribute to the upliftment of their societies but cannot do so because they are not allowed.

Ultimate Reality and Meaning [URAM] and Contemporary African Realities [CAR]

What has the above got to do with the concept of Ultimate Reality and Meaning (URAM)? I am aware of the reasonableness of this question and would address it with a few remarks on the concept of Ultimate Reality and Meaning (URAM).

It seems to me we can approach the concept of URAM from two angles: as an abstract metaphysical concept and as a practical life phenomenon. As the former, URAM is a mental construct with little or no connection with real life concerns. As such, the picture of CAR presented above would seem to have nothing to do with URAM, and the consciousness of CAR, occasioned by the life experiences of Africans would not be an essential presupposition of URAM. Such a conception of URAM would also appear to regard it as an exception to the valid Marxian position that

> Men are the producers of their conceptions, ideas etc -real active men,
> as they are conditioned by a definite development of their productive

forces and of the intercourse corresponding to these, up to its furthest forms. Consciousness can never be anything else than conscious existence, and the existence of men is their actual life-process.[5]

I submit that any interpretation of URAM which may lead to a denial of the validity of this point is inadequate.

The second interpretation in which URAM is seen in practical terms seems to me a more acceptable one. As discussed by Tibor Horvath, URAM is shot through and through with practical real life dimension. According to Horvath, URAM refers to "that to which the human mind reduces and relates everything; that which does not reduce to anything else."[6] It is "what man has most on his mind." However, as he goes further to observe, "All...interpretations (of URAM) are conditioned by each man's particular existence; which in turn is a manifestation of the existing ultimate reality."[7] It follows therefore that URAM has a lot to do with the real existence of individuals since the only road to the realization of "the existing ultimate reality" is via each individual's perception.

In the contemplation of URAM, there is praxis. The individual's contemplation is in a social context and cannot therefore be purely abstract. Furthermore, in the African context, such contemplations, grounded as they are in the social milieu, cannot but have social dimension. Philosophy cannot fail to take the human dilemma seriously. URAM, seen as a practical life concept, is an expression of ultimate reality as depicted in the context of practical living. It is a reflection on the problems of life and the meaning it has for people. The conception of URAM takes a cue from the living experiences of the people. The understanding of the realities of life as lived in a particular historical moment also reflects people's conception of ultimate reality. It is this connection between URAM as practical concept and CAR as the practical life experience, that I have as the justification for presenting this picture of CAR in this context.

URAM and Understanding CAR : Three Views

If the foregoing is accepted, I would now like to highlight further connection between my discussion of CAR and my interpretation of URAM by presenting three explanations of CAR in the light of certain views of URAM. Three views are identifiable in the effort to understand, make sense of and resolve the problems posed for human existence in Africa by these realities. These include the religious view, the cultural view and the politico-economic view. I will take up each of these views in the next three chapters, beginning with the religious view in this chapter.

Contemporary African Realities: The Religious View

By the religious view of URAM, I mean that view which takes God (or any comparable being/concept) as the ultimate reality. Thus, on the religious view of URAM, the ultimate explanation of CAR must be traced to the missing link in the lives of a majority of contemporary Africans: GOD. As the ultimately real, no one can make any headway in life without coming to terms with Him. So any nation or individual that does not take God seriously as the ultimately real and as the one who gives meaning to existence, cannot avoid the kinds of realities which I have highlighted as CAR. In other words, the ultimate explanation for CAR is Godlessness: the refusal to accept GOD as the ultimate reality. This seems to imply that if you accept this *ultimate reality of God*, you are bound to accept His direction and everything will follow. Examples of this view can be found in the writings of Bolaji Idowu, John Mbiti and a host of other African theologians.[8]

Thus in the concluding pages of *African Religions and Philosophy* (1969), Mbiti raises the question whether "in this period of dilemmas and challenges, religion has a place and a role to play in Africa."[9] He answered his question in the affirmative, observing, among other things, that apart from supplying new myths or reviving old ones, religion "should and can provide tools and inspiration to the man of Africa to think afresh the fundamental issues of his life which matter most and to find both meaning and security in that life."[10] Furthermore, Mbiti argues that secularism cannot provide the much needed forum for discovering the meaning of life because it only reduces "man to a statistical robot, casting votes for politicians, producing more goods in the factory for capitalist, a figure in population census for communist revolutionaries or just a competitor in the classroom, bus or queue for a dish of rice."[11] Obviously, Mbiti does not see humans finding the meaning of life in any of these activities, and he concludes that "only religion is fully sensitive to the dignity of man as an individual person and creature who has both physical and spiritual dimensions... It is only religion which contains the area and tools for everyone to search for and fathom the depths of his being."[12] It follows from these observations, therefore, that Mbiti would regard the present predicament of Africa, as depicted in my elaboration of contemporary African realities above, as emanating from a gradual elimination of God and religion from the lives of Africans.

But what exactly does this mean? Mbiti's characterization of Africa's dilemma is that of traditional societies rooted in traditional solidarity but increasingly being exposed to modern change, which makes the foundation of their existence and sense of solidarity shaken and undermined. This calls for new values, new identities and a new self-consciousness; and it is to this need that he believes religion has a response. How? Mbiti's answer is as ingenious as it is paradoxical. First, as he concedes, Africa has almost every religious system that the world has ever known represented on her soil. If religion has a role to play, then it must either be a combination of all those religions through a cooperative effort, or by some process of elimination [on what ground?], some of these systems will be discovered inappropriate and one may be seen to have the most desirable prospect of contributing to the resolution of the African dilemma. While Mbiti tosses with the former approach, it is only to reject it in favor of the second, and the pride of place is, not surprisingly, given to Christianity.

The thrust of Mbiti's position may be reconstructed as follows:

Contemporary African Realities: The Religious View

1. Every religious system is represented in Africa. However, for a religious system to be relevant to the resolution of the problem of contemporary African realities, it must be capable of adapting to the needs and values of modern societies.

2. The main strength and contribution of African traditional religions lie in the past - a period when each society evolved its own religious system and it in turn shaped the evolution of the society.

3. Traditional religions [including ancient Christianity in Egypt and Ethiopia, as well as Islam and African traditional religion] have become dangerously institutionalized, and involved with every department of human life.

4. Institutionalization prevents these religions from playing an effective role in the face of new challenges: the disintegration of the old social order means the disintegration of the institutionalized religion.

5. Ancient Christianity, legalistic and orthodox Islam and African traditional religions are not sufficiently ready for radical social changes.

6. Yet that these religions are not thus ready for change and cannot keep pace with it does not mean that such changes can do without a basically religious orientation: since traditional Africans are in all things religious, any movement for change must take this into account.

7. The problem with traditional religions is that while they make appeal to Zamani myths, they are not rich in future myths and, yet, both are needed.

8. There are Sasa and future (myths) in Negritude, African personality, African socialism, Christian ecumenism and Muslim brotherhoods.

9. Muslims and Christians have purely futuristic expectations such as paradise and messianic hopes. They are therefore able to supply new myths to go along with the new and radical changes.

10. But this is not enough. Religion should and can provide tools and inspiration to the man of Africa to think afresh fundamental issues of life which matter most, and to find both meaning and security in that life. Here is the area in which religion can hope to make a lasting contribution to modern Africa. It is only religion which provides a common denominator for all in origin, experience and

destiny, which contains the areas and tools for everyone to search for and fathom the depths of his being.

11. From 10, it seems to follow that all religions, whether singly, jointly or in competition have a contribution to make in creating new standards, morals and ethics for a changing society.

12. Such contributions can be most effectively made at the level of *Transfused Religion*: a non-institutionalized level where religion is akin to social uniformity, more like the Rousseauian civil religion, "tolerant and indifferent", best injected in the homes and schools.

Mbiti sees this religious transfusion as a basis for the forward movement of African societies, based as it is on the religious traditions of Africa, but now infused with modern needs and values. It is, so to say, a civil religion exploiting the religiosity of traditional Africans. In the light of such a great religious heritage, institutional and orthodox religions need not be apprehensive if their inner and professing adherents are few. They should be able to take comfort in the fact that they will have shepherded a portion of humanity from secular to sacred history, from the slavery of formal religiosity to the freedom of self-hood.[13]

This is inspiring indeed. For if such a concept of civil religion can be worked into the social life of citizens of African nations, we may, at least hope for some relief from the problems we have highlighted here. For one thing, it is a means of infusing a sense of patriotism in the hearts of citizens. If those who do not now believe that they owe anything to their country can, by such a transformation, be made to see their misconception of life, part of the battle will have been won. This is why Rousseau brought up the idea of civil religion, and it is the basis of his recommendations to political leaders as presented in his *The Government of Poland*. But as inspiring as this is, it is not really what Mbiti wants and so, the process of elimination must continue.

13. Transfused religion is a "long mythological route to come to the reality." The idea that people can embrace a civil religion does not appear real to Mbiti and so a shorter path is called for: Christianity "which is also 'indigenous', 'traditional' and 'African' like the other major religious systems considered here, holds the

greatest and the only potentialities of meeting the dilemmas and challenges of modern Africa, and of reaching the full integration and manhood of individuals and communities."[14]

Mbiti observes that the other religious systems are not saying anything radically new or different from what is already embedded in Christianity. The point then is that other religious systems are incapable of resolving the problem of African realities. Traditional religion is eliminated because, according to Mbiti, it concerns itself only with the Zamani [past] and not with the future. Islam and Christianity are relevant because they are capable of supplying new myths, and providing tools and inspirations for thinking afresh the issues of life. It would seem then that traditional religion is found wanting in both of these vital areas. I do not know what it means to say that no future myths are supplied by traditional religion when most of the variants have conceptions of not only an after-life, but also of immortality and reincarnation which tend to restrain human beings from a life of greed, avarice and wickedness-the major banes of our present decadent societies. Thus Mbiti himself notes that because "the sense of corporate life is so deep [among traditional Africans], it is inevitable that the solidarity of the community must be maintained, otherwise there is disintegration and destruction...If a person steals a sheep, personal relations are at once involved because the sheep belongs to a member of the corporate body...As such it is an offence against the community..." In the circumstance, there are many laws, customs and regulations. "Any breach of this code of behavior is considered evil, wrong or bad, for it is an injury or destruction to the accepted social order and peace. It must be punished by the corporate community of both the living and the dead...."[15] As we know, nobody wants to be the target of communal anger, and so people have that constraint to serve as curbs against anti-social behavior.

In the matter of provision of tools and inspirations for thinking afresh the fundamental issues of life, I imagine that this has to do with the contingent paraphernalia that came along with missionary activities - schools, health care systems, etc. There is no doubt that this has helped in many ways to improve the conditions of humankind in Africa. Of course, we also know that the improvement of life does not also go along with the eradication of greed, corruption and wickedness and that, many public officials, for instance, would rather take advantage of loopholes in statutes to defraud their nations even when they have sworn on oath to protect the constitution. The imported legal system, with its emphasis on proving a crime beyond reasonable doubt, is therefore not as effective in this regard as the traditional oath system.

Islam is eliminated because it has not itself fully awaken to the demands of the day due to its legalism and tardiness while Christianity is consciously responding and contributing to the realization of human needs. The problem with all these is that Mbiti has not substantiated his views well enough. For it is one thing to assert the superiority of a world-view, it is another thing to present arguments to back up the assertion and it is here that Mbiti has not been adequate. It may very well be, however, that Mbiti does not want to rest his views on arguments. For as he goes on to suggest, the uniqueness of christianity does not rest on all the points that have been made thus far.

14. The uniqueness of Christianity is in Jesus Christ. He is the stumbling block of all ideologies and religious systems; and even if some of his teaching may overlap with what they teach and proclaim, His own Person is greater than can be contained in a religion or ideology....It is He, therefore, and only He, who deserves to be the goal and standard for individuals and mankind.[16]

15. Traditional religions, Islam and the other religious systems are preparatory ground in the search for the Ultimate. But only Christianity has the terrible responsibility of pointing the way to that ultimate identity, foundation and source of security.

This is, therefore, the direction in the search for the ultimate as Mbiti sees it. He concedes the fact of religious pluralism. Indeed, the final optimistic note he leaves us is that until christianity is able to point us to the ultimate, "there is sufficient room for religious co-existence, cooperation and even competition in Africa."[17]

Mbiti's position is typical of the official orthodox position of christianity in its evangelistic garb in which salvation of the soul is the focus of the search for the ultimate. This position raises two basic issues. Africa has been exposed to christianity and islam for quite a while. African bishops, missionaries and lay men and women are numerous. Even when religious enthusiasm is fading fast in Europe and America, Africa seems to have provided a safe haven for the gospel and it seems that the continent may even boast of having more christians now than any other continent. Not only this, since the early seventies, numerous varieties of new religious and evangelical movements have sprung up with full commitment to the revitalization of the message of the gospel. So our problem is not lack of religiosity. There has not been a dearth of resources for the spiritual development of our people. The real question is how relevant the christianity of the missions has been for the resolution of the impasse created by CAR. How can we account for CAR in the light of the religiosity of our people. Has christianity lived up to the expectations of salvation conceived in its widest possible terms as liberation from sin and servitude? If it does not profit a person to lose their life while gaining the whole world, does it benefit them to live a life of indignity and misery now in the hope of gaining eternal life later? Why, indeed, can they not avoid misery now and still gain eternal life? What is the reason for this inevitable disjunction that permits only one and not both? These are questions which mission christianity fails to address. But if the motive is understandable [though not justified] in the case of mission-controlled colonial-inspired christianity which had to serve the interests of the masters of commerce in the metropolis, an African clergy has no business perpetrating the same old dogma when there are the pressing problems of hunger for food, knowledge and freedom.

The argument against traditional religion is weak if we approach the issue from this perspective. Indeed, one problem with the mission-sponsored christianity is that it presents God as an apolitical being who is indifferent to the misery and suffering of people in this world as long as their eternal life is guaranteed by grace. This is certainly strange to most traditionalist whose gods are interested in their well-being here on earth. *Ogún*, the Yoruba god of iron and war, is always ready to fight on the side of his people. *Osun*, the god of fertility, listens and provides for the barren. *Sàngó*, the god of thunder is responsible for dealing with the *amòòkùn ja'lè*'s those who commit atrocities in the dark hoping that no one sees them. They and those who break oaths of loyalty to their land and those who betray trust are given instantaneous judgements. The point is that the gods of traditional religion are politically alert. Interestingly, this is also true of the god of Israel, supposedly the same as the christian God. If Yahweh stands with the oppressed and is always eager to protect them and to set free the bound [Isaiah 61:1-2], a position which Christ also affirmed [Luke:4:18-19], from where then do we get our model of christian gospel in Africa which seems to sentence our churches to the unenviable task of defending the oppressors and neglecting the cry of the oppressed? For is it not the case that silence in the face of oppression means acquiescence with it?

Understanding Religion as a Liberating Agent

It is this kind of posture on the part of official christianity that seems to explain, even if it fails to justify, the position of the radical intellectual and humanist who rejects religion, agreeing with Marx that it is the opium of the poor. From this perspective, religion has no place at all in the resolution of the problem created by CAR because religion speaks to the soul whereas the problem we face belongs to the body. In other words, it is not by addressing the heart and soul of oppressors that you will change the system that fertilizes oppression. Rather you have to engage in the praxis of liberation to assist the oppressed in their struggle and, as it has been observed above, mission-sponsored christianity, at least, does not lend itself to this kind of engagement. More seriously, however, the radical intellectuals' justification for their position seems to rest on the observation of concrete episodes in the direction of christian evangelism in Africa. For one thing, even when the church claims to serve the interest of the poor, what it does is to either provide them with spiritual armor against their bodily weakness occasioned by the oppression they are undergoing, or provide them with food basket thus ensuring their continued availability as listeners. Neither of these speaks effectively to the problem which, for its solution, requires the church to stand firm in its condemnation of oppression and to demand, in the strongest terms, an end to it. Yet, it is in this matter of demanding an end to oppression that the church has been found wanting. At best, few preachers, now and then, sermonize on the evils of oppression. At worst, the trend has been for the church to maintain a nauseating neutrality in the face of oppression and injustice. Indeed, in not a few occasions, corrupt politicians get praises from their churches during the various thanksgiving services they organize to celebrate their election victories made possible by bribes, thuggery and rigging. The church aids and abets dishonesty, violence and oppression when it does not stand up to condemn these evils. It is clear then that the radical intellectual who discountenances religion as a solution to CAR has a basis.

Yet this cannot be the end of the matter. Religion, as has been observed in chapter 4, is not an institution separate from other aspects of the lives of the people in traditional African societies. It is a way of life which can only be discountenanced at a very high price. Even if it is true that it is an opium, the problem is to get the people to see it as such. Humanists and secularists are still the underdogs in contemporary Africa and politicians know this well; which is why they often manipulate the religious consciousness of the people for their own interests. In such a situation, not much can be achieved by a radical intellectualism which denies the reality of objects of religious devotion. A more effective approach is to use their belief system as a means of transforming their existential conditions. This is where there is a huge responsibility on the religious leaders to expose the realities of their existence to the people; to use the message of the gospel to mobilize the people for their own emancipation. Mission christianity has failed in this regard because it has collaborated with both the imperial overlords as well as with native oppressors. It has failed to translate the message of freedom from suffering and servitude into concrete praxis in which the people can participate. It has refused to confront the forces of evil even as they devour the beautiful vineyard of God's children. It has therefore itself become a part of the problem that needs to be solved, instead of providing adequate solution.

Yet it is not impossible to transcend this attitude of mission christianity in favor of one which recognizes the place that religion occupies in the life of millions of Africans and which therefore takes it up as an instrument for the liberation of the masses from the forces of oppression and injustice. What is needed is a radical theology which speaks the message of salvation as liberation. "As we bring Christianity face to face with the African reality", Jean-Marc Ela aptly remarks, "we must rethink God."[18]

Rethinking God entails bringing to the fore God's liberating actions and interpreting these for our times and situations. It requires, as Kwesi Dickson puts it, placing " the concrete human situation in the forefront of the church's thinking" as well as "a shift from orthodoxy to orthopraxis."[19] It means involving God in the practical issues of politics and morality: human rights violation, development strategies, work ethics, distributive justice and penal justice. It is perhaps no longer news to recall that in many parts of Africa today, it is the poor and wretched that gets the most brutal punishment for crimes against the state while the rich and powerful get away with the most atrocious crimes against the people. Thus embezzlement of public funds which sentences the people to a life-time of pauperism has become institutionalized and therefore hardly punished since the culprits themselves determine the punishment ahead of time. But in many cases starving people have been summarily executed for stealing, and military decrees, punishing crimes with death, have been pronounced to retroactively take care of offences committed in the past. Should the church be silent in such situations? And from where will that kind of silence be derived if, in fact as we know, the prophets of old cried out against injustice? Could it then be that the model of mission christianity presented to us by the colonial system still controls the thought and practice of the African clergy? Or, could it be that there has developed a coalition of interests between the African clergy on the one hand and indigenous and foreign oppressors on the other? In the face of the church's embarrassing silence when it should speak up against human rights violations, one wonders whether the latter suggestion is not the truth of the matter. But, of course it is not only a betrayal of the people's expectation, it is also a betrayal of the God of the prophets and of the gospels. Did Jesus Christ not declare for the oppressed of this world?

What is required of Christianity to be relevant to the African realities is also required of Islam, more so because Islam, by constitution, does not just concern itself with the spiritual life of devotees; it deals with the social and political aspects of life as well. Thus the jihad of Uthman dan Fodio against the Habe rulers of Northern Nigeria in the nineteenth century was motivated in part by his perception of injustice and oppression against the poor by those rulers. Contemporary Islamic scholars, like their christian counterparts, however, seem more interested in purely spiritual issues. It may be argued that if you successfully appeal to the spirit of a people, you may get them to change their attitudes towards life: shunning riches, avoiding injustice and promoting human rights.

The problem is that those who perpetrate injustice are hardly targeted by our clergy. Indeed, some of the new evangelists pride themselves in their ability to compete successfully with the political elites in the matter of wealth. They are never tired of reminding their congregation that God did not create them to be poor. The blessing of the beatitudes on the poor and weak is lost in the process and the question of how such wealth is to be accumulated is not raised. But given the ways that they themselves, as servants of God, raise money for luxuries beyond their needs, one cannot expect them to preach against corrupt practices. The story is well known of our modern age evangelists who compete with business people in the accumulation of wealth. When they organize crusades, their prime concern is not the salvation of souls which they, theoretically, claim as their task. Rather it is how much offering they are going to be able to collect. They are smart in the art of working up the congregation to give, even when those are the wretched of the earth. Thus at the end of their sermons, members of congregation are invited to close their eyes for the blessing of God. To have these blessings, they are asked to dip their hands into their pockets and bring out all the money they find there. They are to raise such money up for blessing. The evangelist then prays and blesses the money. Thereafter, instruction is given that the money thus blessed cannot go back into their various pockets because it now belongs to God and is to be collected by the messenger of God through the ushers who have been stationed at strategic locations among the crowd of thousands of people. Anyone who put back the money into their pocket stand cursed! While Christ provided food for the hungry, weak and poor who came to hear him, our contemporary prophets feed off the wretchedness of their hearers. How then can one expect them to provide the support needed for the liberation of these wretched masses? Our universities are now centers of new waves of spiritual movements. The young and pliable are fed with doses of suffocating literature in the name of evangelization. They are not only prevented from seeing their long-run situation in its true perspective and thus to take action to redeem themselves from a cursed future; they are also distracted from their immediate goal of attaining the diploma that they need at least to qualify as candidates in the market for jobs that are not always there. The alarming rate at which both faculty and students are recruited into these bands may be explained by the precarious economic and social situations in which people find themselves. It may, of course, also be seen as an inadequate theological response to those situations since it furthers dependency and, in many cases, it also promotes conflict and disharmony which prevents the development of a common front among the youth for the resolution of the problems of CAR. This is especially the case with the Christian and Moslem confrontations in the recent past.

We may then see that Mbiti's characterization of the issues has not taken account of the questions raised above. In addition to this, however, the question of conflict in a religiously plural society is also crucial in our assessment of the role of religion in the resolution of CAR. But Mbiti does not seem to pause to address the question whether religious coexistence in peace is possible and whether the peaceful co-existence of the peoples of Africa is not necessarily jeopardized by the existence of these religions. The need for addressing such a question arises from the recent developments in some parts of Africa and the role which religion has played in violent conflicts. Where such conflicts were not originally caused by religious differences, they were fuelled and aggravated by such differences. Yet it is true that all these religions rest on some notion of peace, tolerance and mutual understanding. As has been observed in Chapter 4 above, it is also interesting that the African traditional religion to which Mbiti gives a grudging recognition seems to have been the one that has shown the least tendency to violence. The relevance of the question whether religion can contribute to peace, to the issue of contemporary African realities raised at the beginning of this chapter, is simply that social conflict and violence are now part of our contemporary realities and conflict and violence, by nature, have a tendency of complicating and aggravating an already bad situation. It seems to me, therefore, that the question of religious pluralism and the quest for social peace deserves to be raised and addressed in this context in which religion is presented as the solution to the problem of contemporary African realities.

Religious Pluralism and Social Peace

When the issue is social peace, our primary interest should be in the area of interpersonal relations among the human beings in a given community or across communities. There is no doubt that the various religions provide the means of inner peace for their adherents. However, the influence of religion on social peace is at best indirect. Yet peaceful coexistence among persons is the real issue; and the question of interest to us in this context is the connection between the existence of many religions and the promotion of social peace. Can religious pluralism contribute to social peace? To answer this question, we have to know, not only that there are many religions, but also the injunctions of these religions, so that the nature of their tendency to contribute to peace could be determined. This brief account will be limited to Christianity, Islam and Yoruba Traditional religions.[20]

Christianity, as we have seen, came as a religion of the poor.[21] It has an egalitarian promise, with the message of divine grace for all, whether rich or poor, Jew or Gentile. It preaches peace on earth and wishes goodwill to all. Indeed, it regards peacemakers as blessed persons. One of the two important commandments, as summed up in Christ's teachings is love of neighbors as oneself. He in fact is the symbol of love: No love is greater than this, that a man would lay down his life for the sake of others.[22] If love of others is a precondition for social peace, then

Christianity which preaches this can be said to have a tendency to contribute to peace. It is remarkable also that Jesus Christ frowned at revenge or retaliation. In fact he says we should love our enemies and pray for those who curse us. Not only this, he instructs his followers to avoid physical confrontation with anyone and if they are slapped on the right cheek, they should respond-not by striking back-but by turning their other cheek. Christ himself was *the* prince of peace.

It would seem then that a society of Christians should be a peaceful society judging from these various injunctions which are essentially favorable to social peace. But this is evidently not so. There is violence even within homogeneous Christian societies due to the politicization of the message of Christ and opportunistic approach to religion. In a world in which it is political power that matters, even those who claim to be followers of Christ have refused to give enough room for his message of peace. In addition, however, we can hardly expect a society of Christians only. There is bound to be mixtures of people of other religions or those without any religion at all. Now, in a normal situation even where there are other non-Christians, injunctions of Christ should see Christians through so that they would live peacefully with their non-Christian neighbors. In other words, they could be passive receivers of all sorts of insults, rather than active pursuers of violence. However, there is one aspect of the Christian injunction which ought to make any christian essentially active aggressors. The great commission commands us to preach the gospel and Christianize the whole world. But in carrying out this instruction, christians are likely to step on certain toes, and those may be very sensitive and unforgiving ones. This has led to many violent encounters.

The Islamic religion is based on the teachings of Mohammed who claimed to be a prophet of Allah-the Most High God.[23] Like the other religions it has an organized followership which is structured in the form of a political set-up. Unlike in Christianity, religion and politics are mingled in Islam and the political power of the prophet is based on his religious mission. The social obligations of devotees derive from and further reinforce their religious duties. Muslims are also enjoined to maintain peace and love their fellow human beings. Leaders are instructed to be righteous, and the creation of social disorder is frowned at and where it is without any adequate reason, it is regarded as a sin. Thus it appears that, like other religions, Islam is a peace-loving and peace-promoting religion. Again, a society of only Moslems should be a peaceful society. This refers to both the promotion of personal peace as well as social peace. But, again, this is evidently not so. Part of the reason has to do again with the politicization of religion and the instrumental conception of its purpose in terms of access to political power. This is in addition to the fact that, like the other religion already touched upon, Islam is a proselytizing religion. The requirement of evangelization is therefore likely to cause friction between believers and non-believers, as well as between conflicting interpretations of its doctrines by believers of different persuasions, thus disrupting rather than promoting social peace. The recent violent clashes between fundamentalists of both Christians and Muslims in several parts of Nigeria also point to this tendency on the part of these agents.

Last to be considered is African traditional religion. As we have observed [Chapter 4] all African traditional religions share a common foundation and structure. With regard to the Yoruba, there is a belief in a supernatural endowment of human life and in the intervention of extra-human powers in human affairs.[24] However, it is difficult to pin down precisely what constitutes the center-piece of the religion. There are many objects of worship, in the sense that apart from the cult of the divinities, there are also nature spirits which are supposed to inhabit objects of nature including trees, mountains, rivers. However, all these religious activities revolve around a belief in a supreme deity - *Olódùmarè* - who seems to occupy the position of the Ultimately Real in Yoruba religious discourse.

As has also been seen, the traditional religion takes interest not only in the personal peace of its devotees, but also in their interpersonal relationships ensuring that they act as a body and live a life of cleanliness. They are instructed to be of good behavior and they are to keep their covenants with one another and with the deity. A serious punishment awaits breakers of covenants. Of course, one cannot fail to mention here at least the most heinous aspects of traditional religion: the issue of human sacrifice which it enjoined in the past. Though the victims of such sacrifice were generally not members of the community [they were aliens or war captives], the fact remains that the toleration of human sacrifice was a stain on an otherwise peaceful and tolerant religion which rests on the idea that the Supreme deity wills the good for all his creatures. But of course, it should be remembered that human sacrifice is not peculiar to African traditional religion; it was a common practice in Judaism, and Abraham, the beloved of God, was to sacrifice his son, Isaac, in obedience to the command of Yahweh.

As we have also observed in Chapter 4, it seems that the main difference between other world religions and African traditional religion in general, may be located in this matter of proselytization and the attitude of fanatics. Indeed, evangelization, *per se* should normally not lead to violence; but from our experience of history, it is so, especially in the recent history of some African countries. It is useful to raise the question why this is so. What is responsible for the phenomena of conflict and violence in the crusading activities of Christianity and Islam? This is a genuine question, the presupposition of which is that even in evangelization, there need not be conflict, if the culture of tolerance can be sustained. There is religious violence and conflict because the various devotees are intolerant of the views of their rivals; and this is so in spite of the fact that all these religions preach tolerance.

How can the phenomena of intolerance be explained? I think it has to be explained in terms of the distorted understanding of devotees concerning their roles in spreading the good news of their religions. Many of them seem to believe that there is great reward for them [if not here on earth, then in heaven] if they successfully convert others to their faith or prevent conversion from their faiths. It then becomes a life and death affair; and this is not always restricted to followers alone. Leaders have their own ways of fuelling the fire of intolerance among their followers, by urging them to defend their faith against 'infidels' or encouraging them to promote the 'superior' truth of their faith.

There is, I think, a further explanation relevant to our peculiar African context. As observed above, religion has come to assume a very important significance in the temporal existence of most people. In other words, it is no longer a question of laying one's treasures in heaven, but more of getting as much as possible of the good things of earthly existence here. Religion has thus been turned into an irresistible source of wealth by many a 'religious leader' in the same [if not greater] proportion as politics in the conception of its practitioners. While some depend on the number of followers within the country for the realization of their mundane objectives through religion, others count on external sources of wealth for as long as they remain in the frontline of the particular religious crusade favored by foreign nations. In the circumstance, devotion to the cause of religion becomes a camouflage for the promotion of the economic interests of such individuals, and they will go any length to sustain it. Since this applies, in particular, to the elites and the so-called religious leaders, it is likely to have a backlash effect on the followers who, in general, do not have the ability to discover the mischief in the pretences of the leaders. This tendency is, again, peculiar to the major religions. Devotees of traditional religions do not, generally, attach great importance to the accumulation of material wealth, either because they lack the kind of drive that it takes, or because there is something in their religious tenets which prohibits such outlook. In fact, many worshippers of traditional religions seem to have a strong belief that should they break their religious vows against involvement in fraud, cheating, dishonesty, stealing and violence, they will suffer instant punishment from the deities.

It follows therefore that if religion is to contribute to the promotion of social peace in Africa, and thus help towards the resolution of our contemporary realities, the various religious leaders have to cultivate the spirit of tolerance that has been a characteristic feature of traditional religion. To do this, however, and get their followers in the right frame of mind, they also need to jettison their selfish instrumental conception of religion in material terms and use it as a means of getting people to cooperate for the resolution of their common problems. This is the only way by which religion can be made relevant to the liberation of humankind in Africa and thus contribute to the resolution of its contemporary realities.

7

CONTEMPORARY AFRICAN REALITIES: THE CULTURAL VIEW

The second approach to the question of ultimate reality is the cultural approach. On this view, the explanation for contemporary African reality can be traced to the fact that majority of Africans have either forgotten or ignored their cultural roots and have assimilated foreign cultures and foreign ideas. These ideas have done an incalculable damage to the social and economic reality of Africa and is responsible for the experience of the moment. There is, on this view, an authentic African personality which is the pillar of African survival in a multi-racial world. When this personality is not developed, or pride is not taken in it, everything goes into shambles. This is when greed and selfish pursuit of wealth and power take over the lives of people. Authentic Africans are their brothers' and sisters' keepers. But with cultural degeneration, he becomes his brother's killer. This accounts for the phenomenon of armed robbery, suicide and murder. An example of the lesson of cultural dependency that is usually cited is the political system. It is claimed that many African nations had highly developed political systems before the era of colonialism. But after independence, instead of reviving these structures in the light of modern times, we now engage in a trial and error method of political system. This is what is partly responsible for our contemporary realities. Indeed on this view, contrary to Mbiti's assumption, God has a cultural root and the God of Africa is quite different from that of other people. So even if you take the Christian God as the ultimately real, you may still fail to grasp the true nature of African realities. Varieties of negritude theories express this view. But so do a number of non-negritude and even anti-negritude approaches.[1] Thus, for instance, both Senghor and Nyerere insist on the need to define an "African road to socialism" by appeal to cultural values which are distinctively African. For Senghor, "culture is the very texture of society" and must not be neglected.[2]

African Socialism fits into the philosophy of Negritude because both are selective rejections of certain aspects of the values of the West and East. For instance, both Senghor and Nyerere reject Western Capitalism and Eastern Communism partly on the ground that they clash with African values of communalism, self-reliance and human equality on the one hand, and classlessness, brotherhood of humankind and the avoidance of conflict on the other.[3] Perhaps, more than any other African scholar, Senghor does a lot to articulate this view. Based on his conviction that Africa has immense cultural values to contribute to the world civilization, he saw his task as highlighting the fundamentals of these values in the light of African cultural realities. Africans are therefore enjoined to assimilate the good in other cultures while they avoid being completely assimilated. To drive his point home, Senghor saw the need for an analysis of the African situation which proceeds from a proper understanding of its cultural and spiritual values.[4]

Negritude.

Senghor undertakes this analysis through the philosophy of negritude. The concept has its foundation in the belief that civilizations differ and that the civilization of the universal must be based on the contributions of all civilizations. Negritude is the affirmation of the distinctiveness of African cultural values, the confirmation of the being of the African. It is, Senghor insists, neither racialism nor self-negation.

Negritude developed as a philosophy of African personality, an expression of the African understanding of ultimate reality and supreme value in reaction to the European denigration of African civilization; especially between the two world wars - as was recalled by Senghor:

> We had been taught, by our French masters at the *Lycee*, that we had no civilization, having been let off the list of guests at the *Banquet* of the Universal. We were "tabula rasa", or, better still, a lump of soft wax which the fingers of the white demiurge would mould into shape. The only hope of salvation you could hold out to us was to let *ourselves be assimilated*.[5]

Paradoxically, it was this policy of assimilation which, by deepening the despair of the young Africans, forced them to probe into the essence of negritude by turning their attention to the findings of ethnologists concerning the wealth of African culture and civilization. Their inquiry showed that before colonization, Africa had been ravaged by the slave trade, which had wiped out images and values in one vast carnage. They learnt that negroid civilization had flourished in the Upper Paleolithic Age and that the Neolithic Revolution could not be explained without them. They further discovered that

> mere discursive reason, the *reason which only sees*, was inadequate to "comprehend" the world, to gather it up and transform it; that it needed the help of intuitive reason, *the reason which comes to grips*, which delves beneath the surface of facts and things.[6]

It was through this philosophy of negritude that Senghor and his fellow black young intellectuals were able to face a hostile world which was bent on killing their self pride and negating their being. Negritude is thus the affirmation and self-confirmation of being. It rests on the obvious fact that peoples differ in their ideas and their language, in their philosophies and their religions, in their customs and their institutions. If so, it follows that Africans too have a certain way of conceiving life and of living it. This is the fact which Negritude attempts to express. As Senghor defines it, it is

> the sum of the cultural values of the black world, that is, a certain active presence in the world, or better, in the universe.[7]

These cultural values, Senghor insists, are all informed by *intuitive reason*. This is one of the essential marks of negritude which distinguishes the black approach to life from the European's, the value of which, according to Senghor, rests on discursive reason and facts, on logic and matter. European reasoning is analytical, discursive by utilization. Negro African reasoning is intuitive by participation.[8]

Negritude and the Rejection of Marxism.

Negritude is presented by Senghor as a philosophy which can respond to the needs not only of modern Africa, but also of the modern world: it is the humanism of the twentieth century. This is because its theory of knowledge corresponds to the new discoveries in science which showed "that facts and matter, which are the objects of discursive reason, were only the outer surface that had to be transcended by intuition in order to achieve a vision *in depth of reality*."[9] In other words, even scientists recognize the inadequacy of discursive reason, that it has to be complemented by intuition to have an adequate grasp of reality. Therefore,

> negritude, by its ontology (that is, its philosophy of being), its moral law and its aesthetic, is a response to the modern humanism that European philosophers and scientists have been preparing since the end of the nineteenth century....[10]

The moral ideas of negritude are particularly relevant for our purpose here. According to Senghor, the universe is made up of life forces each of which is - from grain of sand to ancestor is itself a network of life forces - also a network of elements that are contradictory in appearance but really complementary. On this view, human beings are, for the African, composed of body and soul, matter and spirit. But they are also the virile and feminine element - several souls. Human beings are, therefore, a composite of mobile life forces which interlock. This is the morality in action of negritude. Each of the life forces has a role to play in maintaining the order of the universe and sages, priests, kings and doctors are endowed with relevant knowledge to make use of them "to help bring the universe to its fulfillment."[11]

Senghor emphasizes such features of African civilization as its unity, balance and harmony based both on the *community* and on the *person* in such a way that the group has priority over the individuals without crushing them, but allowing them to blossom as persons. These characteristics of negritude - as the sum of civilized values of the black world - ensured it a place in contemporary humanism and therefore a worthy contribution to the "civilization of the Universal" which is necessary in the divided but interdependent world of the twentieth century. The ontology of negritude, as has been seen is thoroughly humanist - emphasizing the active presence and contribution of human in reinforcing the life forces.

The point that is worth noting here, as in other aspects of Senghor's account is that, for him, negritude represents an elaboration of the black people's contribution to the civilization of the Universal. In the realm of knowledge they have their own method; the sympathetic and sensitive approach to things that come to their consciousness. They are endowed with more emotive response and ability to participate sensuously than the European and, as a result of the belief that the world is composed of life forces in complementary relations and that they all emanate from God to fulfill its purpose, Africans, on this view, would see each object, person or thing as a necessary link in the chain of the universe and treat them accordingly. The relevance of negritude to the resolution of CAR would then appear to be in this original world-view attributed to Africans. The argument appears to be that if we could rekindle and revitalize these ideas in the mind of our people, and thus liberate them culturally from the clutches of western cultural imperialism, we would be in a position to solve other problems. Thus whereas, Nkrumah asked for the political kingdom first, the negritudists appear to be demanding for the cultural kingdom for a start. Indeed, the establishment of the political kingdom is also given a cultural twist.

One of the main objectives of Senghor - as a political thinker is to "integrate Negro-African cultural values, especially religious values, into socialism."[12] To achieve this objective, he felt the need to start with Marx and pose a critique of his "atheistic metaphysics" which, for Senghor, is un-African. Thus he does not mince words in his rejection of Marxism:

> We are not "Marxists" in the sense given the world today, in so far as Marxism is presented as atheistic metaphysics, a total and totalitarian view of the world, a *Weltanschauung*.[13]

But in spite of this outright denial of Marx, Senghor finds it necessary to start with him, and to review his economic theory, his philosophical analysis of alienation and his humanism. This latter Senghor believes to be the positive contribution of Marxian thought: "Humanism, the *philosophy of humanism*, rather than economics, is the basic character and positive contribution of Marxian thought."[14] But even this has its negative aspects. The weakness of Marx's humanism, for Senghor, is that it proceeds from a one-sided conception of man and universe. That is, his ambition was to express the dignity of man and his spiritual needs without ever resorting to metaphysics or ethics or religion. Senghor finds this incomprehensible. For him, Marx is a philosopher in spite of himself: "In the name of whom or of what, after all, does Marx dare to affirm the dignity of man and man's right to appreciate all the products of his labor?"[15] Marx's atheism is therefore rejected as both incoherent and inadequate. Communism which derives from Marxian theoretical practice is also therefore found inadequate by Senghor, for two reasons: theoretical and practical. On the one hand, Lenin's definition of matter proceeds from a one-sided concept, from a purely materialistic and deterministic postulate. On the other hand, "the anxiety for human dignity and the need for reform - man's freedoms and freedoms of collectivities that animate Marx's thought .... are unknown to communism whose major deviation is Stalinism."[16] Marx's weakness is that he placed too much emphasis on materialism and determinism at the expense of ethics and spiritual values.

The rejection of communism is, of course, not a rejection of socialism. Like many of his African colleagues, Senghor opted for African [democratic] socialism which "goes so far as to integrate spiritual values."[17] There is a correspondence between Negro-African philosophy and socialist philosophy. Both according to Senghor are existentialist and humanistic, and that socialism integrates spiritual values. "We would learn that, for the Negro African, the 'vital forces' are the texture of the world and that world is animated by a dialectical movement. We would learn that Negro-African society is collectivist, or, more exactly, communal because it is rather a communion of souls than an aggregate of individuals. We would learn that we had already achieved socialism before the coming of the European."[18]

The rejection of Marxism does not mean an acceptance of capitalism either since neither of them originated from the cultural milieu of Africa. Nor are they compatible with the spirit of that milieu. Indeed, Senghor is emphatic on the rejection of capitalism as one of the contributions of Europe that is incongruent with African tradition. Though it can be seen to have contributed to the progress of Europe, it is now "an out-of-date social and economic system."[19] This is because collectivization of work, which is now the vogue and which constitutes a critical step towards socialization, is not compatible with the extension of private property which capitalism symbolizes. Secondly, capitalism is guilty of alienation in the material and spiritual realms. Finally, Senghor rejects capitalism because it works only for the well-being of a minority. "It is because private capitalism finds it repugnant - or, more precisely, finds it impossible - to transcend its material bounds, it is because of its transformation into colonialist Imperialism that we were converted, after much hesitation to Socialism."[20] Perhaps the hesitation is uncalled for, since in Senghor's own words, negritude, "as a complex of civilized values, is traditionally *socialist* in character."[21] This is why Senghor also insists that socialism means "a return to original sources"[22] and why he believes that Negro African cultural values can be integrated into socialism. So while he disowns Marxism and its "atheistic metaphysics", Senghor accepts a humanist version of socialism. This is also why he considers the philosophy of humanism, rather than economics, as the basic character and positive contribution of Marxian thought. Marx's positive contribution, according to him, is "an incarnate conception of man based on the material and social determinations of man."[23]

Argument for African Socialism.

The inspiration for exploring the way to an African mode of socialism comes for Senghor from his understanding of the definition of the fundamental traits of a socialist society offered by one of is advocates: the state's power is vested in the workers. All means of production are collective property, there are no exploiting classes; the economy is planned, and its essential aim is to afford the maximum satisfaction of man's material and spiritual needs.[24] Senghor finds this definition attractive and it offers the prospect of an earthly paradise for him. "But", he observes, "it has still to come about, the exploitation of man by his fellow has yet to be stamped out in reality, the satisfaction of the spiritual needs which transcend our material needs has to be achieved."[25] And he further observes that this has not yet happened neither in the West nor East. This is the reason for seeking "our own original mode, a Negro-African mode, of attaining these objectives." Senghor's concern is to infuse socialism with African cultural values. For him, culture cannot just be an appendage, it is the basis of politics. Thus any political arrangement that fails to cohere with the cultural values of a community cannot succeed. Negro-African society, for Senghor, is a "classless society", therefore a politics based on the assumption of a class divided society cannot work. It is also "a community based society, in which the hierarchy - and therefore power - is founded on spiritual and democratic values." Again, it follows that a politics based on assumptions of atheism cannot work:

> We are concerned here not with a mere collection of individuals, but with people conspiring together.... united among themselves even to the very centre of their being, communing through their ancestors with God, who is the centre of all centres.[26]

This is his vision of the socialism that is relevant to African cultural tradition, which is existentialist, humanistic and spiritualistic. African socialism, as an extension of African cultural heritage in the socio-political realm, thus offers a bright prospect for Senghor for the resolution of the contemporary realities of

Africa. But as many critics have pointed out, in this arena of life, practice does not always coincide with theory.

Critique of Senghor.

Criticisms of Senghor have been directed against the two strands of his original contributions to the question of value and meaning: negritude and African socialism. Negritude as a concept defines the specificity of black cultural values. Critics have argued that Senghor has overplayed the idea of the homogeneity of black cultural values. Attention is drawn to the varieties of indigenous cultures beside the infiltration of foreign cultures which have been domesticated. Nkrumah, for instance, has observed that African societies can now be seen to have three distinct cultural heritages: Western [Christian], Arabic [Islamic] and Traditional Cultures. The point is to integrate all these in a way that will not compromise the material and spiritual well-being of the African in the technological age. Critics of Senghor think that he is being too traditionalist in his demand for a distinctive Africanity. There are also those who reject Senghor's account on the ground that the idea of negritude is as racist as the idea of assimilation which undermines African civilization. The idea of a black personality based on the peculiarity of blackness [a color] cannot stand serious scrutiny just like white personality cannot.

Furthermore, there are objections to Senghor's negritude on the ground that it is an inadequate way of showing or proclaiming the contributions of Africans to world civilization, or even of announcing its readiness to make an impact. What is lacking is not ideas and theories, but action; and it is in this that Africa has serious deficiencies. Indeed if we look carefully at the practical politics that ensued from this theory, we may be disappointed. Frantz Fanon has alluded to the shocking disappointment that the forces of the Algerian revolution experienced with Senghor's policy of siding with the French:

> It is around the peoples' struggle that African-Negro culture takes on substance, and not around songs, poems and folklore. Senghor, who

is also a member of the Society of African Culture and who has worked with us on the question of African culture, is not afraid for his part either to give the order to his delegation to support French proposals on Algeria. Adherence to African-Negro culture and to the cultural unity of Africa is arrived at in the first place by upholding unconditionally the peoples' struggle for freedom. No one can truly wish for the spread of African culture if he does not give practical support to the creation of the conditions necessary to the existence of that culture; in other words, to the liberation of the whole continent.[27]

This is a very crucial point that has not been well noted by many of the theorists in this group.

Negritude is tied up with African Socialism as its foundation. Culture, according to Senghor, is the basis and precondition of politics. It cannot be treated as an appendage to politics. But if negritude as the cultural foundation has problems, African Socialism, its political fruit, cannot escape unscathed. Thus Senghor's contemporaries, including Kwame Nkrumah, objected to the notion of African Socialism as unserious because it is based on a false impression of traditional African societies:

> Today, the phrase "African Socialism" seems to espouse the view that the traditional African society was a classless society imbued with the spirit of humanism and to express a nostalgia for that spirit. Such a conception of socialism makes a fetish of the communal African society. But an idyllic, African classless society (in which there were no rich and no poor) enjoying a drugged serenity is certainly a facile simplification. There is no historical or even anthropological evidence for any such society. I am afraid the realities of African society were somewhat more sordid.[28]

But Nkrumah himself concedes the presence of a "spirit of communalism" if not a classless structure in traditional African society, and he acknowledges the existence of rich human values in that society. What he rejects, therefore, is the anthropological approach which 'sees' classlessness of structures and not the philosophical approach which seeks to recapture the spirit of 'communalism' "crystallized in its humanism and in its reconciliation of individual advancement with group welfare."[29]

Nkrumah further objects to the Senghorian suggestion that the positive contributions of colonialism such as the economic and technical infrastructure be incorporated and accommodated by Senegal. Nkrumah observes that these can be shown to be imbued with a particular socio-political philosophy which is incompatible "with the philosophy underlying communalism and the desired accommodation would prove only a socio-political mirage."[30] Finally, Nkrumah maintains that to "suppose that there are tribal, national, or racial socialisms is to abandon objectivity in favor of chauvinism."[31]

Apart from these problems with Senghor's position, a more important consideration with the cultural view is the tendency to reify culture, thus making it an abstract entity independent of the struggles that shape a people's life. While Senghor may not be guilty of this, there is no doubt that for many of those concerned with the regeneration of our cultural traditions, the connection between culture and the life struggles of a people has not been given adequate thought. I now want to address this issue by focusing on the Nigerian experience.

On National Culture: The Nigerian Experience

The Nigerian state has been in the forefront in the campaign for the promotion and preservation of African and Black Cultural heritage at least since political independence. Not long ago - in 1977 - Nigeria hosted the widely publicized Second World Black and African Festival of Arts and Culture [FESTAC] at a cost of several millions of petro-naira. Since that time, there have been several national festivals of Arts and Culture all over the country. Foreign heads of states and other dignitaries are usually ushered into the country by beautiful girls with tender voices and graceful steps in demonstration of the cultural wealth of the nation. But the questions remain: in spite of all these, do we now have a national culture? Or do we have only an ideologically distorted and class-linked culture? How can we make culture perform the liberating function which is its destiny and *raison d'etre*?

Conceptions of Culture

There have been various conceptions of culture, some of which are inevitably ideological. For some theorists, culture consists solely of ideas. This follows from the common belief in the "power" of ideas as initiators of action, as if ideas have an independent ontological reality moving in the brains of human beings. Once an idea is present in the mind it influences the bodies of the receptors and urges them to behave in particular ways. So, on this view, the overt behavior we observe - e.g. movement of the arms and legs -and the outcome of this - e.g. rhythmical dances - are just outward manifestations of the real cultural event - a mental phenomenon - going on in the mind. This view is expressed clearly by W. W. Taylor: "Culture consists of ideas, it is a mental phenomenon not material objects or observable behaviour..."[32] Notice that this highly restrictive definition even discounts material objects as culture. But surely this cannot be all there is to the matter. The idea may be there to influence action, but two questions must be raised. First, how does the idea originate in the first place and why has it occurred now? Second, how are we to characterize its end-product if it does not constitute culture? Ideas are derived certainly from the active participation of various individuals in their social interactions in and outside their productive endeavors but all having more or less to do with their efforts to maintain themselves in existence, which of course, does not exclude leisurely existence. Ideas come into the mind from outside, it is not the other way round.

For this reason, the conception of culture as idea is certainly inadequate for it is guilty of treating the dependent as an independent reality. Consider the simple idea of building. Does it just arise in the head without any preceding event? But why do I need a building and what kind do I need? What need is it to satisfy and how can I afford it? These are related matters. The idea of building is therefore a product of human praxis which is itself not static, just as the idea of moonlight story-telling is traceable to the practice of an intensive agricultural system in a rural setting. Of course, this is not to deny that ideas do constitute culture; it is just to correct the view that ideas are all there is to culture which is what Taylor's definition has proposed for our acceptance.

Closely related to the conception of culture as ideas is the view that it consists of abstractions. For some theorists, culture is like an ideal form abstracted from human social behavior but which need not be actually realized in concrete life. It is a conception in the mind of the investigator. From this definition, it would follow that material objects (tools, masks, etc.) are not culture. As Taylor puts it "the concept of 'material culture' is fallacious because culture is a mental phenomenon."[33] Again what we say about the concept of culture as ideas must apply here. This mentalist conception of culture is inadequate because it fails to take account of the material source(s) of cultural phenomena and the involvement of human agents in the development of culture.

Others still conceive of culture as a "superorganic", that is, as "a heritage of ideas which have a transcendent reality of their own, independent of the individuals or societies which happen to bear them."[34] Culture is here treated as a transcendental or metaphysical entity which has made humans what they are and to which they conform as to their historical destiny. Of course, it is partially true that culture is a heritage achieved, retained and passed down from generation to generation. It is also true that culture and its development is not limited by the organic structure of human beings. It is of the essence of culture that it enables human beings to create and develop new methods of living without corresponding changes in their organic make-up. However, these facts do not justify the conception of culture as a transcendental force which acts upon individuals and is not to be understood in terms of their responses to psycho-biological needs. Besides, the idea of culture as social heritage is misleading to the extent that it presents contemporary human beings as passive receivers of culture handed down by a previous generation. But this is a static view of culture and is therefore inadequate. Culture is a dynamic social reality which involves a lot of continuity and change.

All the foregoing are ideologized views of culture. They promote ideas into self-autonomous entities at the expense of human praxis and all are variants of idealist theorizing. Though the realm of culture is the realm of actual life, which is a manifestation of the material conditions of the people, the ideologist represents it as a super-sensible world as if it had an autonomy of its own, independent of the real life of the people.

Culture and Social Existence

An adequate analysis of culture must come to terms with its inevitable connection with all aspects of the social existence of a people and their praxis. The historical, political, economic and environmental conditions of a society are the foundations from which stem its culture. As Ngugi Wa Thiong'O puts it, "culture in its broadest sense, is a way of life fashioned by a people in their collective endeavor to live and come to terms with their total environment."[35] Culture is an aspect of the history of a people, and an adequate understanding of a people's history requires a full grasp of how they have maintained themselves in existence. Cabral has his fingers right on this when he declares that: "Culture is always in the life of a society [open or closed], the more or less conscious result of the economic and political activities of that society, the more or less dynamic expression of the kinds of relationships which prevail in that society, on the one hand, between man [considered individually or collectively] and nature, and, on the other hand, among individuals, groups of individuals, social strata or classes."[36] What is missing in all those idealist theories we have earlier discussed is their inability to see beyond the smoke to discover the underlying fire. They are unable to penetrate the various appearances of social life into the reality that lies beneath. As a result of their obsession with ideas, some even deny the validity of "material culture", regarding it as a fallacious if not meaningless phrase. But surely ideas do not have an independent existence. The analogy of a fruit is apt. A fruit is borne by a plant. But the plant itself has its root firmly in the soil. The richness of the fruit, its robustness or otherwise, is a function of the constituents of the soil. We are aware of the fruit because it is perhaps the only part of the tree which appeals to us. We do not therefore bother about the root of the plant nor about the soil which produces it. However, the farmer will make a mistake if he does not bother, just as the plant scientist must penetrate into this hidden reality which produces the fruit. Culture is the fruit of a people's history which can only be adequately understood if all its determinants, including the ways in which people maintain their material existence, which may give some clue to the kind of cultural expressions specific to the society at any point in time, are taken into consideration.

Of course, culture is more than a product of history, it also contributes to the advancement of history. A cultural achievement normally means an improvement in the level of productive forces which in turn accelerates the historical process of the society in question. To recognize this is to come to terms with the dialectical relationship between creativity and productivity. A conception of culture which emphasizes its basic relationship with production does not thereby ignore what Soyinka refers to as "certain end results of... productive forces whose aesthetic uniqueness made us reach in the first place for the world [sic] 'culture' ".[37] Thus Ngugi again insists that the artistic activities which symbolize the meaning of culture "are derived from a people's way of life and will change as that way of life is altered, modified or developed through the ages."[38] We can see this only if we are able to move beyond the conception of culture which limits it to ideas. Technology is no less a cultural phenomenon than dance and drama. The invention of cassava grinder is a cultural achievement which has exerted a great deal of influence on the nature of social relationship in our societies. It cannot be adequately understood unless we take account of its root and its significance in our historical process. It is of the essence of culture that it *reflects* the material conditions of society while at the same time it advances its social progress, where it is not a victim of the forces that slow down the development of social productive forces. It is along those lines that one may usefully examine the phenomena of culture and its reality in the historical development of the Nigerian state. What should hopefully become transparent is the class-nature of the form and content of culture in a society with class-contradictions. For this purpose we may identify three stages: Pre-colonial, Colonial and Post-colonial [or Neo-colonial] periods of Nigerian history.

Pre-colonial Society and the Phenomena of Culture

Pre-colonial Nigeria has been variously classified and described. Some have adopted Nyerere's claim that pre-colonial Africa comprised of classless communal societies without any distinction between workers and employers. Others have been less charitable, seeing class contradictions as endemic in traditional Africa. The later Nkrumah adopted this later position. There is some truth in both positions. We only need to understand that, due to the dynamic nature of social mode of production, a particular structure does not have to be seen as intrinsic to a society. It is true that in the beginning, neither a complex division of labor nor class distinctions characterized most Nigerian societies. The Yoruba had a communal system of land-holding in which ownership resides in the extended family system rather than in individuals. As land was the major means of production, there was no basis for any serious class distinction. Of course, there was age distinction as well as sexual division of labor and family heads determined access to land on behalf of the members. But such arrangements did not give rise to class distinctions.

Later on, with the development of slavery, things started to change and a modicum of class differences emerged. War-lords who played important roles in the various inter-communal raids became incorporated as part of the nucleus of the ruling class. So were *Babaláwo*'s and *Baasègùn*'s who also became important in the economic and political life of their various communities. Along with the kings and chiefs, they became the custodians of culture and were in privileged positions to determine the forms of cultural expression. But they were more in alliance with the rest of the community. They were mouth organs for the people's concern as they all accepted the direction of the divinities. At this time, therefore, culture was linked with the condition of the people and with their aspirations as they understood them. This is not to say that there were no elements of exploitation, by the ruling class, of the credulity of the masses. A case in point is the philosophy of predestination which the people believe without questioning and which seems to work for the promotion of peace and stability. The important point, however, is that culture, at this stage in the historical development of Nigeria, was still closely linked with the struggle of the masses in a hostile world. The festivals were arranged to celebrate the various seasons and activities connected with them. The New Yam festival coincided with the harvest of yam; *Egúngún* ceremony coincided with the time of new maize and was a period for celebrating the link between the living and the dead. Culture was not separated from life; rather it was a celebration of life and its achievements as well as an expression of human struggle. Of course, since at that time, there was no Nigerian nation, but numerous communities and ethnic groups, we cannot say there was a Nigerian national culture. But we had models of the relationship between culture and a people's struggle which we could have appropriated in the subsequent stages of our development. Culture in traditional society is truly the totality of life, the celebration of life and its vicissitudes. It is the expression of the intrinsic value of work as well as a pride in its fruit. It is not something just made to be enjoyed by the wealthy at their leisure. The colonizers that first started the process of devaluation of our ways of life had a different view of culture.

Colonialism and Culture

Colonialism in any form and society has a distinctive feature vis-a-vis culture: it devalues the culture of the dominated people. All that is needed for the colonialist is the rationalization of its action by denying the existence of any distinctive culture to the colony. But when a people's culture is denied existence, the people themselves are thereby dehumanized and dehistoricized since culture is a fruit of history.

The significance of colonial domination for culture is the assumption of cultural superiority of the colonizer. It is this assumption that suggests to the colonizer the burden of 'civilizing' the subjugated territories. Of course, there has to be some justification of the assumption. Colonizers try to legitimize their otherwise unpopular rule by means of an ideological distortion of the reality that underlies the relationship between the metropolis and the colony. The colony is presented as the home of uncultured, untutored and unproductive beings who need to be helped. The unproductive native needs to be forced, if necessary. In Rousseauian terms, this force, which is usually concretized in forced labor, is nothing but helping the colonized to help themselves. In other words, they are being 'forced to be free.' This is the ideology of colonialism which takes the form of cultural paternalism.[39]

But like all ideologies, the colonialist ideology only serves to conceal its real motive, that is, the economic foundations of colonialism. Lord Lugard does not hide the economic reality behind the ideological smokescreen of the whiteman's burden, as unambiguously put in his *Dual Mandate*:

> Let it be admitted at the outset that European brains, capital and energy have not been and never will be expended in developing the resources of Africa from motives of pure philanthropy, that Europe is in Africa for the mutual benefit of her own industrial classes and of the native races in their progress to a higher plane, that the benefit can be reciprocal and that it is the aim and desire of civilized administration to fulfil this dual mandate.[40]

The ideology of racial superiority is handy for the colonialist imposition of his own culture on the colonized. In colonial Nigeria, this was carried out in differing levels of social reality. Through Western education, for instance, subjects were introduced to the culture of the imperialist with its norms and values which in many cases, conflict with indigenous values. It was part of the intended consequences of exposure to Western education that certain traditional norms which were regarded as repugnant to European ideas of decency and justice should be discarded. There were consequently an initial intellectual and cultural crises created by the conflict between the internalized norms and values of pre-colonial society and the teaching of the schools as illustrated by this type of reflection:

> Government is teaching, now saying that
> *Chukwu* is
> Not fixed to a spot
> That where we go to consult *Chukwu*
> Is a fake
> And we cannot tell
> Whether they are telling the truth
> Or deceiving us...[41]

In order to effectively carry out the program of confusion and cultural alienation of Nigerians, the imperialists had to adopt a policy of divide and rule. They identified a number of intellectual, high bureaucratic officials and petty bourgeoisie whose class interests seemed tied up with the fortunes of the colonial system. The imperialists wooed them and some traditional rulers into the system granting the latter especially material benefits including free education for their children and other pecuniary benefits attached to their position. This class thus became an ally of the colonizer in the task of devaluation of indigenous culture. This further widened the gap that was already existing between the ruling class and the masses and thus prevented the development of a popular culture across the nation.

The ruling class, including the emerging petty bourgeoisie and the top hierarchy of bureaucracy, soon developed sharp tastes for foreign values and culture. As a result of the effectiveness of colonial ideology, the section of the urban populations under the influence of this class of Nigerians soon became impatient about the indigenous culture, treating it as weird and strange. An inferiority complex was created in the psyche of the masses and their cultural originality suffered a serious devaluation.

Even in the dark days of colonialism, however, there was always a silver lining in the sky. Counterpoised against the compromising attitude of the indigenous ruling class and the aggressive policy of cultural imperialism of the colonizer was the cultural resistance of the nationalist movement. This aspect of the socio--political history of Nigeria has been very well documented. What concerns us here is the way in which nationalism promoted the development of national culture. Two points are important to note in this connection. First, the early nationalist movement in Nigeria was primarily bourgeois in character. It was made up of a small class of intelligentsia and merchant class, majority of whom had been exposed to the culture of the colonizer. Many of them had studied abroad and had begun to appreciate the distinctiveness of African cultural traditions. Some of them engaged in writings on the theme of African Culture for the purpose of correcting the prejudiced interpretations of Africa's past by the colonizers and to inculcate cultural pride and self-respect in the mind of Africans.[42] For instance the Zikist philosophy of African personality was incorporated into the program of the Zikist Youth Movement. As clarified by Nwafor Orizu, among the goals that must be reached include the following:

> first, above all loyalties, the African must appreciate his culture - political, social, philosophical and religious. By this I am not suggesting a back to antiquity reaction. I mean that no people can understand the bases of their present behaviour without recalling their cultural background and making the most of its best, while rejecting the bad aspects of it by substituting for these better ways, ways compatible with the ever-changing social horizon.[43]

There is no doubt that these reactions by the early bourgeois nationalists succeeded in creating some cultural awareness on the part of a large portion of the literate population. But it did not lead to the development of a distinctive national culture.

The reason for this failure is contained in the second point worthy of note. The early bourgeois nationalists were concerned more with a continuation of the socio-economic structure as laid down by the colonizers. They were interested in cultural revival because it hurt their ego to be referred to as a people without a culture. At the same time their ambition was to advance to the upper cadre of the colonial administrative and business structure. Most of them did not see anything terribly wrong in the structure of colonial administration and economy as it was. The continuous presence of the colonizers was therefore seen as an obstacle to the realization of their own ambition. But because the structure of colonial political economy was inimical to the development of a true mass culture, the efforts of cultural nationalist could only scratch the surface. As Markovitz has rightly observed: "Focusing on the past and on their cultural personalities had the effect-regardless of the motivations of the intellectuals involved - of diverting attention away from immediate radical political change. Cultural expression proved insufficient to meet persisting and intensifying political difficulties."[44]

Indeed there was no consensus among the Western-trained intellectuals concerning the need for, and the method of, achieving the revival of Nigerian culture. Thus A. O. Alakija once wondered aloud if we should say that "the African ceases to be African because he finds it more convenient to discard his gabarding for the Bond Street Style."[45] He thought it was quite unhelpful to believe so:

> There are some who say that the African will be de-Africanized if he eats with a fork and knife, or sits at a table for his meals instead of using his hands and squatting on the floor as he was wont to do. One extremist has been trying his varying experiments in a well-known school in West Africa in the hope of preventing the Africans from becoming Europeanized. This idea must be dismissed as unhelpful.[46]

The early bourgeois nationalists also had problems mobilizing the masses in the rural areas for cultural revival. This was mainly because they [the bourgeois nationalists] had their own share of superiority complex. Indeed, many of them had no contact with the peasants in the rural areas. The first nationalist movement was limited to the urban areas of the south and to a small class of professionals and middle class workers who felt superior in taste and values. For instance, the Nigerian Youth Movement which was about the first nationalist movement in the country was restricted to Lagos and other Southern cities in its early years. It was therefore not in a position to mobilize the grass root for the development of an authentic national culture to counter the colonial devaluation of indigenous culture.

By the time the Nigerian Youth Movement was ready for real nationalistic pressure, the other bane of Nigerian social life had set in. This is ethnicism.

Within the rank of the bourgeois nationalists, there emerged ethnic consciousness and the myth of cultural diversity was allowed to take the heat off the march toward the development of a national culture. For instance, the Nigerian Youth Movement (NYM) which was by 1938, the foremost nationalist movement in the country, became the first victim of ethnic politics as a result of a factionalization of interests within the emerging indigenous bourgeoisie. It was cheap to appeal to the ethnic consciousness of followers for support against perceived victimization from an out-group. This was what ruined the chances of the NYM to raise the national consciousness of Nigerians. Ernest Ikoli, an Ijo man and Samuel Akinsanya, an Ijebu - Yoruba man had both contested for the seat on the Governor's Executive Council vacated by Dr. K. A. Abayomi in 1941. Ikoli and Akinsanya were President and Vice-President of the NYM respectively. Ikoli won the contest. Naturally Akinsanya was unhappy. But so was Azikwe who had supported him, and both saw their defeat as a manifestation of the general hatred and contempt others had for the Igbo and Ijebus. They in turn appealed to the sympathy of members of their groups and this was the beginning of the end of the NYM as a potential nationalist party.[47]

The significance of the NYM crisis for the development of national culture should not escape us. The myth of cultural heterogeneity and the perception of ethno-cultural prejudice is always an effective weapon against national culture. It was utilized effectively, even if unconsciously, within the NYM and the succeeding political parties. Leaders wasted no time in exploiting the so-called cultural-linguistic difference among the populations. Differences, rather than similarities, were highlighted to the extent that the seeds of ethnic discord were sown and germinated even in places where common members of different ethnic groups had lived together in peace before the era of nationalism and had gone through mutual assimilation. This is in spite of the fact that many Nigerian poor workers and peasants had a common experience of poverty, colonial exploitation, disease and racial prejudice under the colonial system. These poor Nigerians would have benefitted from a revolutionary leadership concerned with changing the relations of production and launching the country on a really sustained path of growth and self-reliance. The petty bourgeois nationalists were not concerned with changing the relations of production. Rather they were interested in sustaining it, but changing the relations of distribution in their favor and against their British counterparts. In the circumstance they were not able to contribute effectively to the development of a truly national culture.

Post-Colonial Society and Culture

The disease that afflicted the pre-independence nationalist struggle and which made it impossible for there to emerge a truly national consciousness soon proved to be drug-resistant. It survived and persisted in the post-independence political game and is still a potent force to reckon with now. The point is that ethnicity has proved to be an effective and cheap weapon for the pursuit of class and personal interests and many political leaders are using it to their own advantage even if to the detriment of building a truly strong nation. Though Nigeria is politically independent, it is a common knowledge that she is not economically independent. The import-export economy inherited from the British imperialists and their financial associates continue to dominate the economic life of the country and is being perpetuated by the ruling class. Ethnicity is being used to mask the reality of the rich-poor gap and the struggle that is going on and this accounts for the persistence of the ideology of cultural diversity and for the apparent retardation in the growth of a national popular culture.

From the beginning of the First Republic through the first Military Interregnum to the end of the Second Republic "Contractocracy"[48], the Nigerian state existed as a conglomerate of organisms without a unifying soul. The ruling class was not bothered about infusing the sentiment of nationalism. The idea of a national culture, which could only be born out of a common struggle for true national liberation from the claws of imperialism and neocolonialism, did not mean anything to them. The national bourgeoisie was concerned with sharing the "national cake" equitably among themselves. To do this, they each had to strengthen their regional political bases, create imaginary stories of victimisation and hatred, thus poisoning the minds of innocent peasants and the younger generations with nationalist outlook and clipping their revolutionary wings. The ruling class of the First and Second Republics were self-seekers who paraded themselves as national patriots. Their philosophy of maximizing individual profits made it impossible for them to develop a true national ethos. It was something beyond the politics of self-interest to develop national institutions. Yet it is the absence of national institutions and national ethos, which could be a rallying point for the masses, that is responsible for the aping of foreign cultures which is fast becoming a vocation especially among the youth. As Rousseau once observed, it is National institutions that give "form to the genius, the character, the tastes, and the customs of a people, that arouses in it that ardent love of fatherland that is founded upon habits of mind impossible to uproot; what makes unbearably tedious for its citizens every moment spent away from home - even when they find themselves surrounded by delights that are denied them in their own country."[49] Without such institutions, patriotic sentiments cannot be developed; and without patriotic sentiments, the urge to contribute to the development of the nation cannot be developed. This accounts for the phenomena of discontent and alienation that seems now to be the lot of many would-be patriots, which compares unfavorably with the genuine sense of community nurtured in traditional societies.

Our position thus far is that the ruling class in post-colonial Nigeria did not encourage the development of national institutions which are essential for true patriotism and national consciousness. It is quite compatible with this position to observe that various governments since independence have paid lip-service to the issue of cultural development. However, it is a fact that until very recently, there was no Federal Government cultural policy for Nigeria. But this is not the important issue. All it shows is that even with a situation such as we are in, where the ruling class is sustained by bourgeois ideologies, the effectiveness of which depends on the formulation of necessary programs and policies for conditioning the masses, the bankruptcy of the ruling class still prevented it from formulating such a program until recently and also during a military administration.

As I have mentioned, however, the non-existence of a cultural policy until recently is not the issue. For even if it existed, as we have argued, it is not the determinant of national culture. The issue is that in spite of the non-existence of a national cultural policy for a long time, there have been various cultural programs and government agencies have been established for the purpose of preserving our rich cultural heritage. These include the establishment of the Museum of Arts, Department of Antiquities and the emphasis on the teaching of cultural heritage in schools, organization of Festivals of Arts as a potential agent for developing a sense of national consciousness and of course, the organization and hosting of the Second World Black and African Festival of the Arts and Culture (FESTAC). With all these, it cannot be argued that the ruling class has not encouraged the development of a true national culture. After all, these are all geared towards the rejuvenation of our cultural heritage. Indeed, but for these institutions, it cannot be guaranteed that we would still have our various languages intact, nor our traditional arts and craft in place. The Department of culture deserves every credit for preserving the cultural heritage of the various ethnic groups through its various programs.

Yet, there is much that is missing. What is promoted in the various programs and festivals could be widened in scope so that we do not emphasize too much of what separate us or what is pleasing only to outsiders, but more importantly those cultural values which we share. We should not just be interested in digging up traditions which inevitably will reveal the cultural differences among the various ethnic groups with a view to generating the myth of cultural diversity which could then be displayed to further mystify the people and prevent the heightening of their common struggle. This is why Frantz Fanon has rightly insisted that:

> A national culture is not a folklore, nor an abstract populism that believes it can discover the people's true nature. It is not made up of the inert dregs of

gratuitous actions, that is to say actions which are less and less attached to the ever-present reality of the people.[50]

One of the problems with Nigeria is the absence of national leadership with a patriotic bent. The political ruling class consists mainly of a self-interested people whose major preoccupation is to accumulate wealth for themselves at the expense of the nation. It has no conception of a desirable future for the masses but to keep them mystified as a means of effective exploitation and oppression. In such a situation, it presents a simplified view of culture to the people, urging them to preserve what they have for posterity. But culture is not static; it is the dynamic synthesis of the social reality of a people. Again, Fanon's account is illuminating: "A national culture is the whole body of efforts made by a people in the sphere of thought to describe, justify and praise the action through which that people has created itself and keeps itself in existence. A national culture in underdeveloped countries should therefore take its place at the very heart of the struggle for freedom which these countries are carrying on."[51] The essential points in this position should not be missed. Fanon refers to national culture as the whole body of efforts made by a people in the sphere of thought. But he does not thereby identify culture as just ideas or thought. This practice in the sphere of thought is geared towards, among other things, praising the *action* through which the people have created themselves. There is therefore a dialectic of thought and action. In the universe of culture, thought and practice are inseparable; and as Okot p'Bitek puts it, culture is philosophy as lived and celebrated in a society.[52] It follows therefore that national culture in the true sense is absent in a situation where a people are denied the freedom to struggle for their true liberation. A people whose lives are controlled by forces outside of themselves cannot boast of real national independence. And since it is in the struggle for freedom that national culture has meaning, a people cannot boast of a national culture without the involvement of all the sectors in the national struggle. National culture has meaning in the popular struggle of a people to shake off oppression and exploitation and become truly free. In a situation where the political class makes it difficult for the people to be truly liberated, but continues to mystify them by all sorts of cultural ideologies, there can be no true national culture. Culture has to be used in the service of genuine national liberation and, it is in the process of such a struggle that a true national culture emerges. Perhaps this is what Senghor means by the claim that cultural liberation is the precondition for political liberation. But the matter of which is prior is not easily determinable. As Aime Cessaire has also rightly observed, "a political and social system that suppresses the self-determination of a people thereby kills the creative power of that people."[53] That is to say that the influence of political liberation cannot be denied. Ngugi Wa Thiong'o puts it more unambiguously: "It is wrong to think of culture as prior to politics. Politics and economic liberation are the essential conditions for cultural liberation, for the true release of a people's creative spirit and imagination. It is when people are involved in the active work of destroying an inhibitive social structure and building a new one that they begin to see themselves. They are born again."[54]

For culture to be of service in the resolution of CAR, therefore, it has to be put in its proper place. Reification has to be avoided. The political struggle for true emancipation must be given its due so that cultural dynamics may be given a free rein. Culture must take its place in the process of true liberation. This means that the cultural expression in its various forms cannot be tied to the apron string of the state as long as it is itself an agent of oppression. In a colonial, neo-colonial dependent state, cultural expression cannot serve its purpose if it takes the side of the state. There are, from our history, worthy examples of the use of culture by individuals and groups as a means of protest against oppression. The late Hubert Ogunde may be singled out. He was exemplary in his use of culture as a liberating agent in both colonial and post-colonial Nigeria. He saw beyond the ideology of colonial exploitation and used the forum of the theater to deal with it. It is this kind of insight that is needed to deal with the present crisis of CAR through culture. The problem with the cultural view is that it does not take this dialectic of national culture and national liberation seriously.

8

CONTEMPORARY AFRICAN REALITIES:
THE POLITICO-ECONOMIC VIEW

The politico-economic view on contemporary African realities [CAR] in their relation to ultimate reality and meaning [URAM] sees CAR as a socio-economic issue which has little or nothing to do with religion or culture except in so far as the latter may also be given a politico-economic interpretation. On this view, an adequate understanding of CAR must take account of Africa's experience of colonialism and neo-colonialism and the natural consequence of its being drawn into the world capitalist system. A neocolonial state is one which is politically independent but economically dependent on its erstwhile colonial masters or other foreign interests. In such a state, the economy is controlled from outside, either directly or by the multinational corporations [MNC's] whose interest is mainly in the maximization of profits for developing the metropolis. The effectiveness of neocolonialism depends highly on the cooperation of the native agents in the neocolonial state. The domestic policies of the government must be tailored to the needs of the foreign controllers. Of course, the native agents have much at stake. They are not just being nice to foreign controllers. Rather they are partners in the business of exploiting the human and material resources of the country for their own interests. Thus the policy of indigenization cannot succeed because there are native agents who perceive their interest as lying in the continuation of foreign domination of the economy. Since these agents are either in government or have representatives in government, the policies of government are reflective of those interests. Criticism will stand in the way of good business; therefore, it cannot be tolerated. This explains why oil boom unnaturally passes into oil doom.

The justification for this position on the problem of CAR has its root in the history of Africa's association with industrial west, an association which has not been anything other than forced dependence. From the devastation caused by the atlantic slave trade to the exploitation that came with the colonial experience, Africa has not known a period of real independence. Flag independence promised all the good things of the world for the masses only to turn out to be one big disappointment in the matter of delivery. Flag independence does not bring liberation from the suffocating grip of the metropolis. African nations become one big television screen whose remote control is in the hands of the industrial nations. What appears on the screen at any one time is what the west wants to see. It is a case of independence without autonomy.

It could have been different. Immediately after flag independence, African nations could have taken a path of self-reliance; one that does not tie their fortunes to the apron string of their erstwhile colonizers. They could have chosen to develop on the basis of their resources, focusing on agro-based industries, developing the potentials of the peasants and investing in their human resources. But eternal dependence seemed to be the fate and they chose to continue with the path to which they were drawn by colonialism, producing raw materials for foreign exchange and using same to import manufactured goods. With this approach, the former colonial powers lost virtually nothing by giving up their colonies. It was not just that capitalism was adopted by most of the newly independent nations; the point is that they adopted a dependent capitalism. It was, as in colonialism, market-oriented, with no independent indigenous bourgeoisie, no entrepreneurial class and, therefore, the hope for economic prosperity can only be dependent on the "good will" of the west.

This "good will" is usually expressed in the form of loans, aids and, most especially, prescriptions for "sustained" development from the World Bank and the International Monetary Fund [IMF]. In recent times, such recommendations have led to the adoption of structural adjustment programs [SAP] by various African states. The basic premise of these programs is that the economies of African nations have developed out of alignment principally either because of the inability of the ruling class to manage it or because of external factors, including world-wide recession, or a combination of these and other factors. To bring them back to alignment, the World Bank-IMF- sponsored structural adjustment programs prescribe, among other things, the devaluation of the currencies to promote export production for foreign exchange, removal of subsidy on several items including food, education, health care; reduction in the number of government employees and a ban on further employment in the public sector. What many countries have discovered, however, is that this adjustment program has created more problems- economic, social and political- than it has been able to solve.[1] It has aggravated the situation of the vulnerable members of society, including children, the poor, and the elderly while, at the same time, it has further improved the condition of those well-off members. By placing emphasis on production for exports, the poor peasants are edged out of agricultural production since they cannot afford the input. The removal of subsidies on fertilizer leads to the same conclusion. So does the removal of subsidy on petroleum product which has the additional impact of raising transportation costs and therefore food prices. In short, SAP, from the perspective of the politico-economic school of CAR, is part of the problem, and not so much of a solution to CAR. It is another reminder of the dependency status of Africa since the World Bank and IMF are now dictating the tune.

For this politico-economic view of URAM, then, the explanation of CAR is to be found in the neocolonial, dependent capitalist formations upon which most African nations are built. Africa's URAM is National Liberation - which is principally the liberation of the socio-economic forces from the claws of neo-colonialism. National liberation, as Cabral puts it, "is the phenomenon in which a given socio-economic whole rejects the negation of its historical process. In other words, the national liberation of a people is the regaining of the historical personality of that people, its return to history through the destruction of the imperialist domination to which it was subjected."[2]

Obafemi Awolowo on the Problem of Africa

Obafemi Awolowo was one of the few African leaders who saw the problem of CAR from a politico-economic perspective, but who also insisted that, any proposed solution which is based on a concept of African socialism that rests on a geographical or cultural restriction, is inadequate. He therefore rejects Senghor's account of African socialism on the ground that socialism is a universal concept:

> Socialism... is a normative social science... it must (therefore) be of universal application. If any principle is purely and strictly peculiar to a given institution, region, or state, it may be a custom, practice or even theory, but it cannot lay claim to the status of science. Just as there can be no African Ethics qua Ethics as a science, or African Logic, so there can be no African Socialism.[3]

But Awolowo also shares Senghor's sentiments against certain features of Marxism: dictatorship of the proletariat, revolutionary struggle and the attitude towards religion. On the question of the idea of dictatorship, he argues that:

> if the proletariat who are now in power [following election victory] are truly representative of the masses, and if the objectives being pursued by them are truly socialist and, therefore, more in harmony with the immutable law than not, then every effort on the part of the displaced capitalists to recapture power by foul means is doomed to fail and sure to rebound catastrophically on them... .[4]

In late 1976, Awolowo gave the first series in the Kwame Nkrumah Memorial Lectures. He rightly devoted the series to a reexamination of the problems of Africa because, as he put it, "the greatest preoccupations of Kwame Nkrumah in his lifetime were the problems of Africa and how to solve them. Even the problems of the country of his birth, Ghana, were seen and tackled by him within a strictly Pan-African context."[5] In these lectures, Awolowo analyzes the causes of the problem of Africa along with the different phases of African historical development: pre-colonial; contact with the White Race; foreign rule and decolonization and the period of independence.

In the period before contact with the White Race, the problems of humankind in Africa included ignorance, technical backwardness, superstitious beliefs, poverty, unproductive methods of cultivation, war and insecurity of life. Awolowo adopts what amounts to a Marxist approach to the analysis of these problems. Let us examine his account.

First, according to Awolowo, "pre-Palaeolithic African, like his primitive counterparts in other parts of the earth, had very few patent problems [i.e. problems of which they are aware but the cause of which they do not know.]"[6] This African had need for food, shelter, and clothing. He adopted the means available to him to satisfy these needs. These means were the crudest because he was still "untutored and his subjective mind still extensively uninformed and infantile, he could not comprehend, let alone interpret his surroundings."[7] His life was most unhealthy and terribly short. "Whenever he suffered ill-health, he never, in the initial stages, knew objectively what to do to restore himself to good health, except insofar as he might be guided by instinct to partake of certain herbs which had curative properties."[8] These, as should be recalled, are features of existence which characterize all primitive peoples and not just Africans. For Awolowo, therefore, the bane of primitive existence consists of ignorance, poverty and disease.

Second, however, improvement gradually came in the matter of invention of crude tools for hunting, food-gathering and root-digging. Indeed, among primitive peoples, Africa was in the lead in the matter of this "technological" revolution. Agriculture is by far, the most revolutionary of the discoveries of the primitive. For with it came settled village life, greater productivity made possible by division of labor and preservation and storage of food. It is also interesting that in most parts of the continent now, storage of food has not proceeded beyond this stone age level! What should be noted thus far is that the locus of human activity is some kind of group or family life. For as Awolowo maintains elsewhere, even if the Hobbesian individualist assumptions are applicable to Europe, they have no place in Africa.[9] So we are here concerned with a socio-economic order in which people are involved as groups [of families] and not as individuals.

The next stage of the analysis suggests an ambivalence in Awolowo's view of the matter. For one is not sure whether the account of "group or class" struggle which is subsequently developed from this historical analysis does not make use of an individualist framework which Awolowo has rejected. To make this point more clearly, it is worth quoting Awolowo at length:

> In the pursuit of these ends [accumulation of goods, etc.], he [the neo-palaeolithic African] became greedy - that is, insatiable in his longing for wealth - and was absolutely ruthless in the elimination of any obstacle, including his fellowmen, that stood between him and the realization of his objective. In other words, because of his many years of nasty, savage and beastly living, the concepts of human dignity, human life, and the like, which as we know them today, were inalienably inherent in man from the emergence of *homo sapiens*, were distant to his thoughts and consciousness. In his utter ignorance of those human virtues, he trampled upon his fellowmen with undisguised, unashamed, and unmitigated savagery, for the promotion of his self-interest and greed. In the brutish situation that ensued and prevailed, in which one family, clan or tribe regarded the other as an obstacle to be demolished at any cost in order to clear the way for the ownership of more and more land for cultivation, and also in which one family, clan or tribe regarded the others as tributaries, or slaves and, therefore, means to the enjoyment of more and more leisure, it was inevitable, and so indeed it happened in all parts of Africa, that two distinct groups of people should, in due course, emerge - the strong, who were in the minority and who became the dominant and exploiting group, and the weak, who were in the majority but went under and became the exploited and enslaved group.[10]

From this passage, three main points seem to emerge as Awolowo's view of the human condition in Africa in the beginning:

1. The neo-palaeolithic African was greedy, ruthless, violent and savage, lacking ideas of human dignity and human life.

2. Economic activities were carried on in family units and family struggle and hatred was part of the order.
3. In the process of struggle between families for economic ascendancy, two distinct groups of people emerged: the dominant exploiting group, and the weak, exploited group. The former were in the minority; the latter in the majority.

There seems to be a great need for clarification here, especially since the historical ground for this account is not very clear. It is also not clear what historical stage in the development of human life in Africa this account is supposed to recapture. It seems clear, however, that at the very beginning, the intercourse between human beings must be very limited even when they developed settled family units and agriculture had been discovered. For the availability of large expanse of land for cultivation made peaceful coexistence possible and therefore there was virtually no basis for violent interactions. Greed, as a concept, also appears inapplicable in such a situation where there was no urge for people to be greedy. The basic needs of life - food, shelter and clothing were still met at the most rudimentary level. Food storage was not available, so there could be no point in accumulating a lot. The need for shelter was met by building huts with available materials; and of course, clothing was not more than what was needed to keep warm. In such a situation, one wonders what could be the basis for greed and ruthlessness.

In *The People's Republic*, Awolowo's view is that "man is a social animal. He was never and could never have been 'solitary'."[11] Human beings live as members of families. There is love and mutual affections in such family units. The affairs of the family, which is not just the nuclear, but the extended family, were presided over by the *paterfamilias* and/or the *materfamilias* who set the rules, sometimes by appeal to the family gods' wishes and sometimes by the "rational conscious thoughts of the *paterfamilias*." Such rules are "invariably motivated by affection for, and the best interests of the entire family."[12] This appears to me to suggest that at least there was love, affection and loyalty in the family units. It is also important to note that the family units were large groups occupying a parcel of land or territory without any near neighbors. So the possibility of violence was minimized.

So Awolowo cannot mean that greed, ruthlessness and violence marked the condition of human beings in the beginning in Africa. All these were later developments and it is not now certain what exactly were the conditions that gave rise to them. Part of it must have to do with the satisfaction of needs as they grew more complex and as population increased and the resources got thinner on the land. The aspect of this that deserves to be noted, however, is that even at such a time, violence was more external than internal. That is, it was not a question of a dominant group developing within a particular family or *community* of families to attack its weaker members. Rather, it was one community of families attacking another community. It was also not in every case that such an attack was for economic reasons. In some cases, it had to do with a perceived need to right a wrong. At any rate, even such violent interactions were not the rule; for different families might live together as peaceful neighbors and later decide to unite for mutual benefits.[13] Indeed, city-states emerged from this mutual love of peace among families as Awolowo also suggested:

> it was the passionate desire for peace among them, and for mutual defence or protection against those outside their union, as well as for the procurement of economic benefits, which led to the emergence of, first, the village-states, then the city-states followed by the nation-states or multi-nation states.[14]

The difference between Awolowo's positions in *The People's Republic* (1968) and in *The Problem of Africa* (1976) is that in the latter, he has adopted a model of class analysis to interpret the African situation which he did not use in the former. He now talks of a dominant group which he equates with dominant class and of the seeds of class struggle:

> ...each group or class now came to regard the other as a patent problem. The dominant group had no doubt in their minds that the dominated group were created to serve them and to bolster their

enjoyment of more abundant life and more comfortable living.... On the other hand, the oppressed class regarded the dominant group as an obstacle to their personal freedom of action, and to their enjoyment of those good things of life to which the dominant group openly asserted claim. In the midst of these counter-vailing and counter-acting objectives on the part of the dominant and suppressed groups, the seeds of class struggle and class hatred were sown.[15]

This appears to be a Marxian interpretation of history; but Awolowo rejects the kind of conclusion that Marx and Engels derived from it, namely, the inevitability of revolutionary transformation which may have to be violent.[16] His rejection of this conclusion may be accounted for by looking again at how he developed his concept of a dominant group. It seems clear that, for him, this group is not a bunch of individuals who happened to dominate others within their group. Rather, it appears to be a term that refers to a dominant family or community of families in the struggle for economic ascendancy. His basic unit of economic life is the family [within which there is love, affection and loyalty]. It is the family struggle for land that "led to interminable inter-clan, inter-tribal and inter-ethnic wars.[17] It is families, therefore, that become dominant or dominated, at least in the first instance.

It would seem that subsequent to their initial victory in their struggle for more land, the dominant family units or community of families also resolved themselves into groups of dominant and dominated. There now arose a "dominant land-owning group" who had to contain the "hatred, resentment, and occasional hostility of the exploited and enslaved class." How might this division within loving, affectionate and loyal family members arise? Awolowo does not give the details. But he glosses over this kind of transition which, I think, may be explained as occasioned by the addition of external populations of defeated families to the original stock. Where wars become institutionalized means of expansion, there would develop a class of warriors as social elites in virtue of their perceived importance. They may also come to see themselves as indispensable and others as existing at their mercy. If this is the case, then from a situation of mutual love and loyalty, there could develop mutual strife and resentment. This seems to be the basis of the dominant-dominated group in Awolowo's account. He also presents an interesting account of how the dominant group resolved the problem of resistance:

> ...they created a large number of gods and made them abide in the skies, well out of mortal view; they created spirits with which they filled the earth and its atmosphere. Since the gods and the spirits were invisible, the dominant class facilitated the emergence of priests who were capable of holding dialogues with these gods and spirits, were qualified to act as spokesmen and interpreters for them through oracular pronouncements and the laying down of taboos and were versed in the rituals for appeasing them when angry. Above all, they created the institution of divine Kingship. While the priest was the spokesman, the interpreter and appeaser of gods and spirits, the King was their divine representative on earth. For this reason, he was clothed with the same halo as the gods and spirits, and his powers over his subjects were absolute and unquestionable.[18]

As may be observed, this is also a strictly Marxist account of the basis and origin of religion. Men make the gods to assist them in their exploitation of others. It would seem then that such a theory should be applicable to all religions and God or gods, including the Christian God. It appears, however, that Awolowo believes in the reality of the Christian God which he identifies with the Universal Mind:

> We see then that the body of man is indeed the temple of God or the universal mind; and we can now find no difficulty in agreeing with the Psalmist when he says that man has been made "a little lower than God." This, in our view is the truth - the only truth.[19]

Indeed, it is knowledge of this truth and conviction derived from it that, for Awolowo, enables one to "automatically enter into the regime of mental magnitude" in which one is "free from: (1) the negative emotions of anger, hate, fear, envy or jealousy, selfishness or greed; (2) indulgence in the wrong types of food and drink, and in ostentatious consumption; and (3) excessive or immoral craving for sex."[20] Here, we see then that Awolowo acknowledges the existence of God as presented in the Bible and that this God made man in His image. On the other hand, his account of African God(s) is that they are made by man to dominate his fellow beings. There has to be a way of explaining this apparent shift. First, it is possible that between 1968 and 1976, Awolowo changed his views about the reality of God, and that he later held the view that all God(s) are man-made. I am not sure about this in view of his continued adherence to the Christian faith until his death. Second, it may be that he really believed that the Christian God is more real and more genuine than the African god; perhaps because it is based on the idea of special revelation. If this is the case, he has not defended the position thoroughly, for both seem to rely on the perceived need by human beings for some power to help them live and survive in a hostile world. While I understand Awolowo's point that the problems of Africa are "real earthy problems (which) cannot be solved by creating gods in the skies, filling the atmosphere with spirits and imposing despots on the community,"[21] it is also true that all societies at one point in their history, rely on such devices to keep them going and intact. I also do not think that the use of incantations at the expense of herbal preparations to effect cures can be attributed to traditional Africans. As we have observed in Chapter 5, the people recognize the existence of germs and viral infection which require herbal cure. Incantation has its own focus and may sometimes be used in conjunction with herbal cure.

Awolowo's analysis of the problem of Africa before contact with Europeans raises anew the question whether Africa experienced class conflict before the incursion of colonialism. His analysis of this, though vague at some points, seems to me to be on the whole valid. Families enter into conflict, and while such conflicts cannot be strictly regarded as class conflicts, they prepared the ground for and sew the seeds of class conflicts which had just begun germinating shortly before the period of foreign rule. For even before the coming of the "White Race", there had been contacts between Africa south of the Sahara and the Mediterranean regions through the Trans-Sahara trade route. People dealt in all sorts of merchandise, including slaves. This also aggravated the inter-ethnic strife as raiders aggressively invaded alien communities. It was, however, motivated by external agencies. Whatever its motivation, the circumstance led to several other problems, including the emergence of social stratification and its consequent effect on social mobility.

It was about this period that contact with the Whites occurred. At first, it was an economic relationship, with the Whites dictating the terms, being in absolute control and the African was made a beast of burden. The rivalry between the Whites over the control of Africa was resolved in Berlin in 1884 when "Africa was portioned among those countries of Europe which later became Colonial Powers on our Continent."[22] The legacy of this Foreign Rule was (i) the ruthless economic exploitation of the continent and (ii) the political subjection of Africans to external authority which, through a policy of divide and rule, sewed the seeds of instability and disunity for the continent. Economic underdevelopment and political disunity and instability are the two problems carried over by African states to the dawn of independence. They are problems which combine to form the core of the horrid state of affairs referred to in Chapter 6 as contemporary African realities. According to Awolowo, our ancestors hardly recognized the enormity of the problems, hence could not do anything about them. What is his own solution?

As a prelude to offering a solution, Awolowo summarizes the problems of Africa under four heads:

(1) The problem of underdevelopment - which includes
    (a)- economic under-development
    (b)- disease
    (c) - economic exploitation
    (d) - underdevelopment of the subjective mind.
(2) The problem of individual freedom and of sovereignty
(3) The problem of constitution-making
(4) The problem of African unity.

I have discussed most of these problems under my category of contemporary African realities in Chapter 6. However, there is one which is original with Awolowo's analysis: Underdevelopment of the subjective mind. [1(d)]. To explain this concept, Awolowo identifies two levels of a man's mind: The subconscious, or, in the language of psychology, the unconscious level. This is what he refers to as the subconscious mind. Second there is a conscious level, which he refers to as the conscious mind. The former may be regarded as the indwelling God or as the seat of Supreme intelligence or as the Idea, etc. depending on who is looking at it - whether a theist, a psychologist or a Hegelian. The important point about it is that the subconscious mind is complete and self-sufficient at birth and cannot be educated or improved.

The conscious mind has two phases: the objective and the subjective phase which he refers to as the objective mind and subjective mind respectively. The objective mind consists of the five faculties while the subjective mind is completely blank at birth. It is the only educable part of the human mind, capable of performing such functions as interpretation, recollection, conception, imagination, inductive and deductive reasoning, volition, cognition, conation, affection and aspiration.[23] Educational standing depends on the level of subjective mind, and it should therefore be the focus of attention. Awolowo's view is that this subjective mind of the majority of Africans is underdeveloped. By this, he does not imply biological inferiority of the African vis-a-vis the European. Rather he means that with regard to the activities of the subjective mind listed above, traditionally Africans are behind the Whites. It is not a difference in kind of mentality but a difference in degree of achievement. One problem with this view is the basis for evaluation, which is not supplied. Presumably illiteracy in Western education is one.[24] But this need not be an adequate yardstick. The functions of interpretation, recollection, conception and imagination, even including inductive and deductive reasoning cannot be tied to literacy in the Western culture. The elaborate scheme of ideas incorporated in the Ifa divination system is possible through a combination of several of these functions of the subjective mind. And, of course, volition, conation, affection and aspiration are even less tied up with literacy in the Western sense.

Awolowo's solution to the problems relies on the efficacy of ideology of an appropriate kind for "curing Africa's politico-economic maladies;" as opposed to religion or culture. He asserted and defended three propositions which he considers fundamental as a prelude to a solution:

1. Man is a sole creative and purposive dynamic in nature: everything else is in a state of inertia. In other words, man is the applied force, the prime mover in every economy; other things are passive agents ready to be moved by man for desired effects.

This is regarded as true in both states of human beings: as material beings, they initiate, innovate, accelerate, invest and produce. As spirit or mind, they are superior to all other beings in the universe, having a living soul similar to, but less in degree than that of, the supreme being.

2. The central problem of man is economic: all other problems are ancillary.

That is to say, the satisfaction of economic needs - food, shelter, clothing is the basic motivation for human beings doing whatever they do. Loyalty to state is derived from this, and Awolowo even proffers an economic motive for religious devotion: human beings serve God mainly because they believe that their economic problems may, by religious devotion, be more easily and quickly solved. It would seem then that the problems that have been identified as African problems may be traced to some economic foundations. Indeed, the state can only have a justification in terms of economic advantages for its citizens:

> the sole justification of a state is the economic advantages which division of labor and exchange of goods and services can confer on the inhabitants of the state. Families do not aggregate and unite in one community or state just for the love of one another. The compelling motivation is economic.[25]

3. Every multi-ethnic or multi-nation state that has come into existence, has done so as a result of coercion by one of the constituent ethnic units, or by the act of a colonizing power, and not as a result of

voluntary agreement for a union on the part of the constituent ethnic or national units.

This is to suggest a principle for constitution-making in such states; a principle that will make use of language or ethnic affinities and therefore avoid creating unitary constitutions for multi-ethnic states.

Following these basic propositions, Awolowo's next move is to examine the two major ideological positions of the contemporary world: capitalism and socialism and their adequacy for solving the problem of Africa. Capitalism is analyzed in terms of its concepts and techniques. Its concepts include the right to private property, free choice, equality and egoistic altruism. Awolowo does not find any of these concepts attractive. Indeed, he finds the characteristic features of capitalism indefensible. These include its exploitative and corruptive feature and its planlessness, both of which make it an unacceptable ideology for resolving Africa's problems. For given its tendency to promote fierce division and to foster the law of the jungle among men, and to trample the rights of men under foot in the name of competition, Awolowo does not see how it could adequately solve the problems already highlighted. It could only aggravate them.[26]

Socialism presents a more attractive means of solving the problem. But Awolowo also marks a distinction between the concept of socialism and its characteristics as it has been demonstrated in socialist regimes. First is the concept of oneness of man which rejects division into classes and is out to abolish it. Second, is the concept of the public ownership of land and of the means of production. Land as the gift of nature cannot belong to any one family or individual to the exclusion of others. Other natural resources are the subject of labor which expends its human powers to fashion them. Capital is produced in this way and should be regarded as the result of the combined effort of a large number of people. It is therefore necessary to emphasize the social character of those means of production by bringing them under social control.[27] The third concept of socialism is ''from each according to his ability and to each according to his deed." Awolowo also finds this acceptable because it recognizes differences in innate talents and ability. He identifies three propositions flowing from this concept:

(i) All men have innate talents or latent ability; and should be given equal opportunity to develop them.
(ii) When all the talents have been developed to the fullest possible limits, each one must be given equal opportunity to contribute to social development.
(iii) When all talents in society are not fully developed, it is not the individuals that are adversely affected alone who suffer; the society as a whole also suffers.

While the above are acceptable to Awolowo, none of the three "characteristics of socialism" are. These include, according to him, civil war, the dictatorship of the proletariat and the extermination of the bourgeoisie. For him, none of these need be a necessary concomitant of socialism in Africa. His reason is that the premise on which they rely are inapplicable in the case of Africa: class struggle is not pronounced; there are no emperors, no absolute monarchs, no opulent aristocrats, no big land-owners, no war lords and no capitalists with vast financial empires. He therefore thinks that socialism can be introduced by democratic processes in Africa. It should be noted that it need not be an essential part of socialist transformation that it must be violent. Awolowo is therefore right about this. However, given his own presentation of life in traditional Africa prior to contact with Europeans, and life in independent Africa with sit-tight rulers who, having tasted the forbidden fruit of corruption, refuse to give up power, it seems the basis for the position that Awolowo now takes is already removed. In other words, were reality different from how he presents it, his argument would be sound.

Awolowo's final summation of the problem of underdevelopment is that it is multi-faceted, comprising of

1) underdevelopment of the subjective mind, typified by ignorance, illiteracy and deficiency in techniques and organization;

2) underdevelopment of the body, typified by disease, calorie deficiency, bad water, bad housing, and filthy environment;
3) underdevelopment of agriculture and excessive under-employment of the rural population, typified by lack of savings and of capital formation.[28]

His proffered solution consists in full development and full employment of every African - man or woman, child or adolescent. Full development means in concrete terms that the state must accept full responsibility for the provision of education at all levels and health facilities free of charge for all its citizens. Full employment means the provision of adequate jobs for every citizen without discrimination. These are well-thought out suggestions and certainly deserve the attention of African leaders. Awolowo himself was at the forefront of the crusade for free education at all levels in Nigeria. To his credit, he was the first to introduce Universal Free Primary Education Scheme in Nigeria while he was premier of the Western Region of Nigeria. His political party [Unity Party of Nigeria], during the Second Republic of Nigeria, 1979-83, also introduced free education in all institutions under their control in Ondo, Oyo, Ogun, Lagos and Bendel States.

There is no doubt that investment in education is a profitable one for the society. This is what many of the so-called African leaders do not realize when they consider the monetary implications. But as Awolowo rightly noted, we have examples of world powers like U.S.A., U.S.S.R and Japan to go by. Education has contributed to the phenomena growth of these countries in various ways. Of course, with education comes enlightenment and awareness of one's rights and responsibilities. The ruling class may be wary of such a development since it is a potential threat to their continued domination of the masses. But this is a fear derived from an unenlightened self-interest. For the phenomena that we have characterized as contemporary African realities do not just affect the masses. Leaders are sometimes subject to violent reactions from a hungry and therefore angry mass. The spates of violent demonstrations that have been the rule in many parts of Africa in recent times are not unconnected with the deplorable situation under which many human beings live. People who are not given opportunity to improve themselves through formal education are most likely to end up as burdens on society. At worst they are likely to become social deviants. With such a development, leaders are not safe too. The same goes for those who found means of sponsoring themselves to acquire education, but were later denied the means of employment. This is even more frustrating and therefore more dangerous. This is why efforts have to be made to provide employment for all. Of course, the goal of full employment is an ideal, but a situation in which firms and companies declare huge profits and still rejoice in laying off workers is simply one that should strike us as odd. This seems to me to be Awolowo's insight in these matters.

With regard to the problem of political instability, Awolowo appeals to states to look into their foundations and adopt appropriate principles for constitution-making. This again goes back to the historical account of the origin of the state which Awolowo has presented in *The People's Republic*. According to that account, the state derives its existence from the coming together of different families in search for peace. The family is the focus of individual loyalty and the *paterfamilias* or *materfamilias* remains its head even after several families have combined resources to form a state. The latter is therefore an instrument devised for the promotion and protection of the self-interest of its members - family units. And Awolowo thinks that linguistic or national groups come to live together in a multi-national state for the same reason as brings families together in a uni-national state.[29] When families come together in this way, either voluntarily or through the mediation of an external force, it must be assumed that there is an implied social contract to the effect that each of the groups will enjoy equal treatment, and that their interests and rights will be protected on equal basis. Failure to abide by this principle is bound to be disastrous for the existence of a multi-national entity.[30]

Following these beliefs, Awolowo formulates his basic principles of statehood as follows:

(a) There can be no state without some distinctive objectives or political ends. This is what distinguishes a state from a nation.

The latter is a natural community based on blood relationship, and does not therefore have to espouse any formal objectives.
(b) The objectives of a state must include the provision of a full and happy life for all its members. This must be their motivating force in belonging to the state.
(c) To attain these objectives, the state must have a suitable constitution and an adequate economic arrangement.
(d) The suitable constitution for a state depends on its nature and composition. It must conform to certain universally valid principles. But whatever its form the best form of government is democracy.[31]

The universally valid principles to which a constitution must conform depend on its composition, and are as follows:

1. If a country is uni-lingual and uni-national, the constitution must be Unitary. Examples: France, Italy, Portugal, Poland and Greece.
2. If a country is uni-lingual or bi-lingual or multi-lingual, and also consists of communities which, though belonging to the same nation or linguistic group, have, over a period of years, developed some important cultural divergences as well as autonomous geographical separateness, the constitution must be federal, and the constituent states must be organized on the dual basis of language and geographical separateness. Examples: U.S.A., Argentina, Brazil, Australia, Austria.
3. If a country is bi-lingual or multi-lingual, the constitution must be federal, and the constituent states must be organized on a linguistic basis. Examples: Canada, Mexico, Burma, India, U.S.S.R.
4. An experiment with a Unitary constitution in a bi-lingual or multi-lingual country must fail, in the long run. Examples: United Kingdom of Great Britain and Ireland, Belgium, Spain, Sri Lanka.

These are expected to solve problems caused by mutual distrust in multi-ethnic states. It is interesting that Awolowo does not consider the desirability of a Confederal constitution for a multi-national state like Nigeria. He does not even mention it at all, in spite of the fact that such a proposal has been seriously considered by many observers in Nigeria. A confederal system suggests itself to citizens who are frustrated about the inability of the multinational state to deliver. It seems nowadays to be the last refuge of the patriot who does not want a complete dismemberment of the state. Yet it does not appear to be a desirable solution and I think that Awolowo is right in rejecting it along with other such arrangements that have been suggested for solving our political problems, for I think they all rest on an inadequate conception of the problem and therefore on an unviable political philosophy.

The search for a political philosophy must be tied up with our historical circumstances and our hopes and aspirations for the future. A political philosophy is not an abstract statement. It is a thought-out formula based on the objective realities of a peoples' existence. Though it is usually put in the language of a priori ideals, it is in fact derived from confrontation with experience. The conception of a *de jure* state takes its meaning in the light of the problematics of the *de facto* state. Since a philosophy of politics has to be grounded in the historical situations of a people, any suggestions of one must take into account the problems we have touched upon. It is in the light of this that some solutions propounded thus far should be examined. For many of them have not touched the foundations of our problems. For instance:

(i) Confederacy - This is appears to be based on the erroneous idea that our problem is basically the ethnic or cultural diversity which is a fact of our national life. It is claimed that we differ so much in everything that the prospect of our ever remaining together is an illusion. "Let each section (ethnic group, zone, etc.) go its way but come back to talk common security, currency and customs, and we will avoid the problem of instability and mutual suspicion." But this is quite misleading. The crux of our problem is not ethnic diversity. The majority of Nigerians do not mind mixing with peoples of other languages and cultures even outside our frontiers. Our problem is that ethnicity has been politicized by those same people who are fleecing us and now using the fact of ethnicity as a weapon to fight their own cause. Confederation will make it easier for the local bourgeoisie to build empires for themselves at the expense of the exploited masses. Political instability *may* be checked but social injustice and exploitative relations will hardly be reduced, just as the creation of more states has not stopped the continued poverty and exploitation of the masses.

(ii) Diarchy/Triarchy - This is based on the perception of an increasing influence and/or impatience of the military wing of the bourgeoisie and the frustration of traditional rulers. But rather than solve our problem, this suggestion will exacerbate it because both the military and traditional rulers belong to the class which have brought us to where we are now. Indeed, there is no reason to expect that even the problem of instability will be solved through this suggestion. What prevents the military from staging a coup even when they belong to the administration? It has happened in military administrations too. Counter-coups have been staged by one section of the military against an incumbent military administration. So why can it not happen when the military merely shares power with civilians in a diarchy or triarchy? But assume, for the purpose of argument, that by an unusual show of restraint, contentment and maximum cooperation among the various parties, the system succeeds in curbing instability, the question remains, will this do? What about the problem of social injustice?

(iii) One-Party System - This is a solution which has not taken into account the fundamental cause of the problem. The ruling class is responsible for the economic rip-off of the nation. This same class is inept and unable to cooperate even for the promotion of their own long-term interests. We have experienced constant rifts among political leaders within the same political party, leading to the break-up of such parties. There is no reason to expect that a one-party system will solve that problem. It will aggravate it and remove once and for all any hopes for democracy. What all these suggested solutions have in common is that they are aimed [either consciously or unconsciously] at the preservation and maintenance of the existing social order and the prevention of future disturbances. They assume the inviolability of the existing social structure and its essential nature. This has to be highlighted and any effort to perpetuate injustice should be frustrated. The problems with Nigerian politics are multifaceted; but they are all inseparably linked with the nature of the political class and the absence of genuine leaders committed to the true development of the nation and the real liberation of the people. There is a crying need to deal with the frustration people have with an economy which promises to be the most vibrant in the whole of Africa but whose potentials have not been fully exploited due to the lack of initiatives on the part of leaders and absence of motivation on the part of followers. It is only when this problem is addressed and we formulate an adequate philosophy for the emancipation of the downtrodden and the genuine independence of our nation that we can be said to have resolved the contradictions of our political life.

One major problem is that the Nigerian economy, as with other African economies, is a dependent one. Yet it is a fact of history that a country cannot be self-reliant as long as it is not in full control of its economy; and without a national self-reliant economy, we cannot have a stable political system. Finally, without a stable political economy, we cannot guarantee the welfare of the masses and social justice for all. We operate an unstable system, subject to the vicissitudes of the world economic system. Sometimes it experiences prosperity, at other times, there is recession. But the plight of the masses of the people, relative to a tiny minority, seems to be constant misery. When there is a drop in societal fortunes, the helpless and hopeless masses feel the pinch most. A relevant example is the effect of our government's austerity measures on the masses vis-a-vis the small number of fortunate members of the society many of whom had also contributed to the plight of the nation. The workers and the generality of the people either suffer from increased unemployment which leads ultimately to reduction of wages, or by a cut in benefits that normally apply to them, or yet by an increase in the rate of inflation which is not necessarily cured by their unemployment.

On the other hand, any increase in society's fortunes makes the political class better-off while the masses come out just with the crumbs. For even when wages are increased, there is guaranteed an increased surplus product in excess of their wages and this means more profit to the owners of capital who are generally not sensitive to the need to cater for the welfare of the masses if only to maintain them in existence. This is our predicament. We do not now seem to have a stable system which recognizes the problems of hunger and poverty as a serious one. Neither do we have a system which rewards genuine positive contributions to the development of the society. It appears that what the system favors is not excellence of ability or character, which were the sole basis for reward even in our traditional social systems, but rather cleverness in fraud and skillfulness in sycophancy.

The political class also seems to lack initiative and enterprise. Elsewhere, even in the industrial nations, the ruling class opens up new avenues for investment and initiate viable enterprises and welfare schemes for the working class. That is an illustration of the capacity of such bourgeoisie to pursue its enlightened self-interest with rigor and sense. The Nigerian capitalist prefers to rape the economy in public to feed the industrial growth of other nations. This compounds the problem of general poverty at home and makes it possible for the ruling class to continue to use the poor masses for their individualistic interests by all sorts of patronage. These days, both individuals and governments are the culprits. Because the Nigerian political ruling class has little or no interests in the development of education, mass illiteracy and ignorance is the lot of majority of the people. This makes it possible for the ruling class to use them for the promotion of their interests. Recall here the use of ignorant people to carry ballot boxes during elections and help politicians to rig elections.

The point worth stressing, then, is that the collective humanity of our people have been brutalized continuously by the manipulation of state power for the promotion of the class interest of the politicians and their sponsors. The problem of instability, arising from frequent changes of governments, is not the main issue. For there has been no change of government- civil or military - which has favored the common people since independence. What this means is that instability has been a problem for the ruling class and not a real problem for the masses. We must therefore shift the discussion from that of finding solution to the problem of political instability to that of solving the problems of emancipation and total liberation of the masses. That is the political problem. As we have seen it is also an economic problem.

Towards a Solution

What, then, should be our philosophy in the light of the above considerations? It is clear to me that we need to emphasize two objectives for any future political order in Nigeria namely:

(a) Self-reliance - i.e. a genuine political and economic independence of our nation from all external controls and influences.

(b) Self- actualization - i.e. a true political and economic freedom for all citizens and absence of exploitation of any kind. This freedom requires/entails full active participation of all the productive sectors of the economy in the governance of the nation.

Hitherto our electoral laws have not given us the best in terms of the quality of those who have access to the means of power. We have edged out of consideration, perhaps unwittingly, those who are genuinely committed to the upliftment of the nation. Thus the majority of public servants do not have the motivation to give their service in the political realm for several reasons. First, in order to contest elections, they have to resign their appointments. This is not an attractive option since they cannot be sure that, even when they are acknowledged to be good and acceptable to their people, other factors will not prevent them from being elected. In the context of our political history, such factors usually turn out to be crucial. One of them is the financial strength of a candidate. Another is the rigging ability of the opponents. Second, there is the factor of ethnicity which prevents many public servants from contesting for elections in their places of residence. Thus a public servant may have lived all his/her working life totalling thirty years in a community, yet s/he may not expect to be able to contest an election in that community simply because s/he is not born there. This makes it possible for irresponsible people to get into public positions because all it requires is for them to go back to their villages where they can hope to capitalise on ethnic or sub-ethnic sentiments. This has been partly responsible for the phenomena of corruption because those who have good knowledge of a candidate's ability and character [by being his/her neighbors for a long time], are not in a position to have much contribution to determining his/her suitability or otherwise; while those who get to contribute to his/her election usually do so on ground of sentiment and, of course, also expect to be rewarded with patronage. This is also an important motivation for corruption.

In the political system of the future, therefore, to guarantee the full democratic participation of everyone and avoid the danger that lies in the politicization of ethnicity which has been the bane of our politics since independence, and to eradicate the impression of quick wealth associated with politics, the political representation and participation should not be based on ethnic affiliation. It is time we down-played the significance of ethnicity in our national life. It appears we have been blindfolded for a long time, dancing to the tune dictated by the apostles of parochialism. The criterion for participation and representation should be active participation in the productive sectors. Every one should be involved actively. This is how it was in pre-colonial times. Those who contributed their efforts to the economy were not left out of participation in governance. In some cases, the system of age-grade was adopted such that every age-group made their contributions. We have a democratic tradition which we ought to have explored for the benefit of us all. While we cannot go back to excavate the past traditional structures, we should at least be guided by the spirit behind them. In our present circumstance, age-grades seem to have given way to laboring groups. This is why they should not be left out. Democratic citizenship requires that everyone be given the opportunity to make their contributions to the development of the nation, both economically and politically.

9

THE ETHICS AND POLITICS OF WORK

Contemporary African societies are facing a social problem which, in my view, needs to be understood and resolved. I do not claim that I can resolve it; that is a social task. A social problem, by nature, demands a common effort of all for its solution. My task here is to open up a promising path- by exposing the foundations of the problem- towards its ultimate resolution. I want to formulate the question of what work is and what it is conceived to be, and how our conception of it is influenced by, and in turn affects, the socio-economic structure in which we find ourselves. My thesis is simple: Work- productive activity- is one of the essential aspects of the human condition. However, it is now, in our societies, conceived as a curse- a terrible thing to be avoided. This conception of work, which is manifested in our attitude to work, is inimical to our socio-economic growth, individual well-being and the furtherance of our personal and national self-reliance. For one thing, it is an ideological associate of low productivity. The sad thing, however, is that our socio-economic structures have also contributed in no small way to the development of this conception of work and the attitude it engenders. It would seem then that our socio-economic structures are inadvertently creating the means of their own self- mortification. For, when the majority of workers come to associate any call for increased productivity from them with a call for their increased dehumanization, it does not augur well for the future of our nations; and that seems the point we are in now.

Our economies suffer from low productivity and this is a serious problem in view of its consequences for us all. Without high productivity, we all suffer need frustration, perhaps in different degrees, as the supply of commodities and services fall far short of demand. High productivity is an essential foundation for development, and an unproductive society cannot launch itself on the path of progress. Yet the stark reality is that, as far as this aspect of our national life is concerned, our record is unenviable. In the specific case of Nigeria, a nation with an estimated population of more than 100 million, our per capital gross national product is still under $800, and this itself we owe to the unpredictable oil fortune which has so far been our savior.

Several factors are, no doubt, responsible for this unsatisfactory situation we are in, and these include purely economic and technical ones. With regard to those, experts in the areas know better. However there is also what I consider as the social and human factor too, and this, I am sure, economists would also agree, is a crucial one. Included here is people's conceptions of work and the social relations that influence those conceptions. My interest here is primarily in understanding this factor, what gives rise to it, its influence on productivity and the social transformations required for its supersession.

Work, in general, is human activity. But since there are other types of human activities beside work, there is need for further distinction. Human activity involves the exertion of body and/or mind. It is the interaction between human beings and their environment, whether physical, social or spiritual. Meditation is a form of human activity; so is jogging. Some activities may aim at bringing about an end-product beyond themselves; others may be done for their own sake. There is a sense in which being active-doing things- is of the essence of humans. Living is being active. But while all work is activity, not all activity is work. Indeed, some activities may aim at bringing an end distinguishable from themselves, yet they cannot be characterized as work. There is, for instance, sexual activity, which aims at procreation. But to refer to this as work would be to overstretch the term. One cannot, for instance, compare this with the activity of hewing rock or building bridges. What, then, is the difference between work and other forms of human activities?

Conceptions of Work

Work, as I understand it, is that productive activity, the primary aim of which is the production of the material means of sustaining and reproducing human existence. Through work, nature is transformed in various ways, directly or indirectly, to produce the material conditions of life. All activities that have this as their ultimate aim, whether they deal with nature directly or not, are properly characterized as work. On the other hand, all activities which may indirectly lead to the production of such material conditions of life, but which do not have this as their primary purpose cannot be characterized as work. For instance, a boy plays the farmer, clearing a small circle at the backyard and planting a few seeds of corn. He has thereby transformed nature to a certain extent, and the seed may germinate and produce some corn. But if the production of corn was not his primary aim, if he did what he did for no purpose, if he enjoyed doing it for its sake-for the fun of it- then, his activity is productive only accidentally. His activity is play, not work. His aim is enjoyment and fun, which he derives from the activity itself. His situation is different from that of the farmer whose aim, in tilling the soil, is to transform nature primarily for the purpose of procuring the means of existence. The difference between work and play, then, lies in the primary purpose of the activity. It cannot wholly be, as is sometimes suggested, in the freedom of choice, which is claimed to characterize play but not work. For some works are as freely chosen as play. Nor can it be in the intrinsic satisfaction which is claimed to characterize play but not work. For some works are as intrinsically satisfying as play. Of course, this is not to deny that, in general, work tends to be less free and less satisfying than play. But this is not always or necessarily so; and a lot depends on the institutional structure under which work is done. Here, Dewey's observation is, in general, instructive:

> Both [play and work] are equally free and intrinsically motivated apart from false economic conditions which tend to make play into idle

excitement for the well to do, and work into uncongenial labor for the poor.[1]

What is needed, then, is to put in place those true economic conditions which will make work more play-like than it is now.

Traditionally, work is taken to fall into two categories: manual and non-manual. The former is, generally, more arduous, involves the use of muscles to a greater degree, less satisfying and with lower remuneration than non-manual work. On the other hand, non-manual work generally involves the use of muscles to a less degree, and, some would say, perhaps in justification of wage differentials, that it requires longer period of training, and involves greater responsibility and maximum dedication than manual work. I leave this open since it does not affect my argument here.

Now, each of these categories- manual and non-manual- may be further divided into two according to the degree of freedom of choice and operation which the worker enjoys, as well as the amount of satisfaction s/he derives from work. Thus manual workers fall into two categories of: [a] wage laborers who are the least satisfied and least free. Their work is usually the most arduous and least remunerated; and they have no choice because that is the only means they have for procuring the means of existence. [b] crafts-people, including self-employed artisans, blacksmiths, and subsistence farmers. Members of this set do not sell their labor power for wages, but rather use it to create use-values for themselves or for exchange. For this reason, they have some freedom to organize their work as they wish. Such freedom is, of course, limited by the institutional impediments created by the nature of the political economy.

Non-manual [otherwise referred to as mental] workers also fall into two categories: [a] white-collar labor comprising teachers, clerks, civil servants and managers who also depend on wages- though with a little more freedom of choice and operation than manual laborers, and [b] talents- comprising artists, musicians, inventors and traditional healers whose work consists of the development of unique talents at a pace determined mostly by themselves, and who do not have to sell their labor power to others to procure the means of their existence. This set of workers tend to find more intrinsic satisfaction in their creative work, and, with greater freedom to develop and realize their own potentialities, there is a tendency for them to identify themselves with their work and take joy in it.

The distinctions just drawn- between work and play, and between categories of work- are useful, but it should be pointed out that they do not help us to identify what work means to people and the place it occupies in their lives; yet this is crucial. Indeed, the suggestion that we should struggle for conditions which will make work more play-like may be objected to on the ground that it begs the question whether, by nature, work can become play-like. To decide this one way or the other presupposes a commitment to a particular view of work. If, for instance, we should start from the premise that work is essentially a drudgery then we are not likely to expect it to become play-like. And as I have claimed, the conception of work which we share will, to a great extent, influence our attitude to work.

The truth, of course, is that work has meant various things to various peoples through the ages, and it may well be that our own conception with all its inadequacies, is shared with different historical epochs in different societies. The ancient Greeks, for instance, identified productive activity with manual work and opposed it to contemplative activity, which according to them, is proper to human beings, while the former was regarded as a necessary evil and reserved for slaves. Manual work, on this view, does no good to the mind and was considered a constraint on the practice of virtue. Though Aristotle thought that a virtuous life- which he identified with the happy life- requires exertion and does not consist in amusement, he went on to identify perfect happiness as contemplative activity. For this is what is most proper to man, making him more Godlike: "If you take away from a living being action, and still more production, what is left but contemplation? Therefore the activity of God, which surpasses all others in blessedness, must be contemplative, and of human activities, therefore, that which is most akin to this must be most of the nature of happiness."[2] He even imagined a situation in which labor could be eliminated from the lives of human beings: "if every instrument could accomplish its own work obeying or anticipating the will of others...if, in like manner, the shuttle would weave and the plectrum touch the lyre without a hand to guide them, chief workmen would not want servants nor masters slaves."[3] But as it should be obvious, even if this wish were to become a reality, it would still not eliminate productive activities. For even if instruments were to accomplish their work, these instruments still have to be made; and it would be the task of human beings to produce them. Production of labor saving machines will still be productive activity, though Aristotle may still consider it an evil or [at least] a second-rate activity.

Contrary to the Aristotelian conception, Marx views work as the essence of the human being. Productive activity, for him, is species-activity and productive life is the life of the species. Work is the only activity that expresses and affirms people's essential humanity. For one thing, human need procurement is possible only through work. Even those who enjoy idle excitement must depend on the productive activities of others. In work, use-values are created which serve humanity by making its future existence possible. The potentiality for the continued existence of humanity which is in-built in every human being is actualized in work. Nature has to be transformed, through work, to provide the means of furthering human existence. Whatever differentiates humans from animals and other living beings is clearly manifested in the amazing extent to which human beings have been successful in transforming nature, not only for their continued existence, but also for their improvement. The world has been humanized through work, and it is human productive activities that are also responsible for the subjection of what would have been a hostile universe. Indeed, to think that we are cursed to work is to think that we are cursed to exist, and this seems to show the absurdity of such a conception. Even if it is conceivable that our needs could be procured without much effort, if the fields could provide the crops we need without being tilled, we would at least need to reach for them, to transform them according to our needs.

Besides, as humanity is reproduced through work, so is our human personality expressed. We engage a significant proportion of our human powers in work and since these powers make up our individual personality, it would follow that we express our personality in work. What we do, and how we do it, is normally a reflection of what we are. Not only this, it is only through work that we can realize our human potentialities to the fullest. The world created by human productive activities is the real human world in which human potentialities are actualized. As each of us realizes his or her individual potentialities, the world we thus create is a product of our collective humanity, and it is what makes possible the furtherance of our human existence. To say that productive activity is species activity is to say that it is the essential activity of humans. To do without it is to cease living in a human world, and to cease being human. This is the lesson from the Marxian conception of work, and it is one which we are yet to take seriously in our society.[4]

The main difference between Aristotle and Marx with respect to the concept of work is that while Aristotle draws a distinction between manual and contemplative activity and regards the former as curse and the latter as self-realization, Marx collapses both into the single category of human productive activity and regards such activity as human essence. It seems to me that we may locate the source of this difference in the fact that while Aristotle based his judgment on his observation of his immediate environment with all its deprivations for manual workers, Marx based his account on his assessment of what ought to be the case in a world without deprivations and without class distinctions. Furthermore, for Aristotle, God is the most perfect being and humans have to endeavor to be God-like. Looking at the perfect nature of God from the perspective of a 'damned human being', Aristotle is convinced that the activity of God cannot be as onerous as human activity. His must be blessed and therefore contemplative- as opposed to the manual productive activities of humans.

I would like to suggest that academic work is the closest to Aristotle's concept of contemplative activity in the contemporary classification of work. Notice, of course, that for Aristotle as well as for other Greek philosophers of his time, all learning come under the umbrella of Philosophy which was divided into Moral [including Politics, Economics and Law etc.] and Natural [including Physics, Astrology, Mathematics, Biology etc.] The person engaged in the activity of contemplation in these areas of human learning is, for Aristotle, engaged in a process of realizing his or her true self since he/she is doing what is closest to his/her nature.

Now the goal of contemplation- indeed its *raison d'etre*- is to know. We do not contemplate just for the sake of it. It is the urge to know, to discover the truth that is at the root of the contemplative activity. Socrates' obsessive quest for knowledge of himself and his species led him to the contemplation of nature and human society, in obedience to the commands of the Delphic oracle. In the same manner, the primary goal of the academic profession is the advancement of knowledge. Following from this, an academic staff has the duty to realize this goal through teaching and research. Many academics made a voluntary choice of the profession on the basis of their commitment to the realization of these ends, strong dedication to the cause of true scholarship and their sound judgment of academic work as a calling and a veritable means to self-realization. While, for instance, few other workers in other professions may regard work as a means of amassing wealth and relieving poverty, genuine scholars focus on the most laudable objective of advancing the frontiers of knowledge. It is not uncommon that the results of their inquiries provide the means of wealth for people in other professions; but as academics, they are judged by how well or otherwise they carry out the task of advancing the frontiers of knowledge and not by how much wealth they can accumulate.

This is the way it should be under normal circumstance. However, we do not now have a normal situation in the Nigerian society. For Nigerian academics especially are also subjected to evaluations by appeal to factors alien to their profession. The average person does not appear to understand why academic work should not produce wealth when, in fact, varieties of parasitism in other professions do. The Nigerian academic conception of their work as self-realization is being called into question, and in its place, the idea of academic work as a curse, like others, seems to be taking shape. The system has also, to a great extent, succeeded in demoralizing many members of the academic profession and, being the major group succumbing to the idea of work as self-realization, their gradual abandonment of that conception, and of the conception of work as cure for poverty, seems to complete the process of a general affirmation of the idea of work as curse by Nigerian workers.

It is very easy to discover the conception of work which dominates our political economy today. The facts are conspicuously written all over the face of those who regard themselves as workers. It shows in our attitude to work that most of us conceive our work as a curse, a plague to be avoided as much as possible. There are now virtually no exceptions: blue-collar, white-collar, including even the self-employed artisans and craftsmen, all act as if they regard work as a curse. Freud's observation seems surprisingly to be applicable to our own society here and now, perhaps with more force than to his own:

> as a path to happiness, work is not highly prized by men. They do not strive after it as they do after other possibilities of satisfaction. The great majority of people only work under the stress of necessity, and this natural human aversion to work raises most difficult social problems.[5]

A visit to any work-place will more than confirm this assertion. When some workers are not hissing openly or cursing anyone who disturbs their "peace", they are busy doing nothing, "innocently" waiting and watching the clock to release them form bondage. Supervisors are not different. They resent interference. The same is true of manual workers and tillers of the soil, perhaps with some amount of self-justification. After all, how can one explain to them and justify their having to work with their own hands or eat from the sweat of their brows while others 'toil' in air-conditioned offices? I once visited a village and met some laborers working on the farm. By coincidence, a news item was being relayed on their employer's radio. A state commissioner was quoted as advising young people to stay on the farm on the ground that it is profitable to be a farmer. The news was received with resentment by these workers. "It is not his fault" ran a comment, "if it was so profitable, why does he not stay on the farm himself?" I got the message.

To have to work with one's hands under such miserable conditions and low returns as the farm laborer's is, as far as these men are concerned, not the best deal one should bargain for. It is, as it were, a curse. The so-called self-employed craftsmen are not left out. After all, it is conceivable to them that a person may acquire wealth without work. They even see around them evidence that this is not only conceivable, its probability is extremely high. The economy itself seems to encourage and sanction it. If people around them- perhaps of similar background and age-could amass wealth with no visible work-effort, then it must be a curse for them to exert effort at work. Their attitudes to their work betray their conception of work.

This phenomenon calls for understanding and explanation. We should examine the facts and expose the real source of the problem. This is necessary, especially if one does not share the belief that by nature, work is really a curse. I do not, and it is my view that this inadequate conception can be superseded. But first, we need to account for it.

It is possible and helpful to categorize workers according to the factor[s] responsible for and /or contributing to the persistence of their conception of work as a curse together with the attitude which betrays this conception. I think there are, at least, three such categories. First there are those persons who, most probably, exposed to the Hebrew conception via the Old Testament story of disobedience and the Fall, have come to regard work as an evil, and humanity as cursed to toil. To some Nigerians, perhaps the story, in itself does not justify an indolent approach to work, but the fact remains that a substantial number may find it as a basis for detesting work and regarding it as, at best, a necessary evil. Second, there are those who are frustrated by their persistent poverty in spite of the fact that they work hard, and contrary to the traditional conception of work as cure for poverty. This group find, to their dismay, that work has virtually lost its traditional curative power and that the culture of poverty seems to remain in their domain even when they conscientiously dedicate themselves to its eradication through individual work-effort. Finally, there are those workers who see the socio-economic structure of our nation as an unjust system. They see our system as one which lays emphasis on worker productivity but with no corresponding consideration for workers' well-being. Work is probably conceived as a curse by this set because they feel they are not regarded as persons to be respected, but as things or another factor for increased profit. This seems a hang-over from our colonial experience.

The position of the first group above is, to my mind, indefensible. It seems absurd to suggest that conceiving work as a curse has its origin in the creator. After all, as *Babaláwo* Ifatoogun with whom I had a rewarding discussion on the traditional Yoruba conception of work argued, God's creation of "heaven and earth and all therein" is a kind of work. But does it make sense to say that God cursed Himself to work? Perhaps, the idea is that, on creation there was plenty of food and drinks for the first man and woman. But then, they would at least, have to reach out for the food, and this would be a kind of work. Neither does it make sense to suggest that because work is a thing we must do, therefore it is a curse. After all, we must eat in order to survive. Do we then regard eating as a curse? Marcus Aurelius' injunction, I think, is an adequate reflection on the nature of work:

> In the morning when thou risest unwilling, let this thought be present-I am rising to the work of a human being. Why then am I dissatisfied if I am going to do the things for which I exist and for which I was brought into the world? Or have I been made for this, to lie in bed-clothes and keep myself warm? But this is more pleasant. Do thou exist, then, to take thy pleasure, and not at all for action and exertion?[6]

The other two categories have better cases, and their reasons more relevant in any search for a solution to the problem of work-discontent. Take for instance, the case of those who are frustrated by their continued poverty in spite of their hard work. There was a time when work was conceived as a cure- a panacea for poverty. This conception is summed up in that beautiful Yoruba rhyme which many of us learnt from the cradle:

Isé loògùn isé
Múra sísé òréè mi

Isé la a fi d' eni gíga
Bi a kò ba r'éni fèhìn tì
Bi òle laa ri
Bi a kò ba r'éni gbókànlé
A a te'ra mósé eni.

Work is cure for poverty
Be hard-working my friend
For one can become great
Only through hard work.
When we have no supporter
We may appear lazy
But in such a situation
It only pays to
Keep on working hard.

Many writers have emphasized the role of work in traditional African society, where it is regarded as an indispensable nerve of social life. Thus according to Julius Nyerere, in "traditional African society, everybody was a worker. there was no other way of earning a living for the community."[7] There was no room for loiterers in the political economy of traditional Africa. The saying, " whoever does not work, shall not eat" had a strong foundation in the structure of the society. The communalistic nature of traditional society promoted and sustained the conception of work as a cure. It was clear to everybody that loitering or idleness does not cure poverty, and that one had to engage in useful productive activities. The relative absence of a social division into economic classes also contributed to the growth of this idea. For where there is relative equality in terms of ownership of means of production, and where the existing social relation is not essentially exploitative, then every worker may be encouraged to put in their best for the benefit of themselves and others. One of the reasons many people will not now conceive work as a cure for poverty is that the conditions which seemed to justify such a conception in the traditional society have been superseded. For in the place of communal mode of production in which virtually everyone engaged in useful work, we now have a system which appears to favor parasitism over useful work. Where a person can be seen to be amassing wealth without any visible work-effort, then the conception of work as a cure for poverty has become anachronistic.

This seems to be our situation today. Many have come to the conclusion that productive work no longer cures poverty. They resort to all sorts of tricks and anti-social activities, and those workers who approach work as if it were a plague on their lives seem to be reacting to this reality of our social existence. It should be noticed that the conception of work as a curse is not a prior factor in this episode; rather, it is the structural realities which seem to determine the attitudes. People do not speculate about how they should conceive work. But whether they do or not, the reality they face and to which they are just responding is such that they feel unable to conceive of work as a cure any more. For their work, instead of aiding in the elimination of their poverty, seems to confront them as another constraint on the path of freedom and comfort. How is this so?

Understanding the conception of work as a curse

For the beginning of an answer to this last question, we need to look at the position of the third category identified above: those whose conception of work as curse originates from their understanding of the social structure; and examine their analysis of our economic system and work-structure, first with respect to manual workers and then non-manual workers and self-employed persons. We operate a system in which the reward for most work is wages. But many workers have come to believe that these wages are determined, not by considerations of their needs as persons, but only by reference to their needs as workers. This is how they understand the idea of minimum wage; that it is based on an idea of the minimum subsistence level for workers at work, and beyond that, that which is needed to maintain their families. If we recall that in our system, even this minimum is grudgingly approved by the ruling class, then we can appreciate the position of this category of workers.

Second, as we observed in Chapter 8, the dependent nature of our economy is also cited as part of the problem. Subject to the vicissitudes of world economic system, sometimes it experiences prosperity; at other times, recession sets in. Manual workers, however, seem not to have any better days. Always below the general poverty level, they have a case against a system which has apparently been responsible for their plight.

But if this is true of manual workers, what is the case of white- collar and blue-collar workers who still behave as if they were cursed to work? They also have their own reasons which, again, turn on their understanding of the workings of our society. First, our economic system is not isolated from the rest of our socio-political system; both are interdependent, and mutually supporting. Thus just as the factory worker feels cheated by the system, so does the public servant, university worker and other white-collar workers. They also see around them evidences of exploitation, fraud and open corruption in high places which go unchallenged. It is difficult, if not irrational, to be moral in an immoral society, and while a perfectionist ethics may be practiced in an imperfect society, some moments of frustration will definitely arise when decency will be thrown to the dog. And when those who are otherwise virtually useless to society can grease their pockets with millions of Naira from the public treasury which is being maintained by the sweat of these miserable workers; when loitering and parasitism and cheating seem to pay more than honest hard work, when smart "pen-robbers" display their loots openly and get public praise for it; then it should be clear that those who behave as if they regard work as a curse have their own reasons. Such is the situation of non-manual workers and self-employed persons.

No doubt, a change is required; but we have to be clear as to the kind of change. To my mind, we should be deceiving ourselves if we just call for a change in the attitude to work. I do not think that that is the root of the problem, and I think it is not quite correct to say that all human beings are naturally aversed to work. I am more inclined to believe that we are what society makes us to be. Rousseau once claimed that man in the state of nature may be stupid, but that he is not wicked. I say that he is not lazy either. But society picks him up and intensifies his desires only to have them frustrated; it makes him labor only to exploit him, and the more effort he makes at self-development, the less returns he gets.

Certainly the attitude or conception is not the prior thing then, and should not be the target for reform. The attitude is predicated on the realities of social existence. A call for change of attitude must therefore be predicated on a change of the social realities which led to the conception. After all, as we have seen, there was a time when people had a different attitude to work. What is needed is a total operation on our social and economic institutions. To call for worker productivity under present conditions is not likely to meet the desired response.

Two options are open to us. We may work for either the resuscitation of the idea of work as a cure for poverty, or towards the promotion of the conception of work as self-realization. Both ideas, of course, presuppose a determination to change the social structure which influences and justifies the inadequate conception of work as a curse, and both are superior to that conception. To conceive work as cure presupposes a readiness to exert the requisite effort to free oneself from the shackles of poverty. This would be sound provided that there is a guarantee that the system will not stand in the way of those who make such efforts. The sort of change required in our attitude to work is, in principle, not impossible to effect as long as the guarantee is there and the efficacy of work as cure is not in doubt.

The more serious problem, however, relates to the concept of poverty itself and the efficacy of individual work-effort as its cure. Poverty is a social concept. It is a dynamic one too. A person is judged poor against a standard which is largely determined by society, whether consciously or unconsciously. Thus the poverty line of the United States differs from that of Nigeria because the standards used to determine them differ. In Nigeria, washing machines and even telephones are still luxury items; in the United States, they are not. Poverty is also a dynamic concept. What counts as being poor changes from time to time as the standard changes within the same society. So it is across societies. Poverty is a subjectively determined social relation. For these reasons, it is unrealistic to expect that poverty can be cured by individual work-effort since, in fact, the individuals do not determine the standards according to which they are judged poor. For they may conscientiously make the effort without meeting the standard. Indeed, what should be the target? Three square meals a day for self and family? But children have to go to school, and one needs shelter and clothing, etc. No matter how hard a worker tries, it should be a real task to meet all of the shifting standards society sets to cross the threshold of poverty; and the reason the standard cannot be met need not be the worker's fault. This is why it seems to me inadequate to resuscitate the old conception of work as a cure for poverty. Poverty as a social problem can only be cured by social effort, not by individual work-effort.

Indeed, this point seems to be realized in many societies, including ours, where perhaps as an attempt to dampen the effect of the social determination of poverty on individual workers, they are often urged to be patient, to be contented, to avoid inordinate ambitions to be rich and to be proud of their work and station in life irrespective of how they fare wealth-wise. All these are indications of the fact that, we are also aware of an alternative conception of work; one that does not see it so much as accumulation of wealth, but rather as a process of realizing our individual human potentialities, a process of developing our innate abilities and talents for the benefit of humanity. Self-realization is realizing one's potentialities and this is possible only when one exerts one's body and mind at essentially human productive activities. The more we succeed in changing nature through productive activities, the more we know ourselves. Provided the problem of poverty is taken care of by society through a sustained effort to meet the basic needs of everyone, then it should not be difficult to promote the idea of work as self-realization. For then, workers, not bothered by the problem of accumulating more wealth than they need [perhaps in anticipation of an upgrading of the poverty level] will see their work as a process of developing and coming to know themselves better, and thus contributing to the advancement of our common humanity and the solution of our common problems.

To realize this ideal, and thus effect a change from our conception of work as a curse, there is need for some changes in the structural conditions of work. First, there is need to assure all those who engage in useful and productive activities that they constitute an important link in the chain of our national economy. This should be done, not just by verbal exhortations, but by sustained actions. All levels of workers need to be given adequate representation and effective participation in the making of decisions that affect their work. Frustration arises for workers, not just from low monetary remunerations, but also, and perhaps mostly, from not being counted upon when vital decisions which affect them are being made. It is a surprise that this obvious fact is sometimes neglected even by employers of non-manual labor. A natural desire of human beings is to be taken seriously, to be respected as a person. This is frustrated when a senior officer in an establishment single-handedly takes decisions that affect colleagues without any consultation with them. Such an attitude contributes to worker dissatisfaction and thus to the development of the wrong attitude to work.

Second, efforts have to be made to eliminate all forms of corrupt practices which are a direct effect of the inordinate ambition to get rich quick. This is one of the root causes of the problem. Those who consider themselves smart enough to make money by whatever means display their wealth to the dismay of the confused masses who are thereby forced to question their own condition. The latter may then either find a way of joining in the race or they may resign themselves to their destiny. This is where the philosophy of destiny gets into play. Either way, the result is the development of the wrong attitude to work with its disastrous effect on social life.

This is why we need to make a more serious effort to get rid of corruption in high places from our society. The enormity of the task cannot be overemphasized. For there is a sense in which the foundation of corruption is in the society itself. What society wants from its public officials, it eventually gets. As I said earlier with respect to poverty, I think society also determines the degree of public immorality in general, and corruption in particular. Whether by showering praises on ostentatious display of wealth, the origin of which we do not know; or by ridiculing the honest but modest members of society, or indeed by expecting patronage from public officials, we directly contribute to the high level of public immorality in our society, and indirectly to the conception of work as a curse. This also shows how far away we have moved from the foundations of traditional social life.

Third, we need a radical social transformation which will effectively usher in an era of discipline in all aspects of our social life. Most of our problems, including our attitude to work, arise because ours is, by and large, an undisciplined society. Indeed, at the risk of being accused of over-exaggeration, it seems to me that indiscipline may be put forward as a viable candidate for the Nigerian national character. Senior officers can not effectively coordinate the activities of their establishment due to the lack of discipline of either those under them, or of those above them, or indeed of themselves. In any case, the cankerworm of indiscipline has eaten so deep into the structures of our national life that its effects could be felt in the highest places including the highest political institutions. To remove it, we need a radical operation which can only be successfully effected by the combined effort and commitment of all. To promote the idea of work as self-realization and self development and thereby launch our nation on the path of progress and development, then, we need to initiate policies that will place useful work in its proper place as a worthwhile human activity, by rendering loitering and parasitism unprofitable, by making corruption impossible, by making workers an integral part of the decision-making process and by ushering in an era of discipline and self-control across the board. In short, we need to struggle for the removal of all those structural constraints that seem now to justify the conception of work as a curse.

Unemployment and the Right to Work

Beside the problem associated with work-discontent, however, a more urgent problem for realizing an adequate ethic of work is the sky-rocketing rate of unemployment occasioned by the recent trend in our economy and the policies of government. Workers are being laid off at the prime of their productive life, and young people, just getting out of higher institutions and into the job market cannot find jobs. It seems that policy makers are unsettled about how to solve this problem, and in some cases, higher institutions are blamed for sending unemployable persons to the job market. The irony of this is that, on this kind of explanation, nobody is employable, since unemployment affects both science and humanities graduates alike. Indeed, there are first class students of Industrial Technology roaming the streets in search of job. The problem is this: workers struggle to send their children to school, depriving themselves of the good things of life because they consider it worthwhile to invest in the education of their children since they expect to depend on them in their old age. If in the end, those children graduate from college but cannot get job, there is an additional reason for such workers to be dissatisfied with their lot. To compound this, however, they are also being laid off from work. There are cases in which the husband is retrenched from work, the wife's trading booth is destroyed by sanitation agents because it is aesthetically indecent, and the son or daughter in whose education they invested their whole life savings cannot get a job. This is bound to be frustrating. But what can be done ? Does the society have a duty, and the citizens a right to be provided with the means of work ? This is another crucial question on the issue of the ethics and politics of work.

The constitution of the Federal Republic of Nigeria (1979), for instance, provides in Section 17 (3) that:

> The state shall direct its policy towards ensuring that - (a) all citizens without discrimination on any ground whatsoever have the opportunity for securing adequate means of livelihood as well as adequate opportunities to secure suitable employment.

It appears to me that this provision rests on the assumption that the state has an obligation to provide means of employment for citizens, and that the latter have a right to employment. Indeed this inference seems normal not only to many people, but also to many organizations including the United Nations Organization, which in its Universal Declaration of Human Rights (1948) states that:

Everyone has the right to work, to free choice of employment, to just and favorable conditions of work and to protection against unemployment.[8]

From this declaration, it appears we may identify four variants of the right in question as follows:
- (i) Right to work
- (ii) Right to choice of employment
- (iii) Right to just and favorable conditions of work
- (iv) Right to protection against unemployment.

If these four variants of the right are identifiable, the question then arises: What exactly is it that is claimed when a right to employment is asserted? Is this right identifiable with any of these four rights? Or is it the totality of all of them? The issue centers on the need to determine the real identity and scope of the right to employment and the justification, if any, for claiming it. Along with this is the issue of the practicability of the recognition of the right-claim in the actual circumstance of a poor economy like Nigeria. However, before we get on to the main business, there is a preliminary issue to settle: What, exactly, is involved in claiming any right at all, and a welfare right in particular?

The paradigm case of right is claim-right: To say that "A has a right to X" is to say that:
- (i) A is entitled to X
- (ii) X is due to A.

Thus if X is $10 owed A by B, A has a right to have his $10 back i.e., A has a right to have this amount from B. Claim-rights, in general, thus presuppose the existence of a second party who has the obligation to provide the entitlement. So we need to add a third condition:
- (iii) There is another person, B, who has an obligation to provide A with X.

The statement "A has a right to X" cannot be strictly interpreted in a utilitarian model to mean "If X were given A, it would be a good thing" nor "X is good for, or desired by A." This may be true of A's situation vis-a-vis the having of X; but it is not the meaning of "A has a right to X." A typical claim-right is justiciable. It may be backed by sanctions and B may be coerced to provide A's entitlement if the need arises. Furthermore, if A has a right to X, then the fact that denying A access to X will improve social utility is not a valid reason for that kind of denial.[9]

From the foregoing, it is obvious that I am using right in the stronger sense of Hohfeldian claim-right according to which such rights are logically correlated with duty; and not in the weaker sense of privilege according to which a right is correlated with a no-right state of affairs on the part of others. The ultimate question, then, will be if the right to employment of X is correlated with a duty, whose duty?

A claim-right is a right in the strong sense of the word. In this sense, if it is true that A has a right to (do, have) X, it means that (i) someone else has a duty to A with regard to X, and (ii) it is wrong for anyone to (a) interfere with A's performance of X, or (b) deny or prevent A from having X. Though claim rights in this sense are typically contractual or legal rights, other kinds of rights, (especially human or civic) may be explicated in the same manner. For instance, "A has a right to speak freely" means - in the strong sense - that

(i) There is a duty on the part of others (especially government officials) to refrain from infringing on A's right by interfering with or preventing him from speaking.
(ii) Any such interfering is wrong legally (if it is a constitutional right) or morally (if it is not).

This strong sense of right - which connotes justiciability - is preferable to the weak sense according to which "A has a right to X" simply means that "There is no duty for A to not-do X" or "A does no wrong in doing X."

Let us pursue the difference between the two further because of its implication for our subject. A typical example of a claim-right is the right of employees to have their wages from the employer. This is a contractual right. As long as the terms of the agreement are kept by the employees, the employer has an obligation to pay their salary. This is what is really meant by saying that the employees have a right to their pay. Though it is true that the employees *do no wrong* in getting [or asking for] their pay, and they have no duty to not-have their pay; these are just additional to the real meaning of "the employees have a right to have their pay." In this context where a claim - or contractual right is involved, the primary meaning is that which identifies the obligation correlative to the right as well as the party having this obligation. The other meaning [weak sense] is not a substitute in this regard.

But there are other types of rights in which the weak meaning seems to be primary. Consider, for instance, the right of a person to be recognized by the chairperson at a departmental meeting. This is not a contractual right. It is a liberty-right which carries no strong correlative obligation on the part of the chairperson. For in a situation where there are ten members of staff, each claiming this right, were the chairperson to have a correlative duty, it would be impossible for him/her to discharge it to all.[10] Thus the right to be recognized would seem to mean only that the chairperson does no wrong in recognizing the claimant. It is the sort of claim that may be made in defense of the chairperson's discretion to recognize one out of many intending speakers. So while it is not wrong not to recognize an intending speaker, the chairperson does no wrong in extending such recognition to the speaker.

From what has been said, it would seem that we could have a dichotomy of rights such that all contractual/legal claim-rights carry the strong meaning while others (?) carry the weak meaning. We may wish to fill the gap introduced by the question mark with economic or welfare rights.[11] But the temptation to do this, though very real, should be avoided. The strong-weak dichotomy cannot fit into such a neat categorization. For the main criterion thus far utilized is that rights have correlative duties with identifiable persons. But some of the well-known human or welfare rights would meet this criterion. For instance, the right to freedom of movement is normally conceived as held against other individuals and government as long as the claimant is within the bounds of the law. So the strong meaning would appear to fit in here.[12] Also, the right to work may fit in here with the society, through its government, having the correlative duty.

Right-claims, whether weak or strong, have to be justified because they put the claimant in a relative position of advantage to others. The basis of such a claim must therefore be very strong to justify the preferential treatment or action which the right-claim entails. A worker who claims a right to his pay can justify this on the basis of the existing legal relation between him and the employers. On the other hand, the individual person who claims a right to freedom of conscience may justify this on the basis of his personality as a rational being with fundamental interests and needs which granting this right would promote.

We can now go back to the main question: what is the right to employment, its justification and practicability in a developing country like Nigeria? Having identified four components of the right to employment above, the approach I want to adopt in addressing these questions is to look at one of them, namely the right to work, determine what it means, its addressees, basis and relationship to other components. In the light of this approach, I discuss the meaning of and right to work in the next section. Thereafter, I offer a justification for the right to work and attempt to meet some objections. Finally I evaluate the various ways of providing the means of work, and deal with the question of who has the duty to provide them.

The Meaning of the Right to Work

Work, as an activity one engages in with a prospect of material reward, is not restricted in its coverage. It may be one which persons undertake on their own without doing it for somebody else. But it may also be one which they do for others who are expected to give the reward. For this reason, the question of the right to work is ambiguous. On the one hand, it could mean the right to freely engage in such a remunerative activity without disturbance or intervention. The correlative duty here is for other persons to refrain from disturbing an individual at work. On the other hand, it could mean the right to be provided with such activity [or the means of it] together with the accompanying rewards. The correlative duty here is to provide work for the claimants. The position I would like to maintain is that both meanings are in order. On the first meaning, the individual holds the right against any prospective intruder to prevent unjustifiable disturbance, subject to the observations made in the next paragraph. On the second meaning, the right is held against the society in its corporate existence as represented by the government. It is therefore more of a civic right held by a *bona fide* member of the society who, due to no fault of his, lacks the means of work and cannot function properly as a member, without it.[13] As I would argue below, even if it cannot be shown logically that the right to work entails the provision of means of work by government, it can be argued that the right supports the claim of the right-holder for the means of work to be provided by the government. However, let us attempt some further analysis of the two meanings of the right.

First, let us look at the right to freely engage in a remunerative activity without disturbance or intervention. It should be clear that this has some difficulties. For instance, the scope of such activities has to be defined. Today, armed robbery is a remunerative activity. But do persons have a right to freely engage in it? Should they have such a right? Not many people would defend such a "liberal" interpretation of the right to work! This is one arm of the problem. The other relates to the scope of the correlative duty which is, to refrain from disturbing the right-holder from freely engaging in his remunerative activity. The problem here is to determine what would constitute an infringement of the right or a discharge of the obligation. Suppose I am a wood carver. This is the activity I freely choose to engage in. I need wood to carry out this activity. But there is wood only on your own plot of farm land. Do you infringe my right if you prevent me from cutting the wood? It would seem that for the obligation [to refrain from preventing me from cutting wood] to make sense, the world would have to be different from what it is. It would not be one built on the idea of property. In a sense, then, this meaning of the right to work [and its correlative obligation] would, if pressed fully, conflict with the right to property wherever the latter is acknowledged.[14] This is not all. If the right to work means the right to freely engage in a remunerative activity without hindrance [and no more], the correlative obligation is to refrain from interfering with the claimants. But in case there is no means for them to engage in such activity, there is, on this meaning, no obligation on the part of anyone to provide them with such means. The assertion of the right in such a situation is meaningless.

This seems to be taken care of by the second meaning of the right to work: the right to be provided with [means of] remunerative activity. The correlative duty here is to provide [means of or access to] remunerative activity for those individuals claiming this right. But of course the question must be raised here: why should there be such an obligation on the part of anyone? Granted that a person has a right to freely engage in a remunerative activity, why must s/he also have a right to be provided with [means of or access to] such activity? Notice that these are distinct claims. The right to freely engage in a remunerative activity carries no implication for any one besides the right-holder except of course the negative obligation not to interfere. But if I have a right to be provided with the activity, this carries my freedom further to demand for someone to make something available to me. [Is it the same as the right to be employed?]. What, then, is involved in providing [the means of] remunerative activity to a person and thus discharging the duty correlative to [this interpretation of] the right to work? Second, what could be the justification for this further demand on the addressees of the right-claim? [Who are they?].

To address the former question, first, a remunerative activity may be provided for a person in a number of ways such as:

(i) making land and capital available to them to engage in farming,
(ii) making capital and other factors of production available to them for self-employment in other productive sectors [manufacturing, distributive etc.,]
(iii) giving them job in paid employment requiring no formal education and training,
(iv) giving them formal education and training [with appropriate vocational guidance] to prepare them for, and absorb them into, paid employment in skill-requiring jobs.

While the first two are directed towards providing (the means of) self-employment, the last two are geared towards paid employment by others. So, as it turns out, the right to work could actually entail the right to [the provision of paid] employment. The former is the basic right in this group, while the latter is one of its derivatives. The next question is "What is the justification for the demand for this provision [by others] of the means of remunerative activity as a component of the right to work?" There are two levels to this question. First, "What, if any, is the justification for the right to work itself?" Then second, "What is the justification for this particular interpretation of the right?"

Justifying the Right to Work

Whether interpreted in the weak or strong sense, the right to work can be defended on at least three related grounds. First, work [as remunerative activity] is a means of meeting the basic needs of life; namely, food, housing and clothing. Indeed, as we have discussed above, there is a traditional Yoruba belief that work is a cure for poverty. But even if we do not go this far [since as we have also seen, poverty is a social disease which can only be cured by a social policy], we can at least acknowledge the significance of remunerative work in securing the means of life. To live and think, we must eat, and to eat we must produce, i.e., work. If work is thus so important, there is a strong case for a right to it.[15]

It may be argued, though, that even if the product of work is a means to securing the basic needs of life, there need be no right to it since it is possible for a person to live on charity from society, government or other individuals. Therefore the idea of a right to work, if based only on the existence of basic needs which can be procured by work, cannot be a strong one. This objection however misses the mark. It is true that people can live on charity, but the idea of a right to work does not prevent such. As long as it is recognized that work is still essential [the charitable individuals will still have to work in order to give to the needy and indolent], then the defense of a right to it still holds. On the other hand, defending a right to work does not necessarily mean that the individual must work. S/he may refuse to exercise the right.

On a different ground, the objection to the idea of a right to work on the ground that it is possible to live on charity misses one important moral point. Our self-conception, as well as others' estimation of us, is tied up with our involvement in productive activities to the extent that our sense of self-respect is devalued if we depend on charity from others to acquire the basic needs of life. The right to work is therefore ultimately the right to make autonomous decisions about matters that have to do with our self-respect. Even when one is employed by others for a wage, one's right to work is being exercised [to the extent that one can decide to change jobs] and one's position is certainly far better [because more respectable] than the unemployed who depends on charity. Work is the respectable means to meeting the basic needs of life; therefore, there should be a guaranteed right to it for all those who wish to work.

Finally, work, as we observed earlier, is a means of self-realization. It is a process of realizing and fulfilling our human potentialities and abilities for the harnessing of nature for human benefit. Self-realization is coming to terms with one's potentialities and possibilities, and this is possible only when one is able to exert one's body and mind at work. If this is an important human objective - to realize one's self and fulfil its potentialities, then, it is imperative that one should have a right to the means of achieving it. Work is the means, hence the idea of a right to it. There is no doubt that many see work, not as a means of self-realization, but as a curse. This is due to the negative estimation given to work by those who have identified it with wage [or slave] labor, which is in a real sense dehumanizing. But this can be superseded by transforming the social structure with a view to making work a humane and dignified activity capable of serving as a means of self-realization.

But suppose we agree that there is a right to work on the strength of the preceding argument, it still remains to see why this should entail the demand that the means of work as remunerative activity be provided by some other person(s). How can the strong sense of the right to work [with the correlative duty to provide work] be justified? A Nozickian may, for instance, agree with the first claim in the sense that my having a right to work only means that no one has a right to interfere with my work-effort; but he is not likely to agree with the interpretation of that right as meaning a right to be provided with means of work.[16] To meet this challenge, a first justification that should readily come to mind is simply that if the argument for the right to work is accepted, then this provision should follow as what that right supports. It stands to reason to require that those who cannot provide the means of work for themselves should be helped by others who are in a position to do so. Otherwise the whole idea of right to work becomes meaningless. If I have a right to work, and I choose to farm, but there is neither land nor capital at my disposal, then that right is rendered useless. It is as good as if it did not exist. Here, therefore, is a justification for the demand. This demand makes sense especially in the world of private property accumulation and resultant inequality in which we have found ourselves. As Rousseau once observed, inequality began when one individual was clever enough to enclose a portion of the common land for himself and got others to accept this without complaint. When land and capital are thus privatized and there are persons who have neither on their own, how is their livelihood to be guaranteed except for the right to work to be recognized and the duty to provide them the means of work accepted.

Still it may be objected that this justification does not deal with the moral dilemma raised by Nozick. This is because in an attempt to provide the means of work for the right claimants, the rights of others will be violated. For one means of meeting the demand and providing the means of work for all is for government to nationalize the major means of production and become the sole employer of labor. Is this not a violation of the right of individuals to private means of production and property? To address this objection adequately, one needs to discuss in detail the Nozickian theory of appropriation and highlight the problems with it. Obviously, to do that here would involve unnecessary digression. The important point to note, however, is that Nozick's theory may accommodate such a step in some economies by appeal to the third feature of his theory of entitlement, namely, justice in rectification, if it can be shown that those who own property acquire such property unjustly. In the case of Nigeria, the most committed libertarian should not need any serious argument to be convinced that most of the property owners acquire them through corrupt practices in and out of government and that this tramples on the right of tax payers. Such a libertarian only needs empirical evidence, which is abundant, especially between 1979 and 1983.

Between 1979 and 1983, when a second attempt was made at democratic government, more millionaires were made through contract inflations, kick-backs and commissions than in the previous twenty-three years of our existence as an independent nation. These new millionaires have been able to keep their loots in spite of the various military tribunals which condemned them. It has been suggested that the external debt of over 20 billion dollars which Nigeria incurred between 1979 and 1983 can be settled by the combined external assets of only twelve Nigeria political activists who are now enjoying their wealth in various locations outside Nigeria. Those who now suffer hardship as a result of the economic problems created by the activites of those politicians will not agree that it is wrong to nationalize a wealth so unjustly appropriated.

If Nozick's objection can be answered in this way, there is a far more formidable objection deriving from a conception of rights--the permission theory of rights--which seems to lead to the impossibility of civil and human rights. The permission theory is developed as a component of the task theory of political community. It is necessary, however, to see if there could not be a reconciliation of the idea of a right to work with the permission theory of rights and the task theory of political community as developed and defended by Haskell Fain.

"A normative political community is a community in which at least one person has legislative moral powers with regard to the other members of the community."[17] "The task theory of political community holds that normative political power is derived from the tasks upon which a community is founded."[18] "A right is a normative ability to do something or to have someone else do something. Claim-rights are examples of the latter kind. But rights to *do* something are not claim-rights. Permission rights are rights to do something, not rights to have someone else do something."[19]

Given these views, how should the reconciliation effort proceed? I agree that rights may be conceived in terms of permissions; but I also want to claim that the right to employment is a right to have someone else do something! One way to account for this is the following: In view of its importance, the right to work, conceived as the right to *have* the means of work, may be conceived to be acquired by permission extended upon the constitution of the political community to members to engage in productive activities. The idea here is that establishing a political community on the basis of certain constituting tasks carries with it the idea that members are to engage in activities relevant to the execution of those tasks. But whatever those tasks are, productive activities by members must be relevant. Thus in a political community that is constituted by the task of fishing, we imagine that Jones [to use Fain's characters] may acquire the right to fish by a permission from Smith [his other fellow member of the community]. We expect that Smith will grant the permission to Jones [Or why shouldn't he?] given the fact that the community is constituted by the task of fishing which seems to suggest that neither Jones nor Smith can live meaningfully without engaging in this task. We expect, then, that Smith should know that, should he refuse to grant that permission and therefore refuse to create a right to fish for Jones, the political community can no longer subsist because the task can no longer be performed. And should Smith be silent, it would appear that Jones may as well assume that permission has been granted by the silence.

But granting this does not still give us the idea of a right to employment as a right to have someone else do something. For the right thus granted by Smith's permission is for Jones to do something. So we should proceed further playing the game of permission. Granting permission creates right for the grantee, but not obligation on the part of the grantor. But we need both: it is pointless to have a right to employment without the grantor having a duty to provide the means of access. So, Jones is pretty much aware of the logic of permission and prohibition. He is able to extract permission from Smith, but he also knows that this is not enough. He needs to be assured that Smith will undertake to make the communal vessel available to him without which he cannot go into the sea to fish. He therefore demands from Smith a promise that Smith will make available to him all he needs to fish. Smith has to promise, otherwise his intention becomes suspect with dire consequences for their egalitarian political community. Smith's promise creates a vectorial duty. The point here is that if a political community is egalitarian, and is founded on the moral power of members to direct the execution of tasks, there is a limitation on the kind of models we can use. The temptation to slip into legal conceptualism has to be avoided.

It seems to me then that the task theory of political community can accommodate, at least, the idea of a right to work on the ground that productive activity is necessarily a constituting task of any political community and sustained membership depends on the ease by which permissions are granted and obligations assumed. If this is the case with the model of simple-model political communities, we should expect it to be sustained for complex political communities as well. In other words, just as work as productive activity is a necessary aspect of the constituting task of a simple political community [such as Minerva], it has to be a feature of a complex political community [such as Nigeria]. If permission cannot but be granted to members in simple political communities, it also cannot but be granted to those in complex communities. But whereas, a member of a simple political community can call the bluff of his fellow member if that permission is not forthcoming, by conferring on himself the permission (right) denied him [by defiantly going to fish]; a member of a complex political community cannot really do that because the odds are against him: he does not have the means to call the bluff of society except by becoming anti-social, robber, drug pusher, etc.

What is needed, therefore, is for governments to recognize that (1) productive activity is a constituting task of the political community, (2) every member deserves express permission with the state assuming the obligation - concretized in the provision of employment opportunities, (3) the condition in which one is neither permitted nor forbidden [liberty] is incompatible with the importance of productive activity as a constituting task and can only render members helpless in a situation of scarcity and want, or drive them to working against the very existence of the political community and its constituting tasks. So, even if there are no other civil and human rights, a task theory of political community has to recognize the right to work as right not only to engage in productive activity but also to have the means of doing that provided. This can also be incorporated into the devices for regulating conduct in a political community with regard to its constituting tasks. Thus with respect to a task S in a political community including Jones and Smith:

(1) Jones can give permission to Smith to do S (and vice versa)
(2) Jones can forbid Smith to do S (and vice versa)
(3) Jones can promise Smith that Jones will make available whatever Smith needs [and which Jones can provide] to do S.

While (1) creates right for Smith to do S, (3) creates obligation for Jones with regard to Smith's doing S. If (3) is conceivable, the creation of obligation is feasible.

The Means of Work

Earlier, we have identified some four ways of providing the means of remunerative activity for persons, namely:

(i) making capital and land available to them to engage in farming [and related activity],
(ii) making capital and other factors of production available to them for self-employment in other productive sectors [manufacturing, distributive, etc.],
(iii) giving them job in paid employment [labor] requiring no formal education and training,
(iv) giving them formal education and training to prepare them for and absorb them into paid employment in skill requiring jobs.

It is now necessary to raise some questions: (1) Why [any of] these particular ways? Are they the most desirable or effective means? (2) Who has the duty to provide the identified means? (3) What is/are the prospect(s) for the effective practicalization of the idea in our present circumstances? These are complicated questions, but they are important to resolve in the context of this analysis.

(1) Why [any of] these particular ways for providing means of work? As has been observed earlier, the first two identified ways of providing means of work are geared towards enabling individuals to be self-employed. Historically, the earliest model of work in many parts of Nigeria was for people to engage in private farming activities at the subsistence level. Originally, when land was communally owned, the community would allocate land to families for their use and individuals could in turn secure portions of such lands as they might need for farming. Parents served as "employers" of their offsprings until they were old enough to own their own farms when they are given a portion of land and some capital [equipment and seedlings] to start off. Parents normally felt they had some obligation to do this and in some cases such obligation was extended to finding suitable spouses for their grown up men and footing the marriage bill. Of course, this is not to suggest that the language of right was appropriate to describe this phenomenon. Children certainly did not claim that they had any right to be provided such things by their parents in those days; yet it seems true that parents felt obligated to provide them. This was the situation in many Nigerian communities before contact with Europeans.

Given the stage of society at the time when subsistence farming was widely practiced and was the only available production system, to evaluate the practice of providing land and capital [as means of work] from a normative perspective may be really unwarranted and inappropriate. After all, there was no alternative to it and so, in the prevailing circumstances of low development of production forces, nothing else could have been expected. Times have however changed. Communalism has given way to capitalism with its glorification of the privatization of land and capital. Subsistence farming is fast giving way to large-scale commercial farming with multinationals as entrepreneurs. Children no longer serve parents on the farm and many now go to school [barring increasing costs which have recently shut school gates against them]. But there are still a substantial number of youths and adults who either are unable to go to school at all or drop-out and cannot get paid employment because of their limited formal education. Is provision of farm land and capital a viable way of providing the means of work for them? An adequate answer to this question must come to terms with the present contradictions in our social structure - the dominance of multinationals in agriculture and the gradual, but steady elimination of peasant farmers from the scene. In such a circumstance, a lot depends on the adequacy of what is provided to meet the challenge posed by the advanced capital and high technology of multinationals and their indigenous counterparts. Many states in Nigeria have established agricultural projects for young school leavers, providing them with land and small capital outlay. While the gesture may be commendable, it is important to realize the fact that these young ones are up against great odds. They are to compete with big-time farmers who have all it takes to win. It is true, however, that if the practical problems faced by these young agricultural entrepreneurs are solved, this approach could be a viable means of discharging the duty by the government. This is also true because many would still prefer to be their own bosses as self-employed than to work for others. It is also a way of re-invigorating the traditional value in modern setting. Finally, if such individuals could be encouraged to go into cooperative ventures, this approach could succeed as a means of providing surplus for the nation in the agricultural sector.

What about making capital and other factors of production available to them for self-employment in other productive sectors [apart from farming], e.g., manufacturing, distribution, etc.? This suggestion presupposes a certain type of society, one which has passed through the stage of communalism and subsistence farming, perhaps to one in which industrial and commercial activities have taken shape. Obviously, again, it makes sense only in a particular economic system, one which allows and encourages private ownership of means of production. In such a society, one effective way of providing the means of work will be to make capital available to every individual to start his/her own business. But this is far from feasible as is shown by the history of Western capitalist societies. Not every willing investor can have access to capital. Neither is it desirable. After all, there has to be a crop of work force from which the capitalists can draw labor for their industries.

Of course, it could be admitted that providing capital [and other factors] for some may ultimately provide the means of work for all through a multiplier effect. [For apart from the expectation that those who have capital will employ labor and pay them, other businesses may grow from the initial capital]. This is a typical argument for private enterprise. But it is far from being a feasible option in the present structure of the Nigerian economy. With a labor force of more than 80 million, it is beyond the capacity of government to provide such capital for everyone. On the other hand, there does not exist an aggressive and reliable banking system which can serve as a foundation for the build-up of capital for those who might need it.

The next option we should consider is for society to give him job [as wage laborer] in paid employment which requires no formal education or training. The demand that the addressees of the right to work should provide wage labor in jobs requiring no formal education or training may be defended on some grounds. First, it has been argued that universal access to capital is impossible and that the majority may not have it. On this ground, it may be argued that if those unable to obtain capital on their own have a right to work, and they cannot set up their own business [or are unwilling to do so] and do not have a formal education and training required in specialized jobs, they deserve a job which requires no such training, and the addressee of such a right claim has the obligation to provide the jobs. Second, it may be argued that unskilled wage labor is an inevitable aspect of any economy because skilled and unskilled laboring activities are required in any business or industrial concern. Third, therefore, if there are individuals who have no skills, they should be given jobs requiring no skills. This kind of argument would be directed against the rise of technological unemployment, the cause of which is the use of robots instead of men to do sundry jobs in industries and business. If there is a right to work for everyone, then such practice which may lead to some losing their jobs is morally unjustifiable.

These arguments are strong but it seems to me that the last is the strongest. The first two seem to accept the traditional position with regard to the inequality of access to the means of life: capital and education. It is thus a defense (perhaps unconsciously) of the status quo. On the ground that not all can have access to capital, it seeks to justify the right to wage labor, i.e., the right of those without capital to be employed by those with capital. But how can this be defended without jeopardizing the argument for the right of owners of capital to do whatever they like with their money? If it is legitimate to own capital, and some have it but others do not, what right can the latter press against the former for employment? Beside, if the owners of capital have a title to it as the libertarian would argue, then pressing such a claim on behalf of the unemployed may be said to violate that right and stand in the way of profit-maximization which is the goal of capital. Thus in spite of the fact that some companies, including banks, are now declaring more profits than ever before, they also engage in the business of retrenching workers. One way of resolving this problem is to maintain that, though private capitalists do not have a duty to provide work for the jobless, the government has such a duty and this would require it to create job opportunities and get people into positions for which they are qualified. Why should this be so?

From the foregoing, there are indications of what the answer to this question should be. The duty to provide the means of work for persons belongs to the society represented by the government. Why? One of the fundamental justifications for the existence of a state-political community, following the contractarian tradition, is that without it, life would be nasty, brutish and short [Hobbes] or that individuals would be unable to realize their full potentialities as moral persons [Rousseau] or that they would experience some inconveniences [Locke]. Taking all these together, it seems clear that society through its government is to be justified on the basis of its function, which is mainly to assist the full development [moral and physical] of persons. The task theory of political community, as we have seen, may also arrive at a similar conclusion by attending to the claim that productive activity is an essential task of any political community. If there were no political authority, individuals would fend for themselves in a situation of insecurity occasioned by greed, avarice and violence. The political authority prevents this through the institution of the law. However, it cannot be pretended that all will be well even with political authority if individuals are not protected from the domineering impulse of the smarter and stronger ones. The best way to do this is for the state to provide the means of work and employment for all.

How should this duty be discharged? Most governments would perhaps recognize this duty as theirs, but their approaches to discharging it may be different and may cast doubts on their commitment. There are three possible approaches. First the government may make itself the sole supplier of jobs. This it may do by nationalizing the major means of production so that it assigns people to different tasks according to their training and national needs. Second, the government may create conditions for the creation of jobs by the private sector by deregulating the economy and giving incentive to private entrepreneurs. Thirdly, government may combine efforts with the private sector as employers of labor by embarking on economic and job-creating projects on its own and offering employment to those who want but cannot get from the private sector.[20] What are the chances of each of these approaches effectively providing remunerative activity to all those who need it? The last is a mixed bag of government and private entrepreneurs cooperating for job creation. Under normal circumstances, one would expect a situation in which two are involved in the supply of a commodity to be better than one in which there is only one supplier. However, there is more to the issue of employment than the analogy of supply and demand can capture.

In the case of job provision, the existence of two sources of supply may in fact be a curse rather than a blessing. This may happen if each has expectations that the other is going to act and such action is not forthcoming. This could create an undesirable scarcity in the job market. It is a typical case of everyone's duty ending up as no one's. Unless there is an adequate coordination of efforts, therefore, the combination of government and private efforts may actually turn out not to be an effective way of promoting employment. At present, this is the Nigerian approach; and this fact is a vindication of the skepticism about this approach. For while both private and public sectors are now involved in employment provision, un-employment rate is crushingly high; not to talk of the several cases of inadequate or wrongful employment of persons in jobs other than those for which they are trained.

In the second approach, government does not create jobs on its own; it only creates conditions for the private sector to do so, by the choice of economic policies which are geared towards that end. One of these is the provision of tax incentives to firms and companies to expand. Here the government refrains from controlling the economy through regulations. In fact, a deregulated economy is considered the most effective for job creation. This is a typical *laissez-faire* position. The obligation to provide employment is then off the neck of government. But neither can it be solidly placed on private companies, because they are out to make profit and they can tolerate employment only to such an extent as may not be destructive of their profit motives. So there is no guarantee that a fully deregulated economy with the best package of incentives will lead to full employment. For instance, such incentives may lead to improved technology which may make automation more profitable and this of course will create unemployment. This is the typical case of the conflict between efficiency and rights.

This shows that a fully deregulated economy cannot solve the problem of unemployment, that is, in addition to the other social problems associated with such a policy. Government has a responsibility for the well-being of its citizens, and it cannot transfer that responsibility to industries. There is therefore the need for government to put itself in a position of strength vis-a-vis industrial capitalists who necessarily have their own interests. Where the interests clash, there has to be a way of reconciling them in favor of the well-being of citizens. Suppose, then it is considered more efficient to produce goods by laying off workers than by using them. From what we discussed above, the question must be raised whether the interests of the people will be better served by that kind of approach. The experience thus far, is that they are not being served better. Retrenchment of workers in Nigeria and other African countries has not being matched by any improvement in the provision of goods and services. Inflation and unemployment have gone hand in hand. So the argument from efficiency cannot do the job. What is more important is for the government to assume a more effective position in the structuring of the economy so that it will be able to give appropriate directions for the welfare of the citizens.

Perhaps the argument for the duty of government to provide job opportunities for citizens may be granted on the grounds adduced. But it may also be argued that it does not follow from this that the citizens have a right to employment. Though the arguments above also attempt to sustain the idea of this right, there is an objection which still needs to be met. The experience of some countries which recognize the right of citizens to employment is that worker productivity is dismally low, and the usual reason adduced for this is that such workers are confident that they cannot lose their jobs, since they have a constitutional right to jobs and such a right cannot be forfeited. There are two points to note here. First, to argue for a right to work is not necessarily to argue for an absolute right to work. The right to freedom is a constitutional right in many democracies, but that does not prevent people being sent to jail. The right to employment need not be construed as an absolute right; conditions have to be written into it to indicate when it could be forfeited. Secondly, from what we discussed above, worker productivity may be low even where there is no recognized constitutional right to employment. Other factors are usually involved. If there is a right to self-realization and self-actualization, then there is a right to the means of making this possible. The only means is work; hence the idea of a right to it. The important thing, therefore, is for government to recognize that it has a duty to the citizens to provide them with the means of work, and to use whatever means available to it to effectively discharge this duty.

10

CONCLUDING REMARKS: DEVELOPMENT AND HUMAN VALUES

Many people would agree that the most urgent problem of contemporary Africa is development. Beyond this, however, there is hardly any consensus on either the question of what development is or on the means to achieve it. There is as much controversy over the appropriate socio-political structures required as over the necessary re-orientations, if any, in thought and practice. The question of the relevant educational policies and goals continues to divide people. To focus discussion in a rewarding way, we may approach the issue by addressing three questions that still seem to remain unresolved. [1] What is the nature of development needed by Africa? [2] What kind of political-economic structure is best suited to this development? [3] Does this development require any cultural reconstruction i.e. re-orientation in thought and practice away from traditional outlook? Or should the development effort be reconciled with tradition? I intend, in these concluding remarks, to attempt a very brief review of the problems.

Development is a multi-faceted and complex phenomenon. Any talk of development for Africa must therefore isolate the issues involved. In the various debates generated by the issue, there is a general consensus that there are at least three aspects of any society that is the focus of development:economic, political and social. Thus we talk of economic development, political development and social development. But development itself, in relation to these aspects, suggests positive and sustained growth. It is the movement from a lower to a higher stage of existence. In the context of nations, it connotes the realization of higher capacities for satisfying the needs of the citizens. Thus economic development suggests the capacity of a society to overcome the scourges of poverty, starvation, disease and ignorance. Political development suggests capacity to overcome the problems of instability and disunity; and to have a smooth arrangement for succession while social development suggests the prevalence of humane values suitable for social life.

Of these three, many would also agree that economic development is the most urgent in the African context. This is on the ground that political instability [a veritable sign of political underdevelopment] is a bed-fellow of economic underdevelopment. It is therefore thought that a sustained economic development would be matched by political stability. On the other hand, social development, in the sense defined, seems to be one with which African societies can always take pride in. We should therefore guide against its being compromised in the event of a successful economic development. In other words, as far as social development is concerned, African nations have a good heritage, which they should guard jealously and which they should not be prepared to exchange for anything.

If a sign of economic development is the extent to which a society has been able to overcome the problem of generalized poverty, hunger, disease and ignorance, then a good question to raise is how these can be overcome in contemporary Africa. Again, there seems to be a consensus on industrialization as the most effective means. A country that is mainly a producer of agricultural products as raw materials for foreign industries cannot expect to raise itself up the ladder of development. This was the situation of many African countries at the dawn of flag independence. Industrialization means that a greater proportion of the population be engaged in the manufacturing sector of the economy and a greater proportion of the Gross National Product will flow from the manufacturing sector than from agriculture. What is needed to overcome the problem of generalized poverty is to increase the resources available to the society which can then be in a better position to provide for the satisfaction of basic human needs. But to increase resources, we cannot depend on subsistence farming and related emphasis. The manufacturing sector provides the best avenue for increased output of goods and services for both internal and external markets. Therefore, industrialization is needed. This is the conclusion of many African societies regarding this issue, and no doubt, this conclusion is shared by many western and eastern experts. To be sure, the degree of emphasis varies. Thus many insist that industrialization does not have to be on the basis of big industrial complexes; but that since African countries are primarily agricultural, they should start by developing agro-based industries on small scales. That way, they need not require huge capital outlays which may make them depend on foreign aid. This consensus on industrialization as the means of solving the problem of generalized poverty is, however, not matched by an equal consensus on the kind of political-economic structure that can best achieve it and the economic development with which it is linked. This leads to the next question: what kind of political-economic structure is best suited to the development of Africa?

If, again, we focus on economic development, three major answers have been provided to this question and for various reasons; two of these come from both outside and inside Africa; while the other comes from Africa. First, there is the answer which takes the solution to the problem of African development as that of adopting the social structures and political systems of the capitalist west. An important consideration here is the belief that, given the incentives, people will on their own, embark on productive ventures which will improve the society's welfare. It goes back to the idea of the invisible hand, and the need for minimum regulation of the economic activities of citizens. Of course, one problem as advocates of this approach also recognize is that traditional values of Africa may be swept aside and this may rock the foundation of its social development. Though, there is this possibility, it does not bother its advocates because, after all, that may be one price to pay for development; and in any way, that is how the west was also developed. The emphasis here is on rewarding private efforts as a means of having socio-economic development. Most African countries, at the dawn of independence, were reluctant to go the whole way with this approach. For one thing, because of their historical relationship with African nations, the stigma of being the unwelcome exploiters of African human and natural resources has been a self-imposed lot of the former colonial powers of the west, and many African countries will have nothing to do with whatever is considered the west's economic legacy. Second, many were not ready to substitute indigenous exploitation for colonial exploitation. Thirdly, at the dawn of independence, there was no real class of indigenous bourgeoisie that could be relied upon as catalysts of capitalist development. An eclectic approach combining aspects of capitalism and socialism was the best available to many countries.[1]

The Marxist-Leninist approach regards the backwardness of Africa as a creation of colonial exploitation. Capitalism served the western colonial powers by transferring the wealth of the colonies to develop the metropolis. The only way to get rid of poverty, therefore, is to abandon the capitalist approach. It agrees that economic development requires industrialization; but it maintains that the capitalist approach is full of contradictions that prevent it from achieving the desirable results. To achieve this, there is need to combine the society's resources by nationalizing the means of production so that the state can be in a position to plan. Further, since there has been no indigenous development of a capitalist class, adopting the western capitalist path would mean retaining the western capitalists as partners. But since they have the economic and technological means, this arrangement can only prolong the dependency of Africa on the west. Colonialism will be exchanged for neo-colonialism. For an indigenous path to sustained economic development, therefore, the most effective means is the nationalization of the major means of social production, institutionalization of cooperation and industrialization. This is the socialist path recommended for African development.[2]

Again, while some African leaders sympathized with this approach and even applaud it as similar to the indigenous system, they [except for a few] reject it on three grounds: it is alien; it is based on the idea of class and class struggle and therefore celebrates violence; it is based on atheistic metaphysics. Therefore, instead of going all out for scientific socialism, they introduce the ideas of African socialism, pragmatic socialism etc. The basic assumption in all these is that while socialism is an attractive ideology for organizing social life in Africa, it has to be based on values and structures indigenous to Africa, including the religious values, moral values and the values of community.[3]

The third option is different only in name, not in its basic presuppositions, from this idea of Africanizing socialism. The democratic socialist approach rejects the Marxist approach on virtually the same grounds as African socialists do, except that it does not emphasize the alien nature of Marxism. On the other hand, it also accepts socialism as a "normative science" which cannot vary from place to place. But it rejects the idea of class struggle and revolution as unnecessary features of socialism in the African setting. Democratic socialism, then, also relies on the African values of love and community as a basis for the socialist transformation of African societies.[4]

Which of these approaches is most promising for overcoming the problems of poverty, starvation and ignorance as well as avoiding the problems of social injustice. In view of the fact that majority of African nations adopted one form of socialism or the other upon the attainment of independence, and in view of the fact that none of them has been able to get rid of these problems, it would seem that socialism has been shown as inappropriate for the solution of Africa's problems. Indeed, this is the verdict of the west using the recent experience of Africa's debt to the world. In the place of socialist approach, privatization has been recommended and recently adopted by many countries in the hope that it will get them out of debt and poverty. Besides, the experience of advanced socialist countries including the Soviet Union, which has had to acknowledge problems with its economy, and which is now taking the capitalist path, seems to confirm the inadequacy of socialism. For if we can blame neocolonial and imperialist machinations for Africa's problems, we may not be able to blame such forces for the problem of Soviet Union. Does it mean then that the socialist path to economic development is a dead-end? Many will, again, be reluctant to accept such a suggestion. One major ground for this reluctance concerns the link that many Africans draw between adequate economic development and human values.

African cultures are communitarian as Senghor does not stop observing. The values of community are an important heritage of all Africans. Capitalist path to development does not care to preserve such values; it destroys them with its emphasis on competitive individualism. If African nations therefore go for capitalism because it promises fast economic development, they may have to be content with the loss of such values with its concomitant disruption of social life. Besides, capitalist development necessarily divides society into haves and have-nots, whereas in the indigenous cultures, a society is either poor or rich as a whole. Poverty was not privatized. The argument, therefore, is that if we value the importance of community, cooperation and the ideals of solidarity, we should stay with socialism and sink or rise together. Majority of Africans seem to be in favor of this position which is further strengthened by the consideration that the capitalist path cannot but make African countries dependent. Whatever indigenous bourgeoisie class there is now is made by foreign capital and must depend for its survival on it. In any case, whatever path to development is adopted, there is still the final question: are African cultures an impediment to development?

We have touched on the indigenous beliefs and values of community and fellow-feeling. There are also such cultural beliefs as belief in destiny, causal ideas, and witchcraft. Obviously, development requires an appropriate re-orientation in thought and practice away from negative beliefs. There seems no doubt that the belief in witchcraft may sometimes lead to the development of negative work-ethic. Development requires the establishment of an objective basis for the evaluation and reward for work-effort and competence. This may not be helped if workers generally believe that they are not doing well at work because someone at home is bewitching them. For they will not be urged to take appropriate steps to improve on their performance. So may the belief in destiny promote a negative attitude to work and therefore to development. There is therefore a need for reorientation in some of our beliefs whatever path to development we embark upon.[5] Incidentally, the Marxist "atheistic metaphysics" may have been developed as a reaction to such attitudes.

What about the humane and communitarian values? In a sense, it may be argued that such values are an impediment to development. Industrialization requires breaking of bonds of families. Urbanization, which is a concomitant of industrialization does not take families into account. Individuals are the basic units of consideration and they are the ones reckoned with on assembly lines. But should that ethic be accepted by Africans? Perhaps, here is an example of how traditional African values may serve the west and the east to rediscover such humane values and have them incorporated in their development strategies. There ought to be a way of reconciling communal values which emphasize fellow-feeing, love, humaneness and human welfare with industrial values which emphasize productivity and development since the ultimate goal of development is also the promotion of human welfare. Perhaps one aspect of the alienation that seems an integral part of industrialization may be overcome if more of communal and family values are rediscovered and integrated into the process of development. What is needed is economic development with a human face.

ENDNOTES

Chapter 1

1. Tempels, Placide, *Bantu Philosophy*, Paris: Presence Africaine, 1969, pp.1-2.

2. Paulin Hountondji, *African Philosophy: Myth and Reality*, Bloomington: Indiana University Press, 1983, p.34.

3. Leopold Senghor, "The Spirit of Civilisation or the Laws of African Negro Culture" in *Presence Africaine*, No. 8-9-10, June-November, 1956; *On African Socialism* trans. by Mercer Cook, New York: Praeger, Inc. 1964; "Negritude: A Humanism of the Twentieth Century" in W. Cartey and M. Kilson [ed.], *The African Reader: Independent Africa*, New York: Random House, 1970; J. S. Mbiti, *African Religions and Philosophy*, London: Heinemann, 1969.

4. Mbiti, *op. cit.*, pp.1-2.

5. Gene Blocker, "African Philosophy" in *African Philosophical Inquiry*, Vol.1. No.1., Jan. 1987, p.6.

6. This seems to be the uncompromising position taken by Hountondji. See his *African Philosophy: Myth and Reality*, Bloomington: Indiana University Press, 1983. A few exceptions include Kwasi Wiredu who, in several of his publications, has made room for the coherence of traditional philosophy. See his "On Defining African Philosophy", Paper presented to the Association Ivorienne des Professors de Philosophie, Abidjan, Ivory Coast. Another exception is Odera Oruka who has developed a method for eliciting the philosophy of traditional sages. See his "Fundamental Principles in the Question of African Philosophy" *Second Order* Vol. 4 1975, pp.44-55. More than any of these, however, J. O. Sodipo has been consistent in his position that there is philosophy in traditional thought. See his "Philosophy in pre-colonial Africa" in *Teaching and research in Philosophy in Africa*: UNESCO, 1984, pp.73-80. See also P. O. Bodunrin, "The Question of African Philosophy", *Philosophy*, Vol. 56, 1981, pp.161-81 for a summary of the positions and what amounts to a defence of the school of professional philosophy.

7. John A. Hutchison, *Living Options in World Philosophy*, Honolulu: University Press of Hawaii and the Research Corporation of the University of Hawaii, 1977 p.19.

8. Bodunrin, *op.cit.*; Hountondji, *op.cit.*

9. Robin Horton, "Traditional Thought and the Emerging African Philosophy Department: A comment on the Current Debate" in *Second Order: An African Journal of Philosophy*, Vol.VI, No.1 1977, pp.64-80.

10. Hountondji, *op.cit.* p.47.

11. *ibid.*

12. Hountondji, *ibid.* p. 47.

13. *ibid.*

14. V. Y. Mudimbe, *The Invention of Africa: Gnosis, Philosophy and the Order of Knowledge*, Bloomington and Indianapolis: Indiana University Press, 1988. p.ix.

15. *ibid.*

16. Hountondji, *ibid.* p.63.

17. Gene Blocker, "African Philosophy", in *African Philosophical Inquiry*, Vol. 1, No. 1, January 1987, pp.1-7 [quoting from p.6.]

18. See Olabiyi Yai, "Theory and Practice in African Philosophy: The Poverty of Speculative Philosophy", *Second Order: An African Journal of Philosophy*, Vol.II, No. 2, 1977.

19. Hountondji, *ibid.*, p.48.

20. Yai, *op.cit.*, p.8. See also O. Owomoyela, "African Philosophy: The Conditions of its Possibility", *SAPINA Newsletter: A Bulletin of the Society for African Philosophy in North America*, Vol. III, No. 1, January-July, 1990, pp.14-45.

21. Sandra Harding, *The Science Question in Feminism*, Ithaca and London: Cornell University Press, 1986, pp.182-183.

22. Robin Horton, "African Traditional Thought and Western Science" in *Africa*, XXXVII, Nos. 1 and 2 [January and April, 1967], pp.50-71 and 155-87. See also Harding, *op.cit.*

23. Kwasi Wiredu, *Philosophy and an African Culture*, New York: Cambridge, 1979. See also Harding, *op.cit.*, p.184.

24. Odera Oruka, "Mythologies in African Philosophy", *East African Journal*, 9, No.10 1972; Hountondji, *op.cit.* p.60.

25. Oruka, *op.cit.*

26. G. Niangoran-Bouah, *The Akan World of Gold Weights*, Volume 1, Abidjan: Les Nouvelles Edition Africaines, M. L. B., 1984, p.215.

27. *ibid*, p.217.

28. See Barry Hallen, "Robin Horton on Critical Philosophy and Traditional Thought" *Second Order* Vol.6, No.1 1977, pp.81-92; Kwame Gyekye, *An Essay on African Philosophical Thought: The Akan Conceptual Scheme* New York: Cambridge, 1987; Kwasi Wiredu, *op.cit*.

29. Horton, *op.cit*. p. 64.

30. *ibid*.

31. Wiredu, *op.cit*.

32. *ibid*., p.65.

33. George Chatalian, "Philosophy, The World and Man: A Global Conception" Inaugural Lecture delivered at the University of Ife [now Obafemi Awolowo University, Ile-Ife] Nigeria, on June 28, 1983.

34. Godwin Sogolo, "Options in African Philosophy", *Philosophy*, 65, 1990, pp.39-52 [quoting from p.47].

35. Hountondji, *op.cit*. p.33.

36. P. O. Bodunrin, "The Question of African Philosophy", in Richard Wright ed., *African Philosophy: An Introduction*, Lanham: University Press of America, 1984, p.18.

37. *ibid*.

38. *ibid*., p.19.

39. "What is African Philosophy", presented at the *William Amo International Symposium*, Accra Ghana, 24-29 July, 1978 p.7; cited by Bodunrin, *ibid.*, p.19.

40. *ibid*.

41. See "On Defining African Philosophy" *op.cit*.

42. Arthur Murphy, "Life and Philosophy" [Holograph MS] c.1930, cited by Marcus G. Singer, "Two American Philosophers: Morris Cohen and Arthur Murphy" in Marcus G. Singer ed., *American Philosophy*: Royal Institute of Philosophy Lecture Series 19: Supplement to Philosophy Cambridge University Press, 1985 p.324.

43. Singer, *ibid*.

44. Singer, *ibid*. p.4.

45. Singer, *ibid*., p.11.

46. Singer, *ibid.*, pp.11-12.

47. J. O. Sodipo, "Philosophy in Pre-colonial Africa", *op.cit.*, p.75.

48. Alfred North Whitehead, *Science and the Modern World*, Cambridge: University Press, 1926, cited by Singer, *op.cit.*, p.10-11.

Chapter 2

1. See, for instance, Kwame Gyekye, *An Essay on African Philosophical Thought: The Akan Conceptual Scheme*, New York: Cambridge, 1987; Kwasi Wiredu, "The Akan Concept of Mind", *Ibadan Journal of the Humanities*, No. 3 October 1983.

2. Bolaji Idowu, *Olodumare: God in Yoruba Belief*, London: Longmans, 1962, p.170.

3. cf. Wiredu, *op.cit.*, pp.113-118.

4. cf. *Ori* as physical head, and *ori* as inner head. It appears that for every vital part of the body, there is a conception of a corresponding invisible entity which vitalizes that part.

5. This point is argued forcefully by Olusegun Oladipo in his *An African Conception of Reality: A Philosophical Analysis*, Ph.D Dissertation submitted to the University of Ibadan, 1988.

6. Idowu, *op.cit.* p.171.

7. Wande Abimbola, "The Yoruba Concept of Human Personality", *La Notion de Personne en Afrique Noire*, Paris: Centre National de la Recherche Scientifique, 1971, pp.73-89.

8. On this, see Robin Horton, "Destiny and the Unconscious in West Africa", *Africa*, Vol. 31, 1961, pp.110-116, for a similar concept among the Kalabari. Among other things, Horton observes that the Kalabari understand *teme* [their equivalent of *ori*] as "an immaterial agency which is in existence before the individual is born and which survives his death. Everything that happens in the *biomgbo* is brought about by the wishes of the *teme*; and in this respect Kalabari liken the *teme* to the steersman of the personality". [quoting from p.113].

9. Abimbola, *ibid.*, p.80.

10. Professor Kwasi Wiredu first called my attention to this and several other related questions on this issue in his extremely useful comments.

11. These are further questions raised by Professor Kwasi Wiredu.

12. Gyekye, *op. cit.*, Wiredu, *op. cit.*

13. Wiredu, *ibid.*, pp.119-120.

14. These comments are contained in Professor Wiredu's private exchange with me.

15. Albert Mosley, "The Metaphysics of Magic: Practical and Philosophical Implications", *Second Order: An African Journal of Philosophy* Vol VII Nos. 1 & 2, Jan/July 1978, p.12.

16. Gyekye, *op. cit.*, p.87.

17. Gyekye, *ibid.*, p.88.

18. *ibid.*, p.97.

19. *ibid.*, p.98.

20. *ibid.*, p.98.

21. *ibid.*, p.89.

22. *ibid.*, p.89.

23. *ibid.*

24. See my "Destiny, Personality, and the Ultimate Reality of Human Existence: A Yoruba Perspective", *Ultimate Reality and Meaning: Interdisciplinary Studies in the Philosophy of Understanding* Vol.7, No. 3, 1984, pp.173-188.

25. For some of these problems see my "God, Destiny and Social Injustice: A Critique of a Yoruba Ifa Belief" in Gene G. James ed. *The Search for Faith and Justice in the Twentieth Century*, New York: Paragon House, 1987, pp.52-68.

26. Abimbola, op.cit.; Moses Makinde, "A Philosophical Analysis of the Yoruba Concepts of Ori and Human Destiny" *International Studies in Philosophy*, XVII, No. 1, 1985 pp.53-69.

27. cf. Makinde, *ibid.*, p.58.

28. *ibid.*

29. For more on this, see Wande Abimbola, *Sixteen Great Poems of Ifa*, UNESCO, 1975, pp.178-207.

30. Moses Makinde, "Immortality of the Soul and the Yoruba Theory of Seven Heavens [*Orun Meje*]", *Journal of Cultures and Ideas*, Vol. 1, No. 1. 1983, pp.31-59; Idowu, *op.cit.*

31. See Ola Rotimi, *The Gods Are Not To Blame*, London & Ibadan: Oxford University Press, 1971, p.6.

32. See, for instance, Makinde, *op.cit.*, pp.62-64.

33. For more on this, see my "God, Destiny and Social Injustice", *op.cit.*

34. Abimbola, "The Yoruba Concept of Human Personality" *op. cit.*

35. Gyekye, *op. cit.*, pp.113-118.

36. *ibid.*, p.16.

37. *ibid.*

38. For more on this, see my "Destiny, Personality and the Ultimate Reality of Human Existence: A Yoruba Perspective", *op. cit.* For the Akan view on the normative meaning of person, see Kwasi Wiredu, "The African Concept of Personhood", Paper presented at the Conference on African-American Perspectives on Biomedical Ethics at Georgetown University, Washington D.C. November 1990.

Chapter 3

1. N. A. Fadipe, *The Sociology of the Yoruba*, edited with an Introduction by F. Olu Okediji and O. O. Okediji, Ibadan University Press, 1970, p.150.

2. Recall here the story of Moremi, the Yoruba heroine who sacrificed her only son for the survival of her community.

3. K. A. Busia, *The Challenge of Africa*, New York: Praeger, 1962, p.33.

4. Busia, *ibid.* p.34.

5. Kwame Gyekye, *An Essay on African Philosophical Thought: The Akan Conceptual Scheme*, New York: Cambridge, 1987, p.155.

6. Kwasi Wiredu, "Morality and Religion in Akan Thought" in H. Odera Oruka and D. A. Masolo [eds.] *Philosophy and Cultures*, Nairobi: Bookwise, 1983, p.13.

7. Gyekye, *ibid.*, pp.129-153.

8. Bolaji Idowu, *Olodumare: God in Yoruba Belief* Lagos: Longmans, 1962, p.144.

9. *ibid.*

10. Idowu, *ibid.*, p.144.

11. *ibid.*, p.145.

12. *ibid.*, p.145.

13. *ibid.*, p.145.

14. *ibid.*, p.146.

15. *ibid.*, p.149.

16. *ibid.*, p.150.

17. M. Akin Makinde, "African Culture and Moral Systems: A Philosophical Study", *Second Order: An African Journal of Philosophy* [New Series], Special Issue on Ethics and African Societies, Vol.1, No. 2 July 1988, pp.1-27.

18. *ibid.*, p.2.

19. Makinde, *ibid.*, p.2.

20. *ibid.*, p.3.

21. *ibid.*, p.3.

22. *ibid.* p.4.

23. *ibid.*, p.6.

24. *ibid.*, p.6.

25. *ibid.*, p.10.

26. Wande Abimbola, *Sixteen Great Poems of Ifa*, UNESCO, 1975, p.32.

27. *ibid.*, p.11.

28. *ibid.*, p.12.

29. See Niyi Oladeji, "Proverbs as Language Signposts in Yoruba Pragmatic Ethics", *Second Order: An African Journal of Philosophy*, Vol. 1, No. 2 July, 1988, p.49. For a similar emphasis on the pragmatic nature of Yoruba ethics, see Olatunde B. Lawuyi, "The Tortoise and the Snail: Animal Identities and Ethical Issues Concerning Political Behaviors among the Yoruba of Nigeria", *Second Order*, *ibid.*, pp.29-43.

30. Segun Gbadegesin, "World-view" in Toyin Falola and A. Adediran [eds.], *A New History of Nigeria for Colleges*, Lagos: John West, 1986. pp.227-244.

31. *ibid.*, p.242.

32. My discussion here has benefitted immensely from a series of taped interviews I had with some traditional thinkers: Pa Joseph Olanrewaju Gbadegesin, Pa Adeojo and Gbenle Ogungbenro.

33. Wande Abimbola, "*Iwapele*: The Concept of Good Character in *Ifa* Literary Corpus" in Wande Abimbola ed., *Yoruba Oral Tradition*, Ife African Languages and Literatures Series No.1, 1975, p.393; and Roland Abiodun, "Identity and the Artistic Process in Yoruba Aesthetic Concept of *Iwa*", *Journal of Cultures and Ideas* Vol. 1, No. 1, 1983, pp.13-30. In the following discussion, I draw on these contributions.

34. *ibid.*, p.14.

35. *ibid.*, p.14.

36. Abiodun, *ibid.*, p.15.

Chapter 4

1. John S. Mbiti, *African Religions and Philosophy*, London: Heinemann, 1969; E. Bolaji Idowu, *Olodumare: God in Yoruba Belief*, Nigeria: Longmans, 1962; E. Bolaji Idowu, *African Traditional Religion: A Definition*, New York: Orbis, 1973.

2. Okot p'Bitek, *African Religions in Western Scholarship*, Nairobi: East African Literature Bureau, 1970.

3. Kwasi Wiredu, "Philosophical Research and Teaching in Africa: Some Suggestions", in *Teaching and Research in Philosophy: Africa*, UNESCO, 1984, pp.31-54.

4. Wiredu, *ibid.* p.38.

5. See his "Universalism and Particularism in Religion from an African Perspective", *Journal of Humanism and Ethical Religion*, Vol.3, No.1, Fall 1990, pp.85-108.

6. Idowu, *op. cit.* See also my "Destiny, Personality and the Ultimate Reality of Human Existence : A Yoruba Perspective" in *Ultimate Reality and Meaning: Interdisciplinary Studies in the Philosophy of Understanding*, Vol. 7, No. 3, 1984, pp.173-188.

7. See Wande Abimbola, "The Yoruba Concept of Human Personality" in *La Notion de Personne en Afrique Noire*, Centre National de la Recherche Scientifique No. 544, 1971, pp.73-89.

8. Abimbola, *ibid.*, p.75.

9. Idowu, *op.cit.*, p.51.

10. See Idowu, *op.cit.*, p.55.

11. See M. A. Fabunmi, *Ayajo Ohun Ife*, Ibadan: Onibonoje Press, 1972, p.3. [my translation].

12. Kwame Gyekye, *An Essay on African Philosophical Thought: The Akan Conceptual Scheme*, New York: Cambridge, 1987, p.75.

13. *ibid.*, p.75.

14. *ibid.*

15. *ibid.*

16. W. E. Abraham, *The Mind of Africa*, The University of Chicago Press, 1962, p.54.

17. *ibid.*, p.55.

18. *ibid.*, p 56. Professor Wiredu called my attention to this point.

19. K.A. Busia, *The Challenge of Africa*, New York: Fredrick Praeger, 1962, p.1.

20. *ibid.*, p.41.

21. *ibid.*, p.7.

22. Wiredu, *op.cit.*, p.36.

23. cf. Okot p'Bitek, "On Culture, Man and Freedom" in H. Odera Oruka and D. A. Masolo [eds.], *Philosophy and Cultures*, Nairobi: Bookwise Ltd., 1983, p.114.

24. Karin Barber, "How Man Makes God in West Africa: Yoruba Attitudes Towards the Orisa" *Africa*, 51, 3, 1981, pp.724-745.

25. *ibid.*, p.724.

26. *ibid.*, p.724.

27. *ibid.* p.741.

28. *ibid.*, p.732.

29. Idowu, *op.cit.*, p.40.

30. Idowu, *African Traditional Religion*, p.146.

31. p'Bitek, *op.cit.*, p.50.

32. Idowu, *op.cit.*, Mbiti, *op.cit.*

33. Wiredu, *op.cit.*, p.40.

34. See my "Destiny, Personality and the Ultimate Reality of Human Existence" *op.cit.*

35. Idowu, *African Traditional Religion*, p.105.

36. Idowu, *op.cit.*, p.103.

Chapter 5

1. R. J. Collingwood, *Essay on Metaphysics*, Chicago: Gateway, 1972, p.285.

2. *ibid.*

3. *ibid.*, pp.285-286.

4. *ibid.*, p.291.

5. *ibid.*, pp.296-297.

6. *ibid.*, p.310.

7. *ibid.*, pp.310-311.

8. J. O. Sodipo, "Notes on the Concept of Cause and Chance in Yoruba Traditional Thought", *Second Order: An African Journal of Philosophy*, Vol. 2, No. 2, 1973, pp.16-18.

9. Kwasi Wiredu, "Philosophical Research and Teaching in Africa: Some Suggestions" in *Teaching and Research in Philosophy: Africa*: UNESCO, 1984, p.36.

10. Wiredu, *ibid.*, K. A. Busia, *The Challenge of Africa*, New York: Frederick A. Praeger, Inc., 1962, p.36.

11. K. A. Busia, *Africa in Search of Democracy*, London: Routledge and Kegan Paul, 1967.

12. Wiredu, *op. cit.*, p.37; Busia, *Africa in Search of Democracy*, p. 9.

13. Busia, *The Challenge of Africa*, p. 38.

14. Helaine K. Minkus, "Causal Theory in Akwapim Akan Philosophy" in Richard A. Wright ed., *African Philosophy: An Introduction* Lanham: University Press of America, 1984, p.115.

15. Kwame Gyekye, *An Essay on African Philosophical Thought: The Akan Conceptual Scheme*, New York: Cambridge, 1987, p. 70.

16. E. Bolaji Idowu, *Olodumare: God in Yoruba Belief*, Lagos: Longmans, 1962, pp.43-44.

17. Segun Gbadegesin and Oladimeji Alo, "The Theme of Causation and Contemporary Work Attitude Among Nigerians" in *ODU: A Journal of West African Studies*, No. 31, January 1987, pp.15-31.

18. D. H. Price-William, "A Case Study of Ideas Concerning Diseases Among the Tiv", *Africa*, 23, April, 1960 pp.123-31.

19. *ibid.*, p.36.

20. *ibid.*, p.38.

21. *ibid.*, p.38.

22. *Second Order: An African Journal of Philosophy*, Vol. 7, No. 1 & 2, 1978.

23. I am grateful to Professor Wande Abimbola for this information on the origin of *Ayajo*.

24. M. A. Fabunmi, *Ayajo Ohun Ife*, Ibadan: Onibonoje Publishers, 1972, p.72.[my translation].

25. Fabunmi, *ibid.* p.ix. [my translation].

26. Hans H. Penner, "Rationality, Ritual and Science" in Jacob Neusner, Ernst S. Frerichs and Paul Virgil M. Flesher, *Religion, Science and Magic* [New York: Oxford University Press, 1989], pp 11-24. The quotation is from page 23.

27. *ibid.*

28. For this position, see Sophie B. Oluwole, "On the Existence of Witches", *Second Order: An African Journal of Philosophy*, Vol. VII, No.1 & 2, 1978, pp.20-35; P. O. Bodunrin, "Witchcraft, Magic and E. S. P.: A Defence of Scientific and Philosophical Scepticism", *Second Order, ibid*; pp.36-50.

29. Collingwood, *op.cit.*, p.304.

30. Z. A. Ademuwagun, ' "Alafia"- The Yoruba Concept of Health: Implications for Health Education', *International Journal of Health Education*, XXI, 2, 1978, pp.89-97. See also Godwin Sogolo, "On the Socio-Cultural Conception of Health and Disease in Africa" in *Africa: Rivista trimestrale di studi e documentazione dell'Istituto Italo-Africano*. Anno XLI N. 3, Settembre 1986, pp.390-404.

31. L. Lewis Wall, *Hausa Medicine*, Durham: Duke University Press,1988.

32. Wolfgang Bichmann, "Primary Health Care and Traditional Medicine--Considering the Background of Changing Health Care Concepts in Africa", *Social Science and Medicine*, Vol. 13B, 1979, p.177.

33. Max Gluckman, "Social Beliefs and Individual Thinking in Tribal Society", in Robert Manners and David Kaplan ed., *Theory in Anthropology: A Sourcebook*, Chicago: Aldine, 1968, p.456.

34. Robin Horton, "African Traditional Thought and Western Science", *Africa* XXXVII, Nos.1 and 2 [January and April, 1967], pp.50-71 and 155-87; also reprinted in B. Wilson [ed.] *Rationality*, Oxford: Basil Blackwell, 1970, pp.131-171. This quotation is from p.136 of this book. For a moderate revision of this earlier position, see Robin Horton,"Tradition and Modernity Revisited" in Martin Hollis and Steven Lukes [eds.] *Rationality and Relativism*, Basil Blackwell, 1982, pp.201-260.

35. Peter Morley, "Culture and the Cognitive World of Traditional Medical Beliefs: Some Preliminary Considerations" in Peter Morley and Roy Wallis [eds.], *Culture and Curing: Anthropological Perspectives on Traditional Medical Beliefs and Practices*, University of Pittsburgh Press, 1978, p.16.

36. See A. D. Buckley, *Yoruba Medicine*, Oxford: Clarendon Press, 1985

37. See Wande Abimbola, *Ijinle Ohun Enu Ifa*, Glasgow: Collins, 1968; and *Sixteen Great Poems of Ifa*, UNESCO, 1975.

38. Philip Singer, "Traditional Healing and the Medical/Psychiatric Mafia: An Exclusive Interview with T. A. Lambo" in Philip Singer ed. *Traditional Healing: New Science or New Colonialism?* Conch Magazine Limited, 1977, pp.242-252.

39. Z. A. Ademuwagun, "The Challenge of the Co-existence of Orthodox and Traditional Medicine in Nigeria", *The East African Medical Journal*, Vol. 53, No. 1, 1976, p.21.

Chapter 6

1. David Attah, "Economic Realities in African States", *Daily Times of Nigeria*, November 20, 1972.

2. Obafemi Awolowo, *The Problems of Africa: The Need for Ideological Reappraisal*: Kwame Nkrumah Memorial Lecture, London: Macmillan, 1977, p.48.

3. For more on this, see Ali A. Mazrui, *The African Condition*, New York: Cambridge University Press, 1980.

4. Julius Nyerere, *Ujamaa: Essays in Socialism*, Dares-Salaam: Oxford, 1968, Chapter 1.

5. Karl Marx and Frederick Engels, *The German Ideology* edited by C. J. Arthur, New York: International Publishers, 1947, p.47.

6. Tibor Horvath, "Foreword" to *Ultimate Reality and Meaning: Interdisciplinary Studies in the Philosophy of Understanding*, Vol. 1, No. 1, 1978, p.3.

7. *ibid.*, p.4.

8. Bolaji Idowu, *Olodumare: God in Yoruba Belief*, Lagos: Longmans, 1962, pp.202-215; also John Mbiti, *African Religions and Philosophy*, London: Heinemann, 1969, chapter 20.

9. Mbiti, *ibid.*, p.272.

10. *ibid.*, p.273.

11. *ibid.*, p.274.

12. *ibid.*

13. *ibid.*, pp.276-277.

14. *ibid.*

15. *ibid.* p.205.

16. *ibid.* p.277.

17. *ibid.*

18. Jean-Marc Ela, *My Faith as an African*, Maryknoll, New York: Orbis Books, 1988, p.90.

19. Kwesi Dickson, *Theology in Africa*, Maryknoll, New York: Orbis Books, 1984, pp.124-125.

20. These are indeed very brief remarks. They are accounts of what I consider relevant to the discussion at hand in the injunctions of the various religions. For further accounts of the religions, see the works cited below.

21. See Christ's Sermon on the Mount, [Matthew 5, 6 and 7] which demonstrates the Christian message for the poor in spirit and the down-trodden.

22. St. John 15:13.

23. See, among others, *The Holy Koran*; I. M. Lewis (ed.), *Islam in Tropical Africa*, Oxford: 1966; J. S. Trimingham, *Islam in West Africa*, London, 1959.

24. See Wande Abimbola, *Sixteen Great Poems of Ifa*, UNESCO, 1975; *Awon Oju Odu Mereerindinlogun*, Oxford: University Press, 1977; Bolaji Idowu, *Olodumare: God in Yoruba Belief*, Lagos: Longman, 1962.

Chapter 7

1. See, for instance, Leopold Senghor, *On African Socialism*, trans. by Mercer Cook, New York: Praeger, Inc., 1964; also Leopold Senghor, "Negritude: A Humanism of the Twentieth Century" in W. Cartey and M. Kilson (ed.), *The African Reader: Independent Africa*, New York: Random House, 1970. See also Julius Nyerere, *Freedom and Unity*, London: Oxford University Press, 1967; Okot p'Bitek, *Africa's Cultural Revolution*, Nairobi: Macmillan Books, 1973; and *Artist, the Ruler: Essays on Art, Culture and Values*, Nairobi: Heinemann, 1986; Wole Soyinka, "The African World and the Ethnocultural Debate" in Molefi K. Asante and Kariamu W. Asante eds., *African Culture: The Rhythms of Unity*, Trenton, New Jersey: Africa World Press, 1990.

2. Senghor, *On African Socialism*, p.49.

3. J. Nyerere, "Ujamaa - The Basis of African Socialism", in *Freedom and Unity*, pp.162-171; Senghor, *On African Socialism*, pp.45-46.

4. In what follows, I draw from my "Negritude and its Contribution to the Civilization of the Universal: Leopold Senghor and the Question of Ultimate Reality and Meaning" in *Ultimate Reality and Meaning: Interdisciplinary Studies in the Philosophy of Understanding*, Vol. 14, No. 1, March, 1991, pp.30-45.

5. Leopold Senghor, "Negritude and African Socialism" in *African Affairs*, No.2, 1963. St. Anthony's Papers, No.15, ed. by Kenneth Kirkwood, p.9.

6. Senghor, *ibid*, p.11.

7. Leopold Senghor, "Negritude: A Humanism of the Twentieth Century", *op. cit.*, p.180.

8. Senghor, *On African Socialism*, p.74.

9. Senghor, "Negritude: A Humanism," p.181.

10. *ibid*, p.184.

11. Senghor, "Negritude: A Humanism...", p.185.

12. Senghor, *On African Socialism*, p.26.

13. *ibid*, p.26.

14. *ibid*, p.34.

15. *ibid*, p.36.

16. *ibid*, p.46.

17. *ibid*, p.46.
18. *ibid*, p.49.
19. Senghor, "Negritude and African Socialism", *op. cit*, p.14.
20. *ibid*, p.15.
21. *ibid.*, p.16.
22. Senghor, *On African Socialism*, p.26.
23. *ibid*, p.35.
24. Senghor, "Negritude and African Socialism", p.15.
25. *ibid*, pp.15-16.
26. *ibid.*, p.16.
27. Frantz Fanon, *The Wretched of the Earth*, Paris: Presence Africaine, 1963, p.235.
28. Kwame Nkrumah, "African Socialism Revisited," in Wilfred Cartey and Martin Kilson, ed. *op. cit.*, p.202.
29. *ibid.*, p.203.
30. *ibid.*, p.206.
31. *ibid.*, p.208.
32. W. W. Taylor, "A Study of Archaeology", *American Anthropological Association, Memoir* 69, 1948, pp.98-110 cited by Leslie White, "The Concept of Culture" in F. C. Gamst and E. Norbeck ed., *Ideas of Culture: Sources and Uses*, New York: Holt Rinehart and Winston, 1976, p.64.
33. *ibid.*, p.64.
34. See David Bidney "On the Concept of Culture and Some Cultural Fallacies" in F. C. Gamst and Norbeck, ed., *ibid.*, p.72.
35. Ngugi Wa Thiong'O, *Homecoming: Essay on African and Carribean Literature, Culture and Politics*, Nairobi: Heinemann, 1972 p.4.
36. Amilcar Cabral, "National Liberation and Culture" in *Return to the Source: Selected Speeches of Amilcar Cabral*, New York and London: Monthly Review Press, 1973, p.41.
37. Soyinka, *op.cit.*, p.33.

38. op.cit.

39. I dealt with the impact of colonialism on Nigerian world-views in my "Colonialism and World-view" [unpublished].

40. Lord Lugard, *Dual Mandate in British Tropical Africa*, 1922. See especially the concluding chapter, "The Value of British Rule in the Tropics to British Democracy and Native Races" -reprinted in P. D. Curtin ed., *Imperialism*, Walker & Co., 1972, p.317.

41. Reflections of Ezeuwandez of Ihembosi as recorded by Fr. Raymond Arazu - cited by Elizabeth Isichel, *The Ibo People and the Europeans*, London: Faber and Faber, 1973, p.162.

42. See James Coleman, *Nigeria: Background to Nationalism*, Berkeley & Los Angeles: University of California Press, 1964, p.327.

43. Nwafor Orizu, *Without Bitterness*, New York: Creative Age, 1948, pp.308-9; cited by Nkenna Nzimiro "Zikism and Social Thought in Nigeria" in Onigu Otite ed., *Themes in African Social and Political Thought* Enugu: Fourth Dimension, 1978, p.288.

44. Irving L. Markovitz, *Power and Class in Africa: An Introduction to Change and Conflict in African Politics*, New Jersey: Prentice-Hall, Inc., 1977, p.183.

45. A. O. Alakija, "The African Must Have Western Education" in *Elders Review*, July 1930, pp.94-95, cited by M. Omolewa, "The Adaptation Question in Nigerian Education 1916-1936" in *Journal of Historical Society of Nigeria*, Vol. VIII, No. 3, December, 1976, p.110.

46. ibid, p.115.

47. See Okwuba Nnoli, *Ethnic Politics in Nigeria*, Enugu: Fourth Dimension, 1978, pp.143-144.

48. Contractocracy was first used by a former radical Governor of Kaduna State of Nigeria during the Second Republic, Balarabe Musa, to describe the political system and its fundamental principle. Contractocracy means government of contractors by contractors and for contractors.

49. Jean-Jaques Rousseau, *The Government of Poland*, translated with an introduction by Willmore Kendal, Indianapolis & New York: Bobbs-Merrill, 1972, p.11. See also Abiola Irele, "Culture and the National Idea", *African Philosophical Inquiry*, Vol. 1, No. 2, July, 1987, pp.123-139.

50. Frantz Fanon, *The Wretched of the Earth*, New York: Grove Press, Inc., 1963, p.233.

51. ibid.

52. Okot p'Bitek, "What is Culture" in *Artist, the Ruler: Essays on Art, Culture and Values*, Nairobi: Heinemann 1986, p.13.

53. Aime Cessaire, "Culture and Colonisation", *Presence Africaine*, No. 8-9-10, June-November 1956, p.196.

54. Ngugi Wa Thiong'O, *Homecoming*, p.11.

Chapter 8

1. For case studies of the impact of SAP on African nations and peoples, see Bade Onimode [ed.], *The IMF, The World Bank and the African Debt*, Volume 2: *The Social Impact*, London and New Jersey: Zed Books, 1989.

2. Amilcar Cabral, "The Weapon of Theory" in *Revolution in Guinea*, New York and London: Monthly Review Press, 1969, p.102.

3. Obafemi Awolowo, *The People's Republic*, Ibadan: Oxford University Press, 1968, p.208.

4. Obafemi Awolowo, *Voice of Reason*, Akure: Fagbamigbe Publishers, 1981, pp.195-196.

5. Obafemi Awolowo, *The Problem of Africa: The Need for Ideological Reappraisal*, London: Macmillan, 1977, p.2.

6. *ibid.*, p.7.

7. *ibid.* p.9.

8. *ibid*, p.10.

9. Obafemi Awolowo, *The People's Republic*, p.76: "By his very nature, Man is a social animal. He was never and could never have been 'solitary'."

10. *The Problem of Africa*, p.11.

11. See note 8 above.

12. *The People's Republic*, 1968, p.76-77.

13. *ibid*, p.78.

14. *ibid.*, p.81.

15. *The Problem of Africa*, p.12.

16. See Karl Marx and Friedrich Engels, *The Communist Manifesto*. See also Kwame Nkrumah, *Class Struggle in Africa*, New York: International Publishers, 1970, for a very similar view.

17. Awolowo, *The Problem of Africa*, p.12.

18. *ibid.*, p.13.

19. *The People's Republic*, p.230.

20. *ibid.*

21. *The Problem of Africa*, p.15.

22. *ibid*, p.28.

23. *ibid*, p.49.

24. *ibid.*, p.48.

25. *ibid.*, p.55.

26. *ibid.*, pp.60-61.

27. *ibid.*, p.63.

28. *ibid.*, p.67.

29. Obafemi Awolowo, *Voice of Reason*, p.155.

30. *ibid*, p.156.

31. *ibid.* pp.39-46. For more on this, see my "Obafemi Awolowo and the Politics of Democratic Socialism" in Olasope Oyelaran et.al., *Obafemi Awolowo: The End of an Era?* Ile-Ife: Obafemi Awolowo University Press, 1988, pp.166-177.

Chapter 9

1. John Dewey, *Democracy and Education*, New York: Macmillan, 1916, pp.205-6; cited by Richard Burke in ' "Work" and "Play" ', *Ethics*, 82, No. 1, October 1971, pp.33-47.

2. *Nichomachean Ethics* 117c20-23.

3. *Aristotle's Politics* 125c2-4d.

Notes

4. The connection between work as productive activity and humanity is explored extensively by Marx in *The Economic and Philosophic Manuscripts of 1844*. See also Bertell Ollman, *Alienation: Marx's Conception of Man in Capitalist Society*, Cambridge, 1976.

5. Sigmund Freud, *Civilization and its Discontents*, James Strachey [ed.], New York: Norton 1961, p.27n.

6. Marcus Aurelius, *Meditations* Eks. V and VII.

7. Julius Nyerere, *Ujamaa: Essays on Socialism*, Dar-es-Salaam: Oxford , 1968, p.4.

8. Article 23, par. 1 of the Universal Declaration of Human Rights Adopted by General Assembly resolution 217A (iii) of 10 December, 1948, reprinted in James Avery Joyce (ed.) *Human Rights: International Documents* Vol. 1 , New York: Sijthoff & Noordhoff, 1978, pp. 10-12.

9. See Ronald Dworkin, *Taking Rights Seriously*, Cambridge, Mass., 1977 and Joel Feinberg, "Duties, Rights and Claims", *American Philosophical Quarterly* Vol. 3 1966, pp.137-144.

10. See Marcus G. Singer, "The Basis of Rights and Duties", *Philosophical Studies*, 23, 1972 pp.48-57 (esp. p. 50).

11. For example, Maurice Cranston, in *What are Human Rights*, New York: Basic Books, 1973.

12. See my "The Concept of Inalienable Rights", *Second Order: An African Journal of Philosophy*, [Special Issue: Ethics and African Societies] Vol. 1, No. 2, July 1988, pp.57-77.

13. For this idea of civic right, see Carl Wellman, *Welfare Rights*, Rowman & Allanheld: Totowa, 1982, Chap. 5.

14. Notice, however, that the United Nations Declaration asserts the right to work and to property.

15. See James Nickel, "Is There a Human Right to Employment?", *The Philosophical Forum* X, No. 2-4, 1978-9 pp.149-170.

16. Robert Nozick, *Anarchy, State and Utopia*, New York: Basic Books, 1974.

17. Haskell Fain, *Normative Politics and the Community of Nations*, Temple University Press, 1987 p.119.

18. *ibid.*, p.125.

19. *ibid.*, p.158.

20. See James Nickel, *op.cit.*

Chapter 10

1. For a general discussion of the problems faced by statesmen in their approach to the choice of models, see among others, K. A. Busia, *The Challenge of Africa*, New York: Praeger, 1962, especially, Part 1V; *Africa in Search of Democracy*, London: Routledge and Kegan Paul, 1967; Julius Nyerere, *Freedom and Unity*, London: Oxford University Press, 1967; Kwame Nkrumah, *Consciencism: Philosophy and Ideology for Decolonisation*, London: Panaf, 1970; Obafemi Awolowo, *The Problem of Africa: The Need for Ideological Reappraisal*, London: Macmillan, 1977.

2. See Kwame Nkrumah, *Class Struggle in Africa*, London: Panaf, 1970; *Consciencism*, Obafemi Awolowo, *The Problem of Africa*; *The People's Republic*, Ibadan: Oxford University Press, 1968.

3. Prominent among the advocates of this approach are Julius Nyerere and Leopold Senghor. See Nyerere's "Ujamaa: The Basis of African Socialism" in *Freedom and Unity*, pp.162-171; Senghor's *On African Socialism* trans. by Mercer Cook, New York: Praeger, 1964.

4. See Obafemi Awolowo, *The People's Republic*; and *The Problem of Africa*, for a defence of this approach.

5. For more on this, see Segun Gbadegesin and Oladimeji Alo, "The Theme of Causation and Contemporary Work Attitude Among Nigerians", *ODU: A Journal of West African Studies*, No 31, January 1987, pp.15-31.

BIBLIOGRAPHY

Abimbola, Wande, "*Iwapele*: The Concept of Good Character in *Ifa* Literary Corpus" in Wande Abimbola ed., *Yoruba Oral Tradition*, Ife African Languages and Literatures Series No. 1, 1975.

_____. *Sixteen Great Poems of Ifa*, UNESCO, 1975.

_____. *Yoruba Oral Traditions*, Ile-Ife: African Languages and Literatures Seminar Series, No 1, 1975, *Awon Oju Odu Mereerindinlogun*, Oxford University Press, 1977.

_____. *Ijinle Ohun Enu Ifa*, Glasgow: Collins, 1968.

_____. "The Yoruba Concept of Human Personality" in *La Notion de Personne en Afrique Noire*, Centre National de la Recherche Scientifique, No. 544, 1971, pp.73-89.

Abiodun, Roland, "Identity and the Artistic Process in Yoruba Aesthetic Concept of *Iwa*", *Journal of Cultures and Ideas*, Vol. 1, No. 1, 1983, pp.13-30.

Abraham, W. E., *The Mind of Africa*, The University of Chicago Press, 1962.

Achebe, Chinua, *Morning Yet on Creation Day*, New York: Anchor Press, 1975.

Adedeji, Adebayo, *Towards a Dynamic African Economy: Selected Speeches and Lectures, 1975-1986*, London: Frank Cass, 1989.

Ademuwagun, Z. A., "The Challenge of the Co-existence of Orthodox and Traditional Medicine in Nigeria" in *The East Africa Medica Journal*, Vol. 53, No. 1, 1976.

_____. "*Alaafia*"- The Yoruba Concept of Health: Implications for Health Education", *International Journal of Health Education*, XXI, 2, 1978, pp.89-97.

Aig-Imoukhuede, Frank, "Culture and National Development: Structures, Institutions and Strategies as Concerns of a National Policy", Public Lecture at the Annual Faculty Lecture of the Faculty of Arts, Obafemi Awolowo University, Ile-Ife, Nigeria, July 28, 1989.

Ake, Claude, *A Political Economy of Africa*, Lagos: Longmans, 1981.

Alakija, A. O., "The African Must Have Western Education", *Elders Review*, July, 1930, pp.94-95.

Aristotle, *Politics*.

Aristotle, *Nichomachean Ethics*.

Asante, Molefi K., and Asante, Kariamu W., *African Culture: The Rhythms of Unity*, Trenton, New Jersey: African World Press, 1990.

Awolowo, Obafemi, *The Problem of Africa: The Need for Ideological Reappraisal*, London: Macmillan, 1977.

_____. *The People's Republic*, Ibadan: Oxford University Press, 1968.

_____. *Voice of Reason*, Akure: Fagbamigbe Publishers, 1981.

Ba, Sylvia, *The Concept of Negritude in the Poetry of Leopold Sedan Senghor*, New Jersey: Princeton University Press, 1973.

Barber, Karin, "How Man Makes God in West Africa: Yoruba Attitudes Towards the *Orisa*", *Africa*, 51, 3, 1981, pp.724-745.

Barber, Karin and de Moraes Farias, P. F. eds., *Discourse and its Disguises: The Interpretation of African Oral Texts*, Birmingham: Center of West African Studies, 1989.

Benn, S. I., and Peters, R. S., *Principles of Political Thought*, London: George Allen and Unwin, 1959,

Bichmann, Wolfgang, "Primary Health Care and Traditional Medicine- Considering the Background of Changing Health Care Concepts in Africa", *Social Science and Medicine*, Vol. 13B, 1979.

Bidney, David, "On the Concept of Culture and Some Cultural Fallacies", in F. C. Gamst and E. Norbeck, *Ideas of Culture: Sources and Uses*, New York: Holt Rinehart and Winston, 1976.

Blocker, Gene, "African Philosophy" in *African Philosophical Inquiry*, Vol. 1, No. 1, January 1987.

Bodunrin, P. O., "Human Rights and Democracy in Africa", *African Philosophical Inquiry*, Vol.1, No. 2, 1987.

_____. "Witchcraft, Magic and E. S. P: A Defence of Scientific and Philosophical Scepticism", *Second Order*, Vol. VII, Nos. 1 & 2, 1978, pp.36-50.

_____. "The Question of African Philosophy", in *Philosophy*, 56, 1981, pp.161-181; reprinted in Richard Wright ed., *African Philosophy: An Introduction*, Lanham: University Press of America, 1984.

_____. *Philosophy in Africa: Trends and Perspectives*, Ile-Ife: University of Ife Press, 1985.

Buckley, A. D., *Yoruba Medicine*, Oxford: Clarendon Press, 1985.

Burke, Richard, ' "Work" and "Play" ', *Ethics*, 82, No. 1, October, 1971, pp.33-47.

Busia, K. A., *The Challenge of Africa*, New York: Fredrick Praeger, 1962.

_____. *Africa in Search of Democracy*, London: Routledge and Kegan Paul, 1967

Cabral, Amilcar, "National Liberation and Culture" in *Return to Source: Selected Speeches of Amilcar Cabral*, New York: Monthly Review Press.

_____. "Weapon of Theory", in *Revolution in Guinea*, New York: Monthly Review Press, 1969.

Cesaire Aime, "Culture and Colonisation", *Presence Africaine*, 1964.

Chatalian, George, "Philosophy, The World and Man: A Global Conception", Inaugural Lecture delivered at the University of Ife [now Obafemi Awolowo University], Nigeria, June 28, 1983.

Coleman, James, *Nigeria: Background to Nationalism*, Berkeley: University of California Press, 1964.

Collingwood, R. J., *An essay on Metaphysics*, Chicago: Gateway, 1972.

Cranston, Maurice, *What Are Human Rights?* New York: Basic Books, 1973.

Curtin, P. D. ed., *Imperialism*, Walker & co, 1972.

Davidson, Basil, *Can Africa Survive?*, Boston: Atlantic-Little, Brown & Co. 1974.

Dewey, John, *Democracy and Education*, New York: Macmillan, 1916.

Dickson, Kwesi, *Theology in Africa*, New York, Maryknoll: Orbis, 1984.

Diop, Cheik Anta, *The African Origin of Civilization: Myth or Reality*, Edited and translated by Mercer Cook, Chicago: Lawrence Hill, 1974.

Donders, Joseph, *Non-Bourgeois Theology: An African Experience of Jesus*, Maryknoll, New York, 1985.
Dumont, Rene and Motin, Marie-France, *Stranglehold on Africa*, London: Andre Deutsch, 1983
Dworkin, Ronald, *Taking Rights Seriously*, Cambridge, Mass: Harvard University Press, 1977.
Ebousi-Boulaga, F., *Christianity Without Fetishes*, Maryknoll, New York, 1984.
Ela, Jean-Marc, *My Faith as an African*, Maryknoll, New York: Orbis, 1988.
_____. *African Cry*, Maryknoll, New York, 1980.
Engels, Frederick, *Anti-Duhring*, Moscow: Progress Publishers, 1975.
Fabunmi, M. A., *Ayajo Ohun Ife*, Ibadan: Onibonoje Press, 1972
Fadipe, N. A., *The Sociology of the Yoruba*, edited with an Introduction by F. Olu Okediji and O. O. Okediji, Ibadan University Press, 1970.
Fain, Haskell, *Normative Politics and the Community of Nations*, Temple University Press, 1987.
Fanon, Frantz, *The Wretched of the Earth*, New York: Grove Press, Inc., 1963.
Featherstone, Mike, ed., *Global Culture: Nationalism, Globalization and Modernity*, Sage Publications, 1990.
Feinberg, Joel, "Duties, Rights and Claims", *American Philosophical Quarterly*, Vol. 3, 1966, Pp. 137-144.
Freud, Sigmund, *Civilisation and its Discontents*, James Stratchey ed., New York: Norton, 1961.
Gbadegesin, Segun, "Kwame Nkrumah and the Search for URAM", *Ultimate Reality and Meaning: An Interdisciplinary Studies in the Philosophy of Understanding*, Vol.10, No. 1 1987, pp.14-28.
_____."The Concept of Inalienable Rights" in *Second Order: An African Journal of Philosophy* Vol.1 No.2, July 1988, pp.57-77.
_____."Destiny, Personality and the Ultimate Reality of Human Existence: A Yoruba Perspective", *Ultimate Reality and Meaning: An Interdisciplinary Studies in the Philosophy of Understanding*, Vol 7, No. 3, 1984 pp.165-178.

_____. "Ethnicity and Citizenship", *Second Order*, Vol.10, Nos. 1 & 2, 1981, pp.3-13.

_____. "God, Destiny and Social Injustice: A Critique of a Yoruba ifa Belief" in Gene James ed., *The Search for Faith and Justice in the Twentieth Century*, New York: Paragon Press, 1987, pp.52-68.

_____. "Rousseau, Nyerere and the Politics of General Interest", *Praxis International* Vol.4, No. 2, April, 1984, pp.166-176.

_____. "World view" in Toyin Falola and Biodun Adediran ed., *A New History of Nigeria for Colleges*, Lagos: West Press, 1985.

_____. "Negritude and its Contribution to the Civilization of the Universal: Leopold Senghor and the Question of Ultimate Reality and Meaning", *Ultimate Reality and Meaning: Interdisciplinary Studies in the Philosophy of Understanding*, Vol. 14, No. 1, March, 1991, pp.30-45.

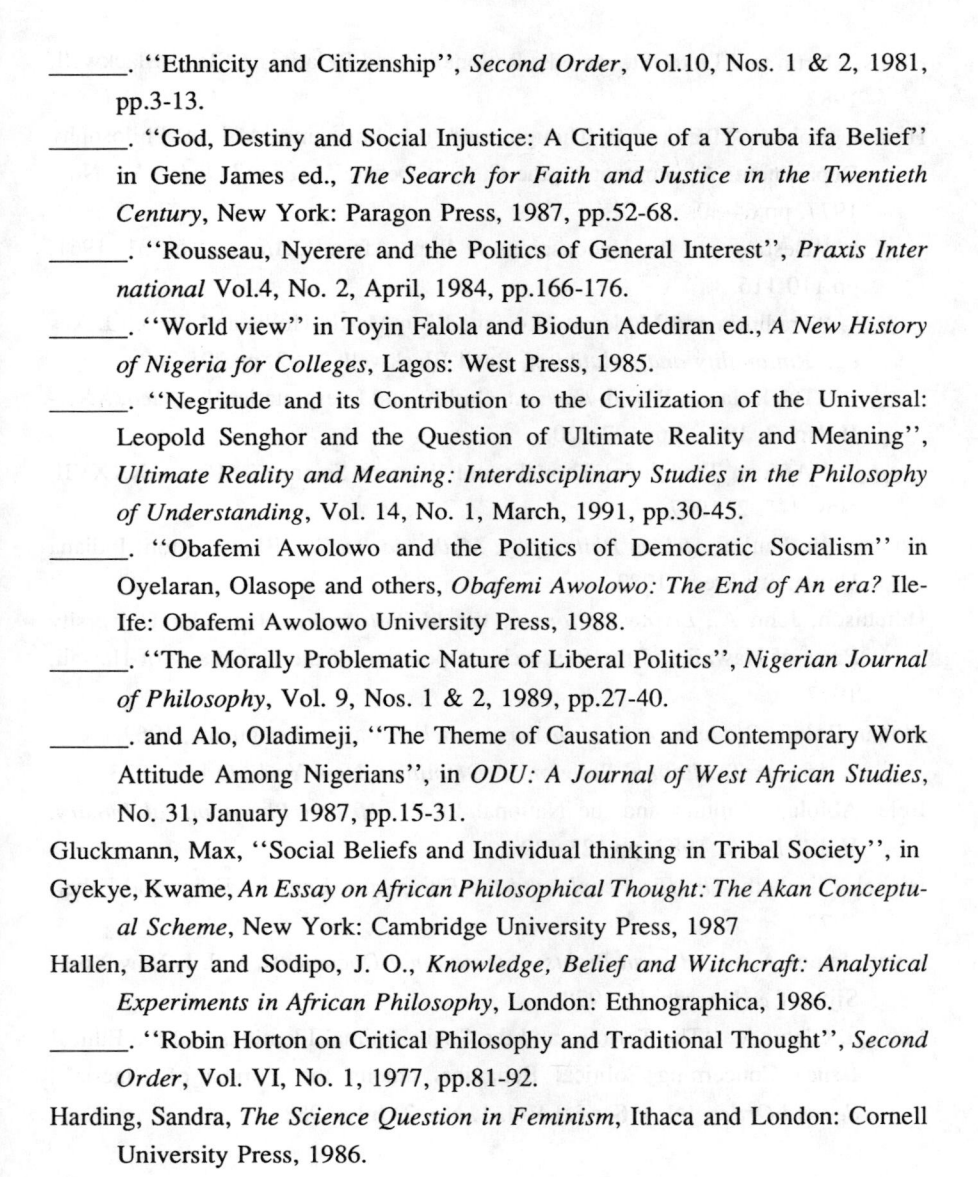

_____. "Obafemi Awolowo and the Politics of Democratic Socialism" in Oyelaran, Olasope and others, *Obafemi Awolowo: The End of An era?* Ile-Ife: Obafemi Awolowo University Press, 1988.

_____. "The Morally Problematic Nature of Liberal Politics", *Nigerian Journal of Philosophy*, Vol. 9, Nos. 1 & 2, 1989, pp.27-40.

_____. and Alo, Oladimeji, "The Theme of Causation and Contemporary Work Attitude Among Nigerians", in *ODU: A Journal of West African Studies*, No. 31, January 1987, pp.15-31.

Gluckmann, Max, "Social Beliefs and Individual thinking in Tribal Society", in

Gyekye, Kwame, *An Essay on African Philosophical Thought: The Akan Conceptual Scheme*, New York: Cambridge University Press, 1987

Hallen, Barry and Sodipo, J. O., *Knowledge, Belief and Witchcraft: Analytical Experiments in African Philosophy*, London: Ethnographica, 1986.

_____. "Robin Horton on Critical Philosophy and Traditional Thought", *Second Order*, Vol. VI, No. 1, 1977, pp.81-92.

Harding, Sandra, *The Science Question in Feminism*, Ithaca and London: Cornell University Press, 1986.

Hollis, Martin and Luke, Steven eds, *Rationality and Relativism*, Basil Blackwell, 1982.

Horton, Robin, "Traditional Thought and the Emerging African Philosophy Department: A comment on the Current Debate", *Second Order*, VI, No.1 1977, pp.64-80.

_____. "Destiny and the Unconscious in West Africa", *Africa*, Vol. 31, 1961, pp.110-116.

_____. "Tradition and Modernity Revisited" in Martin Hollis and Steven Lukes ed., *Rationality and Relativism*, Basil Blackwell, 1982, pp.201-260.

_____. "The Kalabari World-view: An Outline and Interpretation", *Africa*, XXXII, No. 3, 1962, pp. 197-220.

_____. "African Traditional Thought and Western Science", *Africa*, XXXVII, Nos. 1 & 2, 1967.

Hountondji, Paulin, *African Philosophy: Myth and Reality*, Bloomington: Indiana University Press, 1983.

Hutchison, John A., *Living Options in World Philosophy*, Honolulu: University Press of Hawaii and the Research Corporation of the University of Hawaii, 1977.

Idowu, Bolaji, *Olodumare: God in Yoruba Belief*, Lagos: Longmans, 1962

_____. *African Traditional Religion: A Definition*, New York: Orbis, 1973

Irele, Abiola, "Culture and the National Idea", *African Philosophical Inquiry*, Vol.1, No. 2, 1987, pp.123-139

Isichel, Elizabeth, *The Ibo People and the Europeans*, London: Faber and Faber, 1973.

Joyce, James A. ed., *Human Rights: International Documents*, Vol. I, New York: Sijthoff & Noordhoff, 1978.

Lawuyi, Olatunde, "The Tortoise and the Snail: Animal Identities and the Ethical Issues Concerning Political Behaviors among the Yoruba of Nigeria", *Second Order*, [New Series] Vol. 1, No. 2, July 1988.

Lewy, Guenter, *Religion and Revolution*, New York: Oxford University Press, 1974.

Lowie, R. H., *Culture and Ethnology*, New York: Boni and Liveright, 1917.

Lugard, Lord, *Dual Mandate in British Tropical Africa*, 1922.

Makinde, M. A., *African Philosophy, Culture, and Traditional Medicine*, Athens: Ohio University Press, 1988.

———. "Immortality of the Soul and the Yoruba theory of Seven Heavens [*Orun Meje*]", *Journal of Cultures and Ideas*, Vol. 1, No. 1, 1983, pp.31-59.

———. "A Philosophical Analysis of the Yoruba Concepts of Ori and Human Destiny", *International Studies in Philosophy*, XVII, No. 1, 1985, pp.53-69.

———. "African Cultures and Moral Systems: A Philosophical Study", *Second Order* [New Series], Vol. 1, No. 2, July 1988, pp.1-27.

Markovitz, Irvin L., *Power and Class in Africa: An introduction to Change and Conflict in African Politics*, New Jersey: Prentice-Hall, Inc., 1977.

Marx, Karl, *The Economic and Philosophical Manuscripts of 1844*.

Marx, Karl and Engels, Frederick, *The German Ideology*, edited by C. J. Arthur, New York: International Publishers, 1947.

Marx, Karl, *A Contribution to the Critique of Political Economy*, Chicago: Kerr, 1904.

Mazrui, Ali, *World Culture and the Black Experience*, Seattle and London: University of Washinton Press, 1974.

———. *The African Condition*, Cambridge University Press, 1980.

Mbiti, John S., *African Religions and Philosophy*, London: Heinemann, 1969.

———. *Introduction to African Religions*, London: Heinemann, 1975.

———. *Concepts of God in Africa*, London/ New York: Heinemann, 1970

Minkus, Helaine K., "Causal Theory in Akwapim Akan Philosophy" in Richard Wright ed., *African Philosophy: An Introduction*, Lanham: University Press of America, 1984.

Morley, Peter, "Culture and the Cognitive World of Traditional Medical Beliefs: Some Preliminary Considerations" in Peter Morley and Roy Wallis eds.,

Culture and Curing: Anthropological Perspectives on Traditional Medical Beliefs and Practices, University of Pittsburgh Press, 1978.

Mosley, Albert, "The Metaphysics of Magic: Practical and Philosophical Implications", *Second Order*, Vol. VII Nos. 1 & 2, Jan/July 1978.

Mudimbe, V. Y., *The Invention of Africa: Gnosis, Philosophy and the Order of Knowledge*, Bloomington: Indiana University Press, 1988.

Nickel, James, "Is There a Human Right to Employment?", *The Philosophical Forum*, X, No. 2-4, 1978-79, pp.149-170.

Nkrumah, Kwame, *Neocolonialism: The Last Stage of Imperialism*, New York: International Publishers, 1969.

_____. *Consciencism: Philosophy and Ideology for Decolonisation,* New York: Monthly Review, 1964.

_____. *Class Struggle in Africa*, New York: International Publishers.

_____. "African Socialism Revisited" in Cartey, Wilfred and Kilson, Martin, *The African Reader: Independent Africa*, New York: Random House, 1970.

Nnoli, Okwuba, *Ethnic Politics in Nigeria*, Enugu: Fourth Dimension, 1978.

Nozick, Robert, *Anarchy, State and Utopia*, New York: Basic Books, 1974.

Nwala, Uzodinma, *Igbo Philosophy*, Lagos: Literamed, 1985.

Nyerere, Julius, *Freedom and Unity*, London: Oxford University Press, 1967

_____. *Ujamaa: The Basis of African Socialism*, Dar-es-Salaam: Oxford University Press, 1968.

Nzimiro, Nkenna, "Zikism and Social Thought in Nigeria" in Onigu Otite ed., *Themes in African Social and Political Thought*, Enugu: Fourth Dimension, 1978.

Oduyoye, Mercy Amba, *Hearing and Knowing: Theological Reflections on Christianity in Africa*, Maryknoll, New York: Orbis, 1986.

Okot P' Bitek, *African Religions in Western Scholarship*, Nairobi: East African Literature Bureau, 1970.

_____. "On Culture, Man and Freedom", in Odera Oruka and D. A. Masolo ed., *Philosophy and Cultures*, Nairobi: Bookwise Ltd., 1983.

_____. *Africa's Cultural Revolution*, Nairobi: Macmillan, 1973.
Oladeji, Niyi, "Proverbs as Signposts in Yoruba Pragmatic Ethics", *Second Order* [New Series], Vol. 1, No. 2, July 1988.
Oladipo, Olusegun, *An African Conception of Reality: A Philosophical Analysis*, Ph. D Dissertation submitted to the University of Ibadan, 1988.
Ollman, Bertell, *Alienation: Marx's Conception of Man in Capitalist Society*, Cambridge, 1976.
Oluwole, S. B., "On the Existence of Witches", *Second Order*, Vol. Vii, Nos. 1 & 2, 1978, pp.20-35.
Omolewa, M., "The Adaptation Question in Nigerian Education, 1916-1936" in *Journal of the Historical Society of Nigeria*, Vol. VIII, NO. 3, December, 1976.
Orizu, Nwafor, *Without Bitterness*, New York: Creative Age, 1948.
Oruka, Odera, "Fundamental Principles in the Question of African Philosophy", *Second Order*, Vol.IV, 1975, pp.44-55.
_____. "Mythologies in African Philosophy", *East African Journal*, 9, No. 10, 1972.
_____. *Sage Philosophy: Indigenous Thinkers and Modern Debate on African Philosophy*, Leiden and New York: E. J. Brill, 1990.
_____. "What is African Philosophy", Presented at the William Amo International Symposium, Accra, Ghana, 1978.
Oseghare, A. S., "Sage philosophy: A New Orientation in African Philosophy" in Odera Oruka ed., *Sage Philosophy: Indigenous Thinkers and Modern Debate on African Philosophy*, Leiden and New York: E. J. Brill, 1990, pp.249-258.
Otite, Onigu, *Themes in African Social and Political Thought*, Enugu: Fourth Dimension, 1978.
Outlaw, L., "African Philosophy: Deconstructive and Reconstructive Challenges", in Odera Oruka ed., *Sage Philosophy: Indigenous thinkers and Modern Debate on African Philosophy*, Leiden and New York: E. J. Brill, 1990, pp.223-248.

Oyelaran, Olasope and others, *Obafemi Awolowo: The End of An era?*, Ile-Ife: Obafemi Awolowo University Press, 1988.

Penner, Hans H., "Rationality, Ritual and Science", in Jacob Neusner, Ernst S. Fredrichs and Paul Virgil M. Flesher ed., *Religion, Science and Magic*, New York: Oxford University Press, 1989, pp. 11-24.

Price-William, D. H., "A Case Study of Ideas Concerning Diseases Among the Tiv", *Africa*, 23, April 1960, pp.123-131.

Rawls, John, *A Theory of Justice*, Oxford University Press, 1971.

Robert Manners and David Kaplan ed., *Theory in Anthropology: A Sourcebook*, Chicago: Aldine, 1968.

Rotimi, Ola, *The Gods Are Not To Blame*, London & Ibadan: Oxford University Press, 1971.

Rousseau, Jean-Jacques, *The Government of Poland* translated with an Introduction by Wilmore Kendall, Indianapolis and New York: Bobs-Merill, 1972.

Senghor, Leopold, "The Spirit of Civilisation or the Laws of African Negro Culture' in *Presence Africaine*, No. 8-9-10 June-November, 1956.

_____. "Constructive Elements of a Civilization of African Negro Inspiration", *Presence Africaine*, 1964.

_____. *On African Socialism*, translated by Mercer Cook, New York: Praeger, Inc., 1964.

_____. "Negritude and African Socialism" in *African Affairs*, No. 2, 1963.

_____. "Negritude: A Humanism of the Twentieth Century" in W. Cartey and M. Kilson ed., *The African Reader: Independent Africa*, New York: Random House, 1970.

Sindima, Harvey, "Community of Life", *The Ecumenical Review*, Vol 41, 1989, pp.537-551

Singer, Marcus G., "The Basis of Rights and Duties", *Philosophical Studies*, 23, 1972, pp.48-57.

_____. "Two American Philosophers: Morris Cohen and Arthur Murphy", in Marcus G. Singer, ed., *American Philosophy*: Royal Institute of Philosophy Lecture Series, 19: Supplement to *Philosophy*, 1985.

_____. *American Philosophy*, Royal Institute of Philosophy Lecture Series, 19: Supplement to *Philosophy*, Cambridge University Press, 1985.

Singer, Philip, "Traditional Healing and the Medical/Psychiatric Mafia: An Exclusive Interview with T. A. Lambo" in Philip Singer ed., *Traditional Healing: New Science or New Colonialism?* Conch Magazine Limited, 1977, pp.242-252.

Sodipo, J. O., "Philosophy in Pre-Colonial Africa", in *Teaching and Research in Philosophy: Africa*, UNESCO, 1984.

_____. "Notes on the Concept of Cause and Chance in Yoruba Traditional Thought", *Second Order*, Vol. 2, No. 2, 1973, pp.16-18.

Sogolo, Godwin, "On the Socio-Cultural Conception of Health and Disease in Africa", in *Africa: Rivista trimestrale di studi e documentazione dell'Istituto Italo-Africano*. Anno XLI N. 3, Settembre 1986, pp.390-404.

_____. "Options in African Philosophy", *Philosophy*, 65, 1990, pp.39-52.

Soyinka, Wole, "The African World and the Ethnocultural Debate", in Asante, Molefi K. and Asante, Kariamu W. ed., *African Culture: The Rhythms of Unity*, Trenton, New Jersey: Africa World Press, 1990.

Taylor, W. W., *The Study of Archaeology*, 1948.

Tempels, Placide, *Bantu Philosophy*, Paris: Presence Africaine, 1969.

Wa Thiong'O, Ngugi, *Homecoming*, Nairobi: Heinemann, 1972.

Wall, Lewis, *Hausa Medicine*, Durham: Duke University Press, 1988.

Wellman, Carl, *Welfare Rights*, Totowa: Rowman & Allanheld, 1982.

White, Leslie, "The Concept of Culture" in F. C. Gamst and E. Norbeck eds., *Ideas of Culture: Sources and Uses*, New York: Holt Rinehart and Winston, 1976.

Wilson, Brian ed., *Rationality*, Basil Blackwell, 1970.

Wiredu, Kwasi, "Universalism and Particularism in Religion from an African Perspective", *Journal of Humanism and Ethical Religion*, Vol. 3, No. 1, Fall 1990.

_____. "On Defining African Philosophy", Paper Presented to the Association Ivorienne des Professors de Philosophie, Abidjan, Ivory Coast.

_____. "The Moral Foundations of African Culture", Presented at Conference on African American Perspectives on Biomedical Ethics at Georgetown University, Washington D. C. November 1990.

_____. "The African Concept of Personhood", Presented at Conference on African-American Perspectives on Biomedical Ethics at Georgetown University, Washington D. C. November 1990.

_____. *Philosophy and an African Culture*, New York: Cambridge University Press, 1979.

_____. "Philosophical Research and Teaching in Africa: Some Suggestions", in *Teaching and Research in Philosophy: Africa*, UNESCO, 1984, pp.31-54

_____. "The Akan Concept of Mind", *Ibadan Journal of the Humanities*, No. 3, October, 1983.

Wright, Richard A., ed., *African Philosophy: An Introduction*, Lanham: University Press of America, 1984.

Yai, Olabiyi, "Theory and Practice in African Philosophy: The Poverty of Speculative Philosophy", *Second Order*, Vol. II, No. 2, 1977.

Yinger, J. Milton, *The Scientific Study of Religion*, London: The Macmillan Company, 1970.

INDEX

Abayomi, K., 182
Abimbola, Wande, 76, 88 122ff.
Abraham, W. E., 94
Academic work
  as self-realization, 222
Ademuwagun, Z. A., 136
African philosophy
  a conception of, 22
  as communal thought, 7
  as written texts, 7
  and American philosophy, 23
  nature of 1
African proverbs
  as sources of philosophy, 4
  African traditional religion, 83ff.
African traditional thought, 1ff.
Agbo-ilé [compound], 62
Aìlera, 127
Ajala
  and the choice of *orí*, 36
Ajogun, 102
Akan religiosity
  Gyekye on, 93
  Wiredu on, 95
Akinsanya, Samuel, 182
Aláàfià, 127
Alakija, A. O., 181
American philosophy, 9
Ancestors, 88
Ara, 28
Aristotle, 219
Awolowo, Obafemi
  on principles of statehood, 206
  on Marxism, 197
  on African socialism, 192
  on the problem of Africa, 192ff
Ayajó, principles of, 120
Azikwe, Nnamdi, 182
Baalé [compound head], 63
Baasègùn, 176
Babaláwo, 76, 176

Bantu Philosophy, 2
Barber, Karin, 96
Blocker, Gene, 6
Bodunrin, P. O., 19
Bourgeois nationalism, 180
Busia, K. A., 95, 109
Capitalism, 162
Categorical imperative, 74
Causal explanation
  features of, 111
  levels of, 116
Cause
  relativity of, 125
  senses of, 105
Christianity
  and CAR, 148
  and conversion, 97
  and peace, 97
Civil religion, 146
Claim-right, 234
Classlessness, 162
Co-wives, 63
Cohen, Morris, 23
Collingwood, R. J., 105
Colonialism
  and cultural dependency, 161
  and culture, 179
Communalism, 61, 65, 162
Communism, 162
Community
  human dependence on, 58
  in traditional thought, 61
Confederacy, 208
Conflicts
  in traditional societies, 66
Contemplation, as work, 222
Contemporary African Realities
  principles of explanation, 137ff.
  Views of, 137ff.
  the politico-economic view, 189ff
Cultural dependency, 161

Culture
   and social existence, 174ff.
   and national liberation, 187ff.
   Cabral on, 174
   conceptions of, 172ff.
   Fanon on, 185-186
   Nguigi Wa Thiong'o on, 174
   Okot p'Bitek on, 186
Democratic citizenship, 213
Destiny
   Akan conception of, 56
   and immortality, 46
   and meaning of life, 46
   and reincarnation, 46
   and responsibility, 46
   as àkúnlẹ̀gbà, 47
   as àkúnlẹ̀yàn, 47
   as àyànmó, 47
   change of, 55
   choice of, 46ff.
   Yoruba conception of, 56ff.
Development
   and cultural beliefs, 260
   and human welfare, 261
   approaches to, 258
   problem of, 255
Dewey, John
   on work, 217
Diarchy/Triarchy, 209
Diviner, 134ff
Edwards, 23
Eémí, 33
Egúngún [masquerade], 89
Emerson, 23
Emí, 28
Employment, right to, 251ff
Enìyàn, 27ff
Equality, 162ff
Erò [thought], 32
Esè [leg], 56
Ethnophilosophy, 3
Euthyphro question, 75
Evans-Pritchard, 130
Fabunmi, M. A., 122
Fagunwa, D. O., 118

Fain, Haskell, 243
Freud, S., 223
Gbadegesin, Joseph, 120
Gluckman, 130
Golden rule, 74
Gyekye, Kwame, 18, 57ff
Health, conceptions of, 127ff
Herbalist, 129
Hobbes, T., 250
Horton, Robin, 15
Hountondji, P., 4ff
Humanism
   and religion, 150
   in Marxism, 166
Ikoli, Ernest, 182
Illness, 128ff
Imalè [invisible forces], 92
Immortality, and destiny, 46
Incantation, 120ff
Individuality, in traditional thought, 61
International Monetary Fund, 190
ire and ibi, 76
Irònú, 32
Islam
   and CAR, 148
   and peace, 103
Iwà
   as character, 79ff
   as existence, 79ff
   primacy of, 79ff
James, 23
Kádàrá [destiny], 48
Kant, Immanuel, 74
Kantian tradition, 20
Lambo, T. A., 135
Legal conceptualism, 245
Levy-Bruhl, 18, 130
Locke, J., 250
Marcus Aurelius, 225
Marx, K., 220ff
Materfamilias, 195
Mbatsav, 117
Mbiti, J. S. 3ff, 145ff
Mental magnitude, 198
Mill, John Stuart, 75
Moral values, 61ff

Morality
    and religion, 61
    basis of, 67ff
    schools of, 68
    in Yoruba thought, 69ff
    a critique of Idowu, 69ff
    a critique of Makinde, 69ff
    Idowu on, 68
Moremi, 64
Morley, Peter, 131
Mudimbe, V. Y., 11
Multinational corporations, 189
Mythical thought, 15
Myths, 83
Naming, significance of, 61
Natural-supernatural distinction
    Busia on, 110
    Wiredu on, 110
Naturalism, 108
Negritude, 161ff
Nigeria
    national culture, 176ff
    constitution, 233
    economy, 210ff
Nigerian Youth Movement, 181
Nozick, Robert, 242
Nyerere, J., 162
Odù Ifá, 76
Ogún [god of iron and war], 93
Okàn, 28
Okra, 42
Olódùmarè
    and choice of destiny, 49
    as supreme deity, 90ff
One-Party system, 209
Onyame, 57ff
Opolo, 29ff
Oral traditions, 83
Orí, 28ff
    as bearer of destiny, 36
    as determinant of personality, 36
Orisà-nlá, 28
Orizu, Nwafor, 180
Orúnmìlà, 73, 79ff
P'Bitek, Okot, 84

Paterfamilias, 195
Penner, Hans, 124
Person
    Akan and Yoruba concepts of, 42ff
Personality,
    determinant of, 36
Philosophy
    African, 1ff
    American, 19ff, 23-25
    and communal thought, 8-15
    and literacy, 16
    and the African crisis, 22
    British, 19
    European, 20
    Greek, 20
    tradition of, 19-21
    traditional Yoruba, 27-136
    western, 9ff
Pierce, 20
Planes of existence, 87ff
Political community
    task theory of, 245
Political philosophy, 208ff
Poverty, as a social problem, 230ff
Pragmatism, 19-20
Radical theology, 152
Rationality, 124ff
Reincarnation, 46
Religion
    and liberation, 159
    defined, 84
    in Yoruba world-view, 85ff
Religious pluralism, 155ff
Religious violence, 158ff
Right to work
    justification of, 240ff
    meaning of, 237
Rotimi, Ola, 52
Rousseau, J., 250
Sàngó [god of thunder], 97
Second Order, 119
Self-realization, 230
Self-reliance 162
Senghor, L
    and African socialism, 168ff
    and Marxism, 165ff

and negritude, 162ff
    criticisms of, 169
Singer, Marcus. G., 22
Socialization, process of, 63
Sodipo, J. O., 24
Sogolo, Godwin, 18
Spiritual beings, 86
Structural Adjustment Programs, 190
Sunsum, 42
Supernaturalism, 108ff
Supreme deity, in Africa, 99ff
Traditional Africans, defined, 83
Traditional religion, and CAR, 147ff
Ultimate reality
    cultural approach, 161ff
    meaning of 137ff
Underdevelopment, 204ff
Unemployment, 233
Wiredu, Kwasi
    on naturalism-supernaturalism, 109
    on African religiosity, 84
Work
    and play, 219
    and poverty, 229
    and the universal declaration of
        human rights, 234
    as a human right, 234
    as cure, 223
    as curse, 223
    as self-realization, 223
    cateogries of, 218
    conceptions of, 215
    in traditional African societies, 226
    Marcus Aurelius on, 225
    Nyerere on, 226
    Old Testament on, 224
    defined, 216
Work-discontent
    problem of, 232
Yoruba traditional religion
    and peace, 102
Zikist philosophy, 180